THEODORE DREISER

edited by
DONALD PIZER
Newcomb College, Tulane University

THEODORE DREISER

A selection of uncollected prose

Wayne State University Press   Detroit 1977

Library of Congress Cataloging in Publication Data

Dreiser, Theodore, 1871–1945.
  Theodore Dreiser: a selection of uncollected prose.

PS3507.R55A15   1977   813'.5'2   77-771
ISBN 0-8143-1569-0

In Memory of
Wilfried Uhlmann (1934–1972)

CONTENTS

Contents

2

1898–1910

3

1911–1925

4

1926–1945

Contents

ACKNOWLEDGMENTS

At an early stage of this project I benefited from the counsel of Richard Lehan. Mrs. Neda Westlake, Curator of the Dreiser Collection of the University of Pennsylvania Library, has, as always, been of great aid. I owe a special debt to Joseph Katz for making available copies of his unique run of the early issues of *Ev'ry Month*. The American Philosophical Society awarded me a grant which permitted me to undertake the travel necessary to discover and collect Dreiser's periodical publications, and the Tulane University Council on Research aided me with grants in support of transcribing and typing.

For permission to publish material still in copyright, I would like to thank the University of Pennsylvania for Dreiser's unpublished essays: "A Confession of Faith," "Suggesting the Possible Substructure of Ethics," "Some Additional Comments on the Life Force, or God," "It," "O.S. Marden and *Success* Magazine," and "My Creator"; Esquire, Inc., for "You, the Phantom";

11

Acknowledgments

Harcourt Brace Jovanovich, Inc., for Dreiser's introduction to *Harlan Miners Speak*; the *Nation* for "America and the Artist"; the *New Republic* for "The Saddest Story"; and the New York *Times* for "Talks with Four Novelists: Mr. Dreiser" and "Theodore Dreiser." Several paragraphs of the introduction to this edition appear, in different form, in my *The Novels of Theodore Dreiser: A Critical Study* (University of Minnesota Press, 1976), and are published with permission.

INTRODUCTION

Although Theodore Dreiser is best known as a novelist, most of his writing in prose is in forms other than fiction. Besides his eight novels and two collections of short stories, he published two autobiographies (*Dawn* and *Newspaper Days*), three travel accounts (*A Traveler at Forty, A Hoosier Holiday,* and *Dreiser Looks at Russia*), two collections of character portraits (*Twelve Men* and *A Gallery of Women*), a book of New York sketches (*The Color of a Great City*), two volumes of plays (*Plays of the Natural and the Supernatural* and *The Hand of the Potter*), two works of social polemics (*Tragic America* and *America is Worth Saving*), and a collection of philosophical essays (*Hey Rub-a-Dub-Dub*). Moreover, these thirteen volumes contain only a small portion of Dreiser's miscellaneous writing in prose. A professional author for over fifty years, Dreiser produced millions of words in order to make his living and to express his ideas. Much of

13

this work—from a jocular daily newspaper column he wrote for the Pittsburgh *Dispatch* during 1894 to a series of *Esquire* articles on family black sheep in 1944 and 1945—can properly be described as potboiling. Indeed, during two lengthy periods of his career—while a free-lance writer from late 1897 to 1902, and while a magazine editor from 1905 to 1910—most of Dreiser's non-fiction was produced to meet the demands of popular taste. At other times, however, financial independence or a congenial publishing outlet permitted him to write as he wished—to speak out with relative freedom and honesty on topics that interested him. Two such important periods were between 1895 and 1897, when he wrote a monthly column of "Reflections" for the magazine *Ev'ry Month,* and during the last two decades of his life, when he devoted much of his time to philosophical and social concerns.

I have attempted in this book to collect the best and most significant of Dreiser's previously uncollected non-fictional prose. (By uncollected, I mean not collected by Dreiser in book form. A few of the essays I include have been reprinted by others.) One basis of my selection has been to exclude material which deals with areas of Dreiser's life and thought readily available elsewhere. Thus, I have not included autobiographical essays which cover ground well-surveyed in Dreiser's published autobiographies, and I have excluded philosophical and polemical essays which add little to those in *Hey Rub-a-Dub-Dub.* I have rather sought to represent as fully as possible three kinds of writing by Dreiser: that which reveals major moments in the history of his thought and which is not now available in convenient form, such as his *Ev'ry Month* philosophizing and his essays of 1926–45; that which preserves significant commentary by him on the origin and nature of his novels; and that which displays the range of his ideas, from the beginning of his career to its conclusion, so as to provide the material necessary to confront the vexing problem of consistency and coherence in his beliefs.

Some further explanation of my principles of selection is necessary. I have not included material merely to document Dreiser's professional activities and obligations during different phases of his career. If a piece is not of substantive value, I did not consider it for inclusion. I therefore include only one of Dreiser's newspaper stories and articles of 1892–94, only four of the approximately 110 magazine essays he published between late 1897 and the close of 1901, none of his editorials of 1905–1910, and only one of his Communist party-line statements and manifestos of the 1930s and the early 1940s.[1] However, because of their intrinsic value, I have included a number of interviews of Dreiser and several of his hitherto unpublished essays. The interviews reveal Dreiser's ideas and interests with unusual clarity and force at important moments in his career, such as after the suppression of *Sister Carrie* and during 1911–12. The unpublished essays, from "A Confession of Faith" of 1911–14, to "My Creator" of 1943, contain some of Dreiser's most direct statements of his basic beliefs.

Thus, my aim in this volume has not been completeness, for a complete collection of Dreiser's uncollected prose would require some fifteen large volumes. Nor has it been representativeness, since I see no need to rescue from obscurity such evidence of Dreiser's need and enterprise as his article on Japanese home life (April 1898) or his interview with Ty Cobb (February 1925). Nor have I sought uniformity in subject matter, theme, or form. I include material which ranges from reminiscence and prose poetry to reportage and literary criticism to social polemics and philosophy. Rather, my intent has been to present in usable form a body of writing by Dreiser which will aid in the understanding of the mind and art of this complex figure who dominated the American literary scene from approximately 1912 to the late 1920s and whose major work still grips each new generation of readers.

I have divided the material of this volume into four periods not because these represent inclusive phases of Dreiser's thought but because they conveniently outline the configuration of his career as a writer. Dreiser began his career in June 1892, when he became a reporter on the Chicago *Globe*. He was a newspaper man in Chicago, St. Louis, Pittsburgh, and New York until the winter of 1894–95, when he grew disheartened about journalism while working as a space-rate reporter for the New York *World*. In the spring of 1895, Dreiser's songwriter brother Paul Dresser and the music publishing firm of Howley, Haviland & Co. decided to found a magazine in order to publicize the songs of the firm. Dreiser was installed as editor and principal contributor, and the magazine appeared in October 1895.[2] Since women were the chief purchasers of sheet music, *Ev'ry Month* featured columns on decorative and household matters. Dreiser initially had full responsibility for three departments: a lengthy opening column of commentary and philosophizing entitled "Reflections,"[3] a book review and literary news section usually called "The Literary Shower," and theater reviews. In order to avoid the impression that much of each issue was the work of a single writer, the "Reflections" column was signed "The Prophet," "The Literary Shower" was signed "Edward Al" (the first names of two of Dreiser's brothers), and miscellaneous articles and interviews were published under various other pseudonyms of Dreiser. (Only the theater review column appeared regularly under his name.) After a year, Dreiser's contributions to *Ev'ry Month* began to slacken. He published fewer dramatic reviews, the literary column was taken over by another writer, and in the spring of 1897 the "Reflections" section was itself shortened and moved to the back of the magazine, where it appeared untitled and unsigned.

Of Dreiser's extensive writing for *Ev'ry Month,* his "Reflections" column was his major effort and interest. Consisting of three to four thousand words in six to ten unrelated parts, it had a distinctive format and tone. The opening section was usually inspired by an item of national or international news (an election, a war, a monetary crisis). Each column also contained one or more sections on a contemporary social problem (political corruption, slums, trusts) and a relatively short comment on the season of the year. Often, these more temporal reflections would supply Dreiser with a lead into a general discourse on man, nature, and society. Throughout the column Dreiser's tone was that of a shrewd but genial moralist whose concern was to bring home to his perhaps sheltered or unreflective reader some of the underlying truths of life. It is a tone which Dreiser was later to adapt to the chapter opening homilies in *Sister Carrie* on the "true meaning" of clothes, travel, money, and sexual morality. As "The Prophet" explained in one of his January 1896 "Reflections,"

> It is not the purpose of this review to touch upon "timely" or "current" topics, but rather to exhibit them in the light of the higher knowledge, turning the calcium of philosophy upon the negative of the event, and by this means casting a huge picture whose every detail may be discerned and studied to advantage. There is no mad effort here to be beforehand with affairs, but rather to be superior to them, watching, as did the German professor whom Carlyle described in "Sartor Resartus," from a high mental tower in the "Wahngasse" of life, making notes of sights most pitiful, most beautiful, and most ludicrous. . . .

When Dreiser left *Ev'ry Month* in late 1897, he began to contribute to the ten-cent mass circulation journals then displacing the traditional monthlies. He quickly mastered the formula for the preparation of simply written, fully illustrated articles about famous people, well-known places, and current events, and became one of the leading "magazinists" of the day. During the month of September 1898, for example, he published an elaborately illustrated article on "The Sculpture of Fernando Miranda" in *Ainslee's,* a historical and descriptive account of "Brandywine, the Picturesque" in *Demorest's,* an interview with John Burroughs in *Success,* a two-part article on "Haunts of Nathaniel Hawthorne" in *Truth,* a survey of "America's Sculptors" in the New York *Times Illustrated Magazine,* as well as conventionally lugubrious and lachrymose poems in *Demorest's* and *Success.*

Dreiser's breakdown early in 1902, following his marriage difficulties and the suppression of *Sister Carrie,* put an end to this profitable career. When he returned fully to literary work in 1904, it was principally as an editor. For the next seven years he edited magazines ranging from the lowly *Smith's* to the prestigious *Delineator.* His occasional free-lance work during this period sounds a more personal note than his market-oriented writing of 1897–1902. He wrote and published many of the sketches later collected in *Twelve Men* (1919) and *The Color of a Great City* (1923), and in such articles as "The Loneliness of the City," "A Lesson from the Aquarium," and "The Defects of Organized Charity," he expressed themes which were to preoccupy him in his novels.

Dreiser's return to novel writing in late 1910 resulted in a decline in his miscellaneous and occasional work. For six or seven years most of his effort went into his novels and other book-length publications. (From 1910 to 1916 he wrote four lengthy novels, two travel books, two volumes of plays, and most of his autobiography *Dawn.*) Although Dreiser's books brought him fame (as well as notoriety in several quarters), they did not supply him with a living. He therefore again began to produce extensively in various briefer forms—the short story, essay, sketch, and poem. Most of this writing was later collected by Dreiser in the series of miscellaneous volumes he published from 1918 to 1929: *Free and Other Stories* (1918), *Hey Rub-a-Dub-Dub* (1920), *Moods* (1926), *Chains* (1927), and *A Gallery of Women* (1929). Thus, the uncollected material which best records Dreiser's interests and ideas between 1910 and 1925 is often the interview and the unpublished essay.

After the great success of *An American Tragedy* in late 1925, Dreiser continued to publish on a variety of subjects and in a variety of journals. This work differs from his earlier periodical publishing in several ways which help to explain why it was not collected by Dreiser. One large body of publication stemmed from

17

the salability of Dreiser's work after *An American Tragedy*. It consists of much meretricious composition for newspaper syndicates and popular magazines on subjects from "This Florida Scene" in 1926 to "Women Are the Realists" in 1939. Another major kind of writing had its origin in Dreiser's increasing involvement in left-wing movements and causes after his return from the Soviet Union in early 1928 and after the onset of the depression. Much of this publication was both occasional and superficial. That is, it was often written in response to a request for a statement on some contemporary issue or event, and it hewed to the party line. A third kind of writing was related to Dreiser's attempt to express his philosophical beliefs in a lengthy treatise known variously as "Notes on Life," "The Mechanism Called Man," "The Formula Called Life," etc. During the mid-1930s he published a number of almost unreadable excerpts from this work, though the book itself remained incomplete at his death. The best of Dreiser's uncollected work of the last two decades of his life therefore consists of reminiscent articles, semi-popularized explanations of the foundations of his philosophical belief, and attempts to explain and justify his social position and activism.

Much of Dreiser's significant non-fiction prose throughout his career contains two complementary themes. He was preoccupied with his role as artist and seer, as a "genius" seeking both fame and truth in an inhospitable world, and he sought to describe the truth and the world as he had found them.[4] But though these threads—the personal and the philosophical—run through all of Dreiser's work, their presentation differs in clarity and in relative prominence. While writing for *Ev'ry Month,* Dreiser expressed his personal concerns indirectly by means of general comments on the difficulties faced by the genius, and he presented his philosophical views in fragmentary and disconnected form. *Sister Carrie* contains both of these characteristics of the Dreiser of this period. Carrie's career obliquely reflects Dreiser's preoccupation with his own slow emergence as an artist under adverse circumstances, and Dreiser's miscellaneous philosophizing throughout the novel is in the mode and tone of "The Prophet."

Dreiser later became both more articulate and more open in stating his ideas and his ambitions. At first, during the long period from late 1897, when he became a free-lance writer, to his eclipse as a novelist after the suppression of *Sister Carrie,* he was preoccupied by his role as an artist. But with his reemergence as a writer of fiction in 1911, he again played upon the dual themes of art and truth. Thus, the Dreiser of 1911–1925 cultivated the mythic role of the hounded American writer. He was the trailblazer of realism who had opened the way to others while himself suffering the hardships of the pioneer. And the Dreiser of this period was also the formal philosopher of the essays of *Hey Rub-a-Dub-Dub* as well as the informal but pervasive philosopher of the Cowperwood trilogy and his autobiographies and travel books. The two roles merge in *The "Genius."* In that novel the autobiographical central figure not only eventually achieves a successful career as a poetic realist in oils but also crowns his success by attaining a full-blown philosophical interpretation of life. The balance of interest between the personal and philosophical again shifts in Dreiser's final two decades. He was still occasionally concerned with his role as artist, particularly in response to the attack upon him by the New Humanists. But he now devoted himself primarily to expounding in full his philosophical views and in making the social aspect of these views operative in his personal activities.

Although Dreiser was never explicitly autobiographical in his role as "The Prophet," a number of themes in his "Reflections" column nevertheless shape themselves into an autobiographical allegory because of their almost obsessive recurrence and because of their intensity of tone. The allegory centers on the character and experience of the Genius. The Genius as artist is a seeker of "fortune, fame, [and] a beautiful, sympathetic girl." The circumstances of modern life bring him to the city in pursuit of these goals, but the Genius soon discovers that the city contains not only the glorious spectacle which is life at its most compelling but also the struggle for existence which is inseparable from all life. Through his own experience and with the aid of such mentors as Herbert Spencer and Balzac, the Genius becomes aware of the meaning of life. He realizes that though the individual is insignificant in the overwhelming fury of the battle of life, the laws of life are themselves beneficent for the mass of men and for the progress of the race. And the Genius senses that the artist's response to this insight contains three fused emotions: awe toward the vast, impersonal forces of life, compassion for the victims of these forces, and wonder at the "color" or aesthetic appeal of the variation and conflict caused by these forces. But of course Dreiser as Genius in his "Reflections" column was uncertain both of his ability as artist and of his ultimate success. And he was also aware of the comparative weakness of the contemplative mind in the struggle for existence. So a thread of self-pity runs through the allegory. "Alone [the genius] walks, alone labors, alone dreams a great dream," Dreiser wrote in June 1896, in a vein he was to expand into the epilogue of *Sister Carrie,* when Carrie, the incipient artist, sits lonely and unfulfilled in her rocking chair and dreams of the future.

Two of Dreiser's frequent concerns in his *Ev'ry Month* writing—the evils of society and the nature of art—are closely related to this allegory. The faults of American social and political life are many, and Dreiser is properly moral in bemoaning their existence and berating their perpetrators. Yet a note of cynicism, or rather of calm acceptance, accompanies this conventional attitude. Wrong is wrong, Dreiser appears to be saying, but as long as men must struggle to survive, wrong will continue to flourish and reform will accomplish little. No doubt life in the future will be less selfishly rapacious, Dreiser suggests in his September 1896 comment on "Man's Place in Nature," a comment which resembles the well-known philosophical digression on Carrie's imminent fall at the opening of chapter 8. At some distant moment in time man's reason will have evolved to the point at which it can control rather than be controlled by natural forces, and with the dominance of rational choice in human affairs there will come greater harmony and beneficence in social life. The function of art at the present time, however, is not to falsify present conditions. Thus, both the Prophet and Edward Al execrate novels in which authorially manipulated plots solve all dilemmas and in which the consuming human passions are represented as capable of "reasonable and philosophical" resolution. Moreover, art which is either excessively stylized or superficially amusing—as is the art of Beardsley or the stage—is also at fault in its failure to render the underlying truth of life. Balzac should serve as the model of artistic achievement, for his depiction of the seeking heart in conflict with the inexorableness of experience expresses in a single "blend" of "realism and romance" both the spirit of the Genius and the material truth of the struggle for existence. Dreiser later made this aesthetic the underlying theme of such articles of 1898–1902 as "The Real Zangwill," "Curious Shifts of the Poor," "The Real Howells," and "Christmas in the Tenements." In these articles he either praises those writers who have attempted a compassionate identification with man's seeking nature as it comes in conflict with the world or attempts himself to depict the consequences of this basic condition of life.

There is much of the conventional public moralist of the

1890s in Dreiser's *Ev'ry Month* writing. He is like Ames in *Sister Carrie*. Both figures are young men of intelligence and sensibility who are anxious to "further all good causes" and who find in a young girl—Carrie and the typical young girl Dreiser appears to have imagined as a reader of his "Reflections" column—a receptive though unformed convert. Yet present as well in Dreiser's *Ev'ry Month* work are the fundamental ideas and attitudes which were to harden into his characteristic stances as a thinker and writer. With the suppression of *Sister Carrie,* Dreiser cast himself fully into the role of the beleaguered artist whose attempt to tell the truth is thwarted by the blind prejudice and befuddled moralism of conventional belief. This role was confirmed by his later experiences, from his difficulties with Harper's over *The Titan* in 1914 to the full-scale and open suppression of *The "Genius"* in 1916 to his bitter struggle with Paramount over the film version of *An American Tragedy* in 1931. The role was enlarged into mythic proportions by such writers as H. L. Mencken and Dorothy Dudley, who found in Dreiser's career a paradigm of the condition and fate of the artist in a puritan society.

Dreiser began to shape his "reflections" about life into a formal philosophical position between 1911 and 1920, when his energy and productivity were at their peak. He ignored at this point his earlier belief that the destructiveness of the present is to evolve into the rational harmony of the future and stressed the permanent amoral contentiousness of all existence. He used as his central metaphor of life Spencer's idea of rhythm, an idea which Dreiser usually called balance or equation.[5] The world to Dreiser consisted of contending forces—the rich and the poor, the mass and the individual, the strong and the weak—and life was a constant flux as these forces struggled for supremacy. Neither stasis between forces nor victory for any one force was possible, for power always caused a reaction and excessive power caused a reaction even more powerful than the force of its adversary. Man was but a minor element within this inevitable flux, and conventional morality was only a series of labels for actions which had their source in cosmic law rather than individual volition. Dreiser's clearest expression of this belief occurs at the close of *The Titan* in a passage which he later republished under the title "Life Is to Be Learned from Life":

> The world is dosed with too much religion. Life is to be learned from life, and the professional moralist is at best but a manufacturer of

21

shoddy wares. At the ultimate remove, God or the life force, if anything, is an equation, and at its nearest expression for man—the contract social—it is that also. Its method of expression appears to be that
of generating the individual, in all his glittering variety and scope, and
through him progressing to the mass with its problems. In the end a
balance is invariably struck wherein the mass subdues the individual or
the individual the mass—for the time being. For, behold, the sea is ever
dancing or raging.

In the mean time there have sprung up social words and phrases
expressing a need of balance—of equation. These are right, justice,
truth, morality, an honest mind, a pure heart—all words meaning: a
balance must be struck. The strong must not be too strong; the weak
not too weak. But without variation how could the balance be maintained? Nirvana! Nirvana! The ultimate, still, equation.[6]

The idea of equation was immensely useful to Dreiser as a
way of giving shape to many of his underlying beliefs and feelings.
He could use it to express his contempt for conventional morality
while affirming an order in nature independent of human volition;
and he could use its philosophical determinism to attack human
pride while affirming the perceptive and feeling mind which could
sense the beauty of design in a mechanistic world. And always it
was a flexible idea, one which could accommodate his otherwise
contradictory philosophical "moods." For example, he used it for
most of his career to attack moralistic reform movements, but in
the 1930s he adapted it to sanction reform, including reform
through Communism, by arguing that the social balance had swung
too far in the direction of absolute power of the strong and that
reform was the mechanistic response of the social organism to this
imbalance.

The idea of equation was not only flexible but also amor-
phous and could absorb Dreiser's various enthusiasms at different
moments of his career. The mechanism of Jacques Loeb, for example, which he encountered in 1914 or 1915, confirmed in a
specific biological context the mechanism which Dreiser's idea of
equation posited for all life. And in his essay "The American Financier" in *Hey Rub-a-Dub-Dub* Dreiser stated that the ideas of
Nietzsche and Marx were equally significant because their beliefs
represented the two poles of individual and mass power within the
"ever dancing and raging" sea of social flux.

The basic paradoxes and shifting emphases in Dreiser's
thought thus have their permanent center in his belief that life is a
constant flux in which the individual counts for nought as opposites
seek, but never achieve, balance. Although this never-ending

22

struggle may terrify and crush the individual, it benefits the race and has as well a symmetry of design in its components and processes which suggests the presence of an underlying spirit both as its source and as its essential nature. Dreiser's principal shift in the course of his career was from a stress on the destructiveness, turmoil, and impersonality of the "formula" which is life to an emphasis on its wonder, beauty, and beneficence. Put metaphorically, he moved from a stress upon man as a blind figure chained to a huge, relentless engine to man as a figure who, while still chained to the engine, could nevertheless admire its intricate beauty and stand in awe at the power of its maker. Put in terms of Dreiser's characters, he shifted from Carrie's pathetic discovery that we are never satisfied in our pursuit of beauty to Solon's and Berenice's triumphant discoveries at the close of *The Bulwark* and *The Stoic* of the still center of beauty in the underlying design of the processes of life. And, finally, put in social terms, he moved from a stress upon the impossibility of changing the qualities of human nature which are the source of struggle and flux to an emphasis upon the possibility and need of changing the social organism which can control the expression of human nature and thus lessen the extremes of variation within the equation.

Dreiser's ideas resemble those of many late nineteenth-century thinkers—Herbert Spencer, Ernst Haeckel, and Alfred Wallace, for example—whose cosmologies were informed initially by a desire to destroy a conception of the universe and man as supernaturally sanctioned and who therefore posited a world of natural law in which man was but an insignificant tool in the hands of impersonal forces. But these very laws, because of the symmetry and direction attributed to them, became—by implication in Spencer and more directly in Haeckel and Wallace—equivalents of the pantheism of romantic philosophy, in which God is immanent in the laws and substance of nature. In the writings of Spencer, Haeckel, and Wallace, Dreiser encountered early in his career both an attack on the old teleology and an affirmation of a "new" universe of order, purpose, and spiritual unity. The chronology of Dreiser's response to this dual potential in the cosmologies he absorbed in his youth was first to echo the attack and then, later in life, to stress the affirmation.

From as early as the mid-1890s, Dreiser's notion of the world as struggle contained a thread of wonder at the underlying design of nature, as in the closing paragraphs of his "Reflection" on "Man's Place in Nature" in September 1896. During much of

Dreiser's career, these two qualities of mind—the desire to destroy the old supernaturalism and its accompanying system of prohibitory morality, and the desire to affirm a new supernaturalism and its morality of beauty—existed in his thought as alternative but not mutually exclusive responses to experience. Even in *The Financier,* a novel devoted to a figure who successfully defies traditional concepts of order, Dreiser paused to reflect on the impulse of all living things "to arrange themselves into an orderly and artistic whole. . . . It would seem as though the physical substance of life—this apparition of form which the eye detects and calls real— were shot through with some vast subtlety that loves order, that is order."[7] Dreiser summed up the emotional ambivalence which is often the product of this dual view of life in the title essay of *Hey Rub-a-Dub-Dub.* He wrote that when he sees the pattern and beauty of nature, he believes that "there must be some great elemental spirit holding for order of sorts." But when he thinks of the lust and greed and plotting of life, he is "not so sure."[8]

By the late 1920s, however, Dreiser's "reverence before the beauty and wisdom of creative energy"[9] began to be the dominant force in his thought. Loeb's mechanism, for all its usefulness as a confirmation of some of Dreiser's own mechanistic ideas, had proved incomplete because it failed to acknowledge the presence of a "constructive or commanding force" behind and within the laws of life.[10] So for over fifteen years, from the late 1920s to the early 1940s, Dreiser devoted much of his time and energy to gathering a mass of scientific and pseudoscientific data which supported his beliefs and to organizing this material into a large-scale philosophical work which would demonstrate both the insignificance of man and the wonder and beauty of the process of which he was a part.[11] Science thus became to Dreiser both a means of confirming a preconceived "religious" position and a metaphor of that position. He wrote from the Woods Hole Marine Biological Laboratory in 1928 that the scientists there "are not all mechanists. . . . Some are agnostics, some mystics, some of a reverent and even semi-religious turn. Personally I am awed and so amazed by the processes visible to the eye that I grow decidedly reverent."[12] During the late 1920s and early 1930s he wrote many poems (collected in the 1935 edition of *Moods*) in which he substituted for the traditional imagery of external nature an imagery of the beauty of the physical and chemical foundations of life, of electrons and neutrons. By the early 1940s Dreiser frequently expressed his belief in the perfection of the underlying design of life in a quasi-religious form. God, in the guise of creative energy, pervaded all life but was manifest most clearly to those, like the Quakers or Hindus or Thoreau, or like Dreiser himself when admiring a flower or conversing with a snake, who faced life with the searching but intuitive faith of a mystic.[13]

Dreiser's social ideas underwent an analogous broad reorientation. Until the late 1920s, he was usually contemptuous—when not restricted by the obligatory do-goodism of popular journalism—of efforts at reform which ignored the irredeemable Adam in man's nature. "Don't forget," he wrote Upton Sinclair in 1924, "that the brotherhood of man . . . is mere moonshine to me. I see the individual large or small, weak or strong, as predatory and nothing less."[14] Yet coexistent with Dreiser's ready willingness to attack those whom he considered starry-eyed reformers was a broadly based sympathy for the aspirations and needs of the mass despite the weaknesses and limitations of most men. He was no doubt also characterizing himself when he wrote of Cowperwood in *The Titan* that "Individualistic and even anarchistic in character, and without a shred of true democracy, yet temperamentally he was in sympathy with the mass of men more than he was with the class, and he understood the mass better."[15]

By the late 1920s, this predisposition united with Dreiser's increasing responsiveness to specific instances of social injustice to lead him to concern himself less with the impossibility of changing human nature and more with the possibility of ameliorating the effects of unrestrained greed and power. As early as *A Hoosier Holiday* he had written, "I know the strong must rule the weak, the big brain the little one, but why not some small approximation toward equilibrium, just a slightly less heavily loaded table for Dives and a few more crumbs for Lazarus?"[16] In the 1930s, Dreiser believed that this "approximation toward equilibrium" could be achieved by recognizing that society was not merely a static reflection of the permanent in human nature but also an evolving social organism. In 1934, he distinguished between "the inequity of life, which in a general way in the larger sense no one can remedy, but which in a lesser sense such as that which relates to a family, a corporation, or a State or a Nation, can be to a considerable degree modified."[17]

Dreiser's philosophical and social ideas thus underwent a parallel shift from a stress on the limitations placed upon man's understanding and volition by the mechanistic nature of life to an emphasis on the opportunities for insight and action within a mechanistic

25

Introduction

world. So at the end of his career Dreiser was able to indorse
Quaker and Hindu belief on the one hand (at the close of *The
Bulwark* and *The Stoic*) and to join the Communist Party on the
other without a sense of contradiction either between these acts or
between them and his earlier ideas. From a belief that the universe
is a mechanistic equation of forces, Dreiser had moved to a faith
that these forces are part of a divine, though still mechanistic, plan,
and that the need to achieve a greater balance between such opposing forces as strength and weakness or wealth and poverty is sanctioned not only by the mechanism or equation but by the underlying spirit of love—that is, of force as creative energy or God—in all
life. In short, he moved his earlier amoral cosmology up a kind of
ethical slope, and at last found at the height of the slope an emotionally satisfying view of the universe as good and as potentially
better.

Notes to the Introduction

1. For a list of Dreiser's periodical publications, see Donald Pizer, Richard Dowell, and Frederic Rusch, *Theodore Dreiser: A Primary and Secondary Bibliography*
(Boston, 1975).

2. *Ev'ry Month* is extremely rare for the period of Dreiser's editorship, that is,
from October 1895 to September 1897. There are scattered copies in the Lilly
Library, Indiana University; the Dreiser Collection of the University of Pennsylvania Library; and the Yale University Library (on microfilm). The fullest run is in the
private collection of Joseph Katz. Despite the efforts of a number of scholars, no
copies of the first two issues of *Ev'ry Month*—October and November 1895—have
been located. For authoritative accounts of Dreiser's association with *Ev'ry Month*,
see Ellen Moers, *Two Dreisers* (New York, 1969), pp. 32–43, and Joseph Katz,
"Theodore Dreiser's *Ev'ry Month*," *Library Chronicle* of the University of Pennsylvania 38 (Winter 1972): 46–66.

3. The column was initially called "Review of the Month" but became
"Reflections" with the January 1896 issue. From April to July 1897, it was untitled.
Dreiser may have borrowed the title "Reflections" from William Marion Reedy's
use of this title for his column in *Reedy's Mirror*.

4. There are many discussions of Dreiser's basic ideas. Among the most useful
are Robert H. Elias, *Theodore Dreiser: Apostle of Nature* (New York, 1949; rev.
ed., Ithaca, N.Y., 1970); Richard Lehan, *Theodore Dreiser: His World and His
Novels* (Carbondale, Ill., 1969); and J. D. Thomas, "Epimetheus Bound: Theodore
Dreiser and the Novel of Thought," *Southern Humanities Review* 3 (Fall 1969):
346–57. For an annotated discussion of Dreiser scholarship, see Robert H. Elias's
essay in *Sixteen Modern American Authors*, ed. Jackson R. Bryer (Durham, N.C.,
1973). A complete list of Dreiser scholarship can be found in Pizer, Dowell, and
Rusch, *Theodore Dreiser: A . . . Bibliography*.

5. Dreiser's fullest published explanation of the idea of equation occurs in his
essay "Equation Inevitable" in *Hey Rub-a-Dub-Dub*. In expanded and revised

form, this essay would play a major role in the philosophical work which occupied Dreiser from the late 1920s to the early 1940s.

6. *The Titan* (New York, 1914), pp. 550–51; "Life Is to Be Learned from Life," New York *Call Magazine*, July 27, 1919, p.2.

7. *The Financier* (New York, 1912), p. 588.

8. *Hey Rub-a-Dub-Dub* (New York, 1920), pp. 17–18.

9. Dreiser to Ruth E: Kennell, September 5, 1928, in Ruth E. Kennell, *Theodore Dreiser and the Soviet Union* (New York, 1969), p. 222.

10. See Dreiser's story "The 'Mercy' of God," *Chains* (New York, 1927), p. 373. The story was initially published in 1924.

11. Selections from this work have recently been edited and published by Marguerite Tjader and John J. McAleer as *Notes on Life* (Univ. of Alabama Press, 1974).

12. Dreiser to Franklin and Beatrice Booth, July 16, 1928, in *Letters of Theodore Dreiser,* ed. Robert H. Elias (Philadelphia, 1959), 2: 471.

13. For an account of two of Dreiser's mystical experiences of the mid-1930s, see Marguerite Tjader, *Theodore Dreiser: A New Dimension* (Norwalk, Conn., 1965), pp. 72–73, 77.

14. Dreiser to Sinclair, December 18, 1924, Lilly Library, Indiana University.

15. *The Titan,* p. 27.

16. *A Hoosier Holiday* (New York, 1916), p. 60.

17. Dreiser to E. S. Martin, September 4, 1934, in *Letters* 2: 689.

A NOTE ON THE TEXT

The source of the text of each selection is noted at the foot of the opening page of the selection. The text chosen for published material, unless otherwise noted, is that of its first published appearance. Later appearances of a selection in Dreiser's lifetime are also indicated in the note on the source of the text.

I have not normalized or regularized spelling, punctuation, or grammar, with the exception of the normalization of the punctuation of the titles of Dreiser's essays. However, I have silently emended obvious typographical and spelling errors, including the misspelling of proper names. In a few instances I have supplied punctuation or a word or phrase in order to clarify a passage. All such additions are bracketed in the text.

For previously unpublished material, I have reproduced Dreiser's final version. That is, I reproduce the text as revised by him, without any attempt to indicate the occurrence or nature of

28

additions and cancellations. With the exception of the article on O. S. Marden, all of the manuscripts used in this edition are comparatively clean typescripts with few corrections. The Marden typescript contains many marginal corrections and additions by Dreiser.

Dreiser was often a prolix and repetitious writer, and I have therefore cut a number of his more lengthy essays. I have also cut plot summaries and well-known biographical material from the interviews of Dreiser. All cuts are indicated by a line of asterisks in the text. I have cut without indication subtitles and subheads in Dreiser's articles and in interviews of him. This space-consuming material was always the work of editors and does not warrant reproduction. All ellipses in the text are Dreiser's and do not indicate an omission by me.

I have supplied specific titles for material which appeared either as part of a symposium or under a recurrent generic title (such as "Reflections"). All such titles appear in brackets.

All items were signed by Dreiser unless I indicate otherwise. In my headnotes I discuss when necessary the attribution of material not signed by Dreiser and the biographical and historical context of the essay or interview. I have limited annotation to references and allusions not identifiable in a standard dictionary or encyclopedia or not readily understood from the context in which they appear. The full form of all proper names in the text can be found in the index.

1

The Return of Genius

There was born, once upon a time, a great Genius. His younger years were spent in poverty and sorrow. Yet his brain teemed with noble thoughts and grand purposes. One day, his heart filled with sorrow and despair, he wandered about viewing all that was rich and gorgeous, and the iron bitterness of fate entered his soul. He groaned aloud in the depth of his misery.

"Oh, that I was famous. Oh, that fame was mine, and riches, and pleasure. Even the world I would forsake if my name could be assured to posterity."

Musing thus he hurried to the woods and fields and by the side of a silver brook threw himself down and anguish filled his soul.

Then there came to him, above his outcry against fate, a gentle voice, sweet with sympathy, saying: "Thou, poor fool. Hast thou not genius? Is not the world before thee? See, it lies here! Rise! go forth! hew for thyself a path! make for thyself a name!"

He raised up his woebegone face and seeing no one cried, "Who speaks?"

"The God of Genius[,]" answered the voice. "Go and strive and I will assist thee."

The genius only buried his face again and sighed, "would that I had never been born."

Then came the voice again, saying: "What wilt thou?"

"I would that my name may live through all time," answered the genius.

"On one condition shalt thou have glory and an undying fame."

"All conditions will I obey if only my name is hereafter assured."

"I will give thee fame even now, and riches, and ease, and an undying name, only thou shalt not hear nor see thy own glory."

Then Genius arose and was comforted.

"Go, then," said the voice, "and gather from the fields a

Chicago *Daily Globe*, October 23, 1892, p. 4. Signed "Carl Dreiser."

33

handful of poppies. Breathe the perfume from these thrice and thy wish will straightaway come to pass.''

With great joy the Genius went his way gathering here and there from fragrant nooks a handful of poppies, and when these had been gathered he returned to the brook, threw himself by its side and breathed the perfume thrice. Then there came to him a glorious fancy and he was transported to a mansion of silver. In it were ornaments of gold and precious stones, and luxurious furnishings, such as mind could hardly conceive.

All around sounded the voices of birds and the murmur of silver brooks and the air was burdened with the delightful odors of strange and beautiful flowers.

"Oh!" cried Genius, "now am I happy and my fame will be perpetual."

Slaves dressed in gorgeous attire anticipated his every wish and daily brought him tidings of the world without, written on sheets of pure gold. Sweet voices nightly sang his praises from without, saying: "Thy name is forever famous."

Time rolled on and curious longings entered his heart. They were at first as whisperings of some evil counselor, and for a time he spurned them from him. They would come to him, however, and again was Genius unhappy.

"Oh," he thought, "that I might see the world again. What is greatness and glory but to enjoy. That I might see the world bow and smile, that I might feel its glances of admiration and hear its words of praise. Even can I forget riches and ease for that. Had I but that added to my happiness my cup would then be full to overflowing."

Scarcely had the thought come to him than he heard the voice saying: "I have given thee gold and silver and luxurious ease. See! You have delights granted to no other. Thy name is also forever assured. Wilt thou hear voices of praise? Then, insomuch is thy name forgotten. Wilt thou have the admiration of humanity? Then in that degree will thy name be forgotten. Wilt thou mingle with the world and have it bow to thee? Then dies thy name with thee."

The Genius thought long and deeply and was not comforted. No more was there delight in his gorgeous surroundings. No longer murmured the brooks to him in whispering melody. Everything seemed to have lost its harmony. Time brought only a longing to be great among men.

"I will go," he cried. "I will mingle with men and be of them. They are nearer to me than silver and jewels; nearer to me than words of praise and gorgeous luxury. Fling wide the doors! I am through with this life. I will again seek mankind,'' and he hurried from the palace.

On the last step stood a fair maiden bearing a lute and holding in her hand a bunch of poppies. "Breathe of these thrice or thy world will be ever lost,'' she said[,] and the Genius, stooping, inhaled their fragrance.

Then was the brook again as before. Then again he realized his life and its terrors, and looking upward cried, "Oh, that my dream was still," but a voice whispered: "Go! Make for thyself a palace. From it thou canst never leave. In thine own hand is the power—the strength. Achieve thine own glory. It is for thee and thee alone to do this. In effort, will thy genius be sharpened. Aid from the gods would but destroy thee."

And the genius listened to these golden words and returned to men.

[Patronage of Native Genius]

The recent marriages of a daughter of the House of Gould and a daughter of the House of Vanderbilt to noblemen of Europe have given rise to much discussion,* the most important point being whether a young man of excellent family and breeding can ever hope to enter the ranks of wealth and fashion in America and wed an heiress, without having equal if not greater wealth than she. One who knows says no, and he is to be believed. If our American heiresses do not marry foreign noblemen, their parents see to it that if they marry at home they marry well, well in this case meaning wealth. Birth, good position, an untarnished name mean little in society here, if there is not wealth behind them. A rare genius takes his place in the gay ranks occasionally, but not until he has worn himself cynical in the struggle for recognition, usually not until youth has forsaken him and he is leaning sternly upon his talents. Then it is quite too late to think of capturing a tender, petted flower out of the conservatory of fashion. Genius is quite too proud to sue meekly for the hand of some vain innocent who numbers among the suitors for her hand many who have wealth and more who have titles, all humble, and of that cringing mentality that suffers little if any by contemplation of its own satellitic position: this without malice and with the utmost charity.

Fortune, so essential in America, is not so closely inspected in England. What a man is goes for nothing if he be not wealthy here: genius may aspire in more countries than one on the Continent, and with fair prospects of success. But American matrons do not consider that they have reached that high plane in the world where, instead of fluttering after vain titles and alien honors, they might gather about them the children of talent in their own land, and, while aiding them in their efforts, use them to grace the functions of the hour, thus adding a literary and artistic splendor to

"Review of the Month," *Ev'ry Month* 1 (December 1895): 2–3. Signed "The Prophet."

*Anna Gould had married Count Castellane in March 1895, and Consuelo Vanderbilt had married the Duke of Marlborough in early November 1895.

their round of vanities—a condition unknown to-day. They do not know the meaning of the word "patron," and many a graceless young scamp goes a-begging where, were American women really interested in the social charms which they affect, he might become a benefactor of the race and another star in the constellation of genius, so conspicuously absent in the United States to-day. Why, for instance, should not young Townsend (Chimmie Fadden) be taken into the world of fashion, and what would not its votaries gain by contact with him? Where are the patrons of Remington and young Pollard, and why did not some wealthy matron of fashion fasten Woolson Morse to her girdle early enough to have com-pelled recognition of his genius and thus given him hope anew? What kindly matron of millions ever did anything for Eugene Field or James Whitcomb Riley, or John Kendrick Bangs?*

The halls of fashion may be entered again and again and the throng observed: the roll of carriages and the shower of flowers may be ever present, but where midst it all are the poets, the writers, the sculptors, and who among all this host of fashion is proud of them, pleased that they should grace the hour and the occasion by their presence? This adoration of wealth—has it called one single struggling genius into prominence or given one Ameri-can daughter of fashion a love for a child of exalted brain? This hunt for titles—has it gathered together a company of the meritori-ous, or made of all the writers, artists and musicians an even inter-esting showing? Our libraries are filled with strugglers of the bright-est character. Our places of art are attended by a company of pale, thinly-clothed strugglers in the field of science and letters, and men of talent generally are left unnoticed, but little removed from pen-ury and want, while thousands of matrons who might well look after a score of protégés, roll to and from dry receptions to dryer balls, and wonder why fashionable functions are so wearing. American girls are introduced and trained among snobs, are taught to pray with eyes turned Europeward, and are eventually wedded to the highest bidder, while the genius of our land wanders on neglected. Is it any wonder that we are the laughing-stock of the world?

---

*Edward W. Townsend's New York slum stories often featured the character Chimmie Fadden. Percival Pollard and Frederic Remington were just beginning their careers, the first as a critic, the second (at this time) as both a writer of short stories and an illustrator. Woolson Morse was an obscure poet, whereas Field, Riley, and Bangs were well-established as popular poets and humorists.

There ought to be a change here somewhere, and maybe it will be made after awhile. Men of genius once successful will resent in a measure the assertion that they need patrons, looking upon it as an imputation against their sterling qualities; but, nevertheless, their paths could have been made brighter and perhaps their hearts permanently lighter, had their genius been remarked at its early blossom and made the object of some helpful regard. There never was a flower that was not aided by cultivation, and there never was a genius who could not have been aided by those higher in the social scale. Meanwhile, it is not surprising that American society is so exceptionally dull, nor that the American heiress has fewer admirers than the girl in moderate circumstances. The American is still a man and not a fortune-hunter.

[Campaigns for Social Reform]

Mentioning sweatshops recalls the long warfare against this oppression in America, and the additional fact that every city has had its labor investigations and its heartrending exposures, all in vain. Tenement commissions may come and tenement commissions may go, but the sweatshop iniquity hangs on forever. Chicago had a great exposure so far back as 1884, and the *Times,* now the *Times-Herald,* raised its languishing circulation of 15,000 to 95,000 simply by telling how girls worked in small, narrow, ill-lighted rooms over sewing machines, early and late, growing pale and wasting away. Those little side incidents of an apple and a piece of bread for dinner, of thin cotton dresses, faded and worn, doing service as raiment in snow and sleet; those paragraphs about sunken cheeks, and deep, burning, heart weary eyes, so moved the heart of the young city that its prominent residents (Pullman, Armour, Field, Lyman Trumbull) were moved to suggest remedies, and the *Times* began to pay dividends—a thing that had never occurred since the death of its eccentric founder, Judge Storey. There was a great to-do about man's inhumanity to man, and many were the tears and much the momentary sentimentality. Chicago's women were going to organize and begin a crusade. Merchants were going to give money, and preachers were going to go forth and aid these wan strugglers in their awful battle for subsistence. The summer waned, however, and the excitement passed like an autumn breeze. The subject palled and comment grew trite; the *Times* lost its circulation again, and all was as though the pool had never had a pebble cast into it.

Here in New York, also, many "commissions" have come and gone. It was on the 26th of October last that Richard Watson Gilder, the genial poet-editor of the *Century,* appeared before the Reinhard Assembly Committee (engaged in investigating the sweatshop abuses) and duly bemoaned the sweatshops as a crying evil, but could suggest no remedy.* Children, he thought, ought to be

"Review of the Month," *Ev'ry Month* 1 (December 1895): 6–7. Signed "The Prophet."

*See "Reinhard Committee Meets. R. W. Gilder Says 'Sweat-Shops' Are a Crying Evil," New York *Times,* October 27, 1895, pt. 1, p. 9.

taken out of these shops and sent to school. He quoted some law or other, and then someone else said that the sweatshop workers had brought all their trouble upon themselves by agreeing to work cheaper and for longer hours. So the committee separated and went its several ways, Mr. Gilder returning to his books and his poetry.

Dear old Richard Watson! What a poet he is, and how little he realizes that all evils must slowly adjust themselves. It takes many hollow cheeks and consumpted frames, many tearwet faces and broken hearts to right the slightest wrong in this world. All Europe suffered fifty plagues before it learned to wash itself properly, and the hardened heart of Pharaoh unbended only when the tenth horror swept the land and the people clamored loudly to him. Committees cannot do away with sweatshops this year, nor soon, for that matter. Hunting beasts with powder and bullet for pleasure has not been done away with yet, nor will it be soon. So it is with these poor suffering women. The sunshine and rains alternate, the flowers bloom and a thousand pleasures sweep past them, but they are still wan and sickly and lack sufficient food. The snows come and they meet them half-clad. Meanwhile, we sigh, and feel blue, and work up circulations, and finally forget. That is the way of the world.

[Political Corruption]

Every "once in a while," or perhaps they are really continuous, there come reports of exposures of corruption in various cities, and practices the most shameful are aired, so that the public learns a great deal of the tricks and schemes that are current among its servants to pilfer from its coffers for their own enrichment. It appears that men of certain magnetism, but little principle, first obtain ascendency in certain small districts, and then that men of greater magnetism and even less principle gain the good will of these lesser magnates, and by them control the votes of quite large sections, and so dictate who shall be the nominee for any particular office, what he shall do to obtain the said nomination, and, in case he is elected, what he shall do to recompense these leaders through whose influence he has been foisted upon the people.

In perusing the newspaper dispatches from these festering political wounds upon our national corpus, it becomes apparent that every scheme for making money over and above the salary stipulated is at once put into operation by successful officeholders, and that every boon which a city or county or State confers free upon its citizens is at once trammeled and made to pay toll. Whenever a corporation organizes and prepares to develop some local industry it is at once set upon by these greedy wolves of office and made to pay for its natural privileges. The boldest methods are taken by those clothed with official power to obtain money. They pass the most brazen and uncalled-for laws, scarcely draped in rags of honesty, by which they hamper the means of the company seeking to establish itself, and only the most liberal bribes will serve to modify the evil of such sumptuary legislation. The saddest feature of it is that there is scarcely any method of "getting at" these official criminals or of tracing their vile paths and surprising them in the perpetration of wrong. Their methods are secret and they work through agents. Papers are not signed and money is not openly delivered, yet all the time it is passing from the just to the unjust, and no one dare lift his voice for fear of being enmeshed in

"Reflections," *Ev'ry Month* 1 (January 1896): 4–5. Signed "The Prophet."

libel laws and made to suffer for his truthful opinions. Vice stalks about in the guise of contractors and philanthropists, and thieves address election mobs and are carried aloft upon the hands of the populace. What a spectacle to contemplate!

And there is no immediate remedy for it all—that is the pity of it. Human beings are innately greedy—avaricious. They dream of fine clothes and fine homes and of rolling about luxuriously in carriages; and to make their dream come true they are ready and willing to stoop to anything. They steal, and then look at their new clothes gained by so doing, and it is as though oil had been poured upon the slightly troubled waters of their consciences. They take money appropriated to care for the poor, the cripples, the blind and the insane, and the sight of it converted into property and rent makes them hug themselves with delight. They supply cheap, paltry goods when the best was guaranteed, and though many lives are jeopardized and many bodies are unstrung and sent to untimely graves, they do not care, so long as they find that the money they gain contributes to their ease and puts the danger of poverty far from them.

It is absolutely remarkable how slip-shod things can be done when the people as a body pay for them, and how mild the courts can be when it is suspected that some one has money wherewith to buy or exact justice. At the same time that American officials all over the land are piling up money by theft and close bargaining, many a poor lunatic is being starved and beaten by brutal attendants, placed in charge because they could be hired cheap, and because the money so saved could be slipped into a superior's pocket.

At the same time that fires are burning gaily upon the hearths of the influential, thousands in prisons are being detained unjustly, and starved upon fare that has been cheapened by theft and degraded by ill cooking. Get everything you can seems to be the motto of American officials and politicians. The great levy upon the less great, and they in turn demand money from the small fry, who, determined to make something for themselves, beat the beggars and starve the insane. That is horrible, even though it be politics—and we have a Thanksgiving Day every November.

[The Beauty of Everyday Life]

An instance in point of the assertion made in these columns once before, that those painters and sculptors who desire to gain enduring fame must paint and carve the scenes of to-day, is furnished by brilliant Broadway—and a furnishing store at that. In Broadway is everything: windows adorned with rare paintings and crowded with aged bric-à-brac; windows filled with rarest gems and gaudiest trifles, all displayed 'neath a hundred electric bulbs to attract attention. In Broadway surges the cosmopolitan, dallying crowd, and all night the stream of humanity flows past, crowding itself here before a poster and there before a window, where some latest gew-gaw is to show, nothing being quite too trifling to fail to attract some one idler, at least. In Broadway, then, before many trifles, dawdle the mob, and from the size of the crowd and quality of the display one may infer that which is dearest to the popular heart. Before a painting of the nine muses in classic garb, one lone looker-on gives place to another, and before a poster of the latest dancer in red and white some two or three pause momentarily. Before a painting of a Western cow-boy, astride a nervous steed, by Frederic Remington, men and women numbering five and ten at a time linger to study the slightest details of hot sand and blazing sun, casting a strong shadow of horse and rider upon the ground. Before a bronze statuette of a similar character by the same artist, displayed in Tiffany's, an equal number of admirers may constantly be found.

In a haberdasher's window, quite the most glaring of any, with its hundred lights and neckties of yellow and red, was hung recently a copy of the painting by Delorme, entitled "The Blacksmith"—a $50,000 production, though no placard said so.* Before this very modern subject crowded the wayfarers, not five or ten, but as many as could comfortably stand and tiptoe enough to see over each other's shoulders—not the most gaily dressed altogether,

"Reflections," *Ev'ry Month,* 1 (January 1896): 5. Signed "The Prophet."

*The painting, by Hubert Delorme, is reproduced in *Scientific America* 73 (December 14, 1895): 379.

43

nor the most intellectual of eye, quite, but an average mixture of men and women, workingmen and men of leisure, all deeply serious and gaining no little satisfaction from their observation of this work. Comments were frequent, for they noted the warm glow of the fire in the forge and the darkling reflection of the same upon the wrinkled face and brawny, hairy arm of the smith. They studied with evident satisfaction the detail of anvil and hammer, of tool and variety of chains and bolts—in short, the thousand and one minute details which the artist had carefully worked in, filling every nook and cranny. They felt a pang of sentiment as they saw the slightest daub of green as of trees and flowers, through the rude window, where the white daylight contrasted so strangely with the smoky glare of the forge opposite. By the free, serious, willing expression given to the face of the smith they drew the evident moral of content in necessity, and they departed after a while, with a newer life in their heart, however short-lived to be.

This is the instance and this the truth. Let those paint classics who will—here is the fact; and if those so nimble of eye, so masterful of touch, will insist upon shutting their eyes and their hearts to the sentiment and the beauty in everyday life, let them do so. Their punishment shall be oblivion. No work that fails to reflect "today" in that high light of love and God-given beauty unfolded to genius can hope to live. In painting and sculpture we must have truth, though it be, as in literature, told as "fiction."

[The Oligarchy of Wealth]

Dreiser's rhetoric in this "Reflection" is heavily Populist. "Gold" and "silence" would be readily identifiable by a contemporary reader as allusions to a conspiracy by Eastern bankers to control the money supply of the country for their own advantage. More specifically, a financial crisis occurred during the winter of 1895–96 because of the shortage of funds in the United States Treasury. The crisis was resolved in early January 1896, when a consortium of banks agreed to accept a hundred million dollars in United States bonds issued by the Treasury. Dreiser again refers to this crisis in "The Cause of Social Unrest," pp. 49–50.

Practical politicians rise sublime and inspiring at this present period beside the men "out of politics," who never speak with their mouths but signal each other by the "glance significant" and mark their meaning with the sign of gold. They are not of the "common people," these men of silence, nor are they imbued with that national spirit which makes for brotherhood and common interests, and for the welfare of the many in contra-distinction to the opulence of the few. They are not scattered broadcast over the land, nor are they common to all or even any of the States, nor are they known to the people by any of their peculiar characteristics, for they are as fearful of prominence as they are reserved in words, and their way is the path of the exclusive—for they ride in coaches and Pullmans, and are hidden in the depths of the boulevards and the shadows of the swagger resorts of the wealthy. Wherever there is wealth they are gathered, and whenever there tinkles the clink of gold they come silently forward—from nowhere. It is a peculiarity of them that they meet in silent company, unheralded and unsung, and behold! a tremor of unexplainable apprehension is felt through the land. They neither speak nor work openly, and yet at their behest money seems to fade as a shadow from the land, and the people gather and begin to talk panic. There comes but another surreptitious gathering of them, and the banks everywhere find

"Reflections," *Ev'ry Month* 1 (February 1896): 6. Signed "The Prophet."

they are short of gold and cannot pay readily. Large institutions of trade begin to curtail their expenses, and manufacture of all kinds modifies its vigor as though it were crouching in fear of some dread evil. It is as though a blight had fallen upon the land, and men whisper that the "band of the silent" are again at work. There comes yet another meeting, and institutions enter into receivership and idle men become numerous and beg for bread. Uncertainty lays hold upon the very heartstrings of the nation, and panic is whispered far and wide, gold is not and cannot be had except at high rates. Ruin threatens and stalks abroad. In the hour of greatest uncertainty, "the silent" issue forth and betake themselves to Washington. There come secret conferences and secret journeys. Secret coffers of gold are heard of and secret methods of unloading them are broached. Then come contracts and Presidential signatures, with gold for a bargain, when there is a slow upward flow of that commodity, as from wellsprings, and fear and depression fade from the land as though the sun of prosperity had but newly risen. The silent company, so mysterious in its gatherings, so powerful in its aid, slinks, as before, to its bank and its coach, unseen and unsung, there to precipitate another bond issue. About the body of freedom there seems to wrap a coil of snakes.

A Daughter of the Tenements

It is curious to note how many novels are written now-a-days about Bohemia, and the fellows who "move in society" when they choose, and out of it when they don't. They are not bad novels altogether, nor good ones, by several lengths, but they satisfy the craving of those who would "like ever so much" to be society lights and Bohemians, and have a "good time all the time," as Bohemians are currently supposed to do. James L. Ford writes this sort of novel occasionally (they're easy for Ford), as does Hobart Chatfield-Taylor, Richard Harding Davis, and Percival Pollard, though perhaps Percy ought not to be included, seeing that he has only recently brought out his "first offense" in this direction. A good way to write this sort of novel is to first get your Bohemian plot, lay your scenes in well-known cafes, like Delmonico's and Pfaff's, "ring in" an artist's studio or so, a girl raised from the slums into high life, and, presto! there you are, deep in a Bohemian story, and liable to make quite a little money.

It is of this sort of thing that "A Daughter of the Tenements" (N.Y.: Lovell, Coryell & Co.) smacks of, and it is this sort of thing that Mr. Edward W. Townsend has come very near writing, though he has escaped in a measure, owing to some very excellent character touches and some bits of genuine pathos—peculiarities that are entirely wanting in the average "Bohemia" novel—at least, as I have found it. There is nothing deeply human about a ballet girl who marries a musician, who in turn deserts her and leaves her to marry a "slum" Italian and raise her daughter to be a dancer of note, "La Cortese." It isn't very humorous or pathetic, nor even thrilling, that a wealthy society merchant should promote a rascal clerk into full charge of his affairs, and then die just in time to see his fortune dissipated by the said clerk and his sons left poor—in fact, it's rather commonplace; and when one of his sons becomes a *Sun* reporter, and so becomes acquainted with the ex-ballet girl, Terese, and her ("Daughter of the Tenements") Carminella, and the other son goes West and strikes a gold mine, you can't help thinking but that the writer had made it deuced easy sailing for both of them, that's all. When it develops that all of them are to "get along" lovely and

"The Literary Shower," *Ev'ry Month* 1 (February 1896): 10. Signed "Edward Al."

never want, and that Carminella is to become a great dancer on large salary, and that Tom Lyon, her young slum love, is to develop into a great newspaper artist without any "apparent effort," and eventually win her without any other "apparent effort," you begin to think that the novel is "sort of a good thing" all around for everybody. Then, when George Peyton, the son who went West and turned up the mine, also turns up Carminella's mother's first husband "Ettore," and sees him die safely before returning to New York and driving the "base deceiving" clerk, Mark Waters, to the wall, you realize that indeed it is a good novel—so good, in fact that nobody has any trouble at all with anybody, that is, worth talking about.

But for all this, "A Daughter of the Tenements" is still an interesting book, and although quite light, is never wishy-washy. It is by the same author as "Chimmie Fadden," and has some of the touches of curious humor and pathos that characterize those sketches of the Bowery boy. It's very New Yorkish in flavor, fearfully so. Mulberry Bend is spoken of continually, and the Bowery, Stanton Street, Broadway, Washington Square and Park Place are repeatedly mentioned, for local color's sake, no doubt. Then the Standard Theatre is brought in under the *nom de plume* of Mayfair and the Tivoli as plain old Tivoli. Frederic Remington, the *Harper* artist, and a number of newspaper men of the *Sun* staff, are easily recognized at one of the receptions described. Philip Peyton, the newspaper man, who drifts through the novel "on purpose" to help smooth over all little difficulties that may befall the others, and at the same time to sound the praises of the *Guardian* by which the *Sun* is typified, is a very fair representation of the author and on that account interesting. The old rivalry between the *Sun* and *World* is carried into the book, the latter being held up to general scorn under the name of the *Daily Sensation.** There is nothing more to be said of the book, except that it shows that the author has found that a vast difference exists between the conditions that make for novel writing and those that produce good character sketches. No doubt Mr. Townsend has worked hard on "A Daughter of the Tenements," and he has made an excellent start. Some day he will write as great a novel as "Chimmie Fadden" is a great sketch-book. But why call it "A Daughter of the Tenements" when she's not near the most important character in the book?

*The *World,* under Joseph Pulitzer, had challenged the *Sun,* under Charles A. Dana, for supremacy in New York journalism. Townsend's "Chimmie Fadden" sketches had appeared initially in the *Sun.*

[The Cause of Social Unrest]

Now that the bond issue has come and gone, as it were, no more is said of "great depression" and "financial stringency," and the deplorable state of the country.* The door of our national hut has been flung wide to the wolf and a huge chunk of flesh cast it, and it has gone its way growling with hungry joy. There has been a "popular" issue of bonds that is popular in name only. There has been a giving to those who have, and the taking away from those who have not is yet to come, for all things balance and everything works as a pendulum. The banks, the land over, have found a secure investment for their idle surplus, and the people will for the next thirty years pay the three and one half per cent interest which they demand for preserving the treasury. The 500 millionaires and 2000 semi-millionaires will rest comfortably— or will they?

"What is $50,000,000 or $100,000,000 to a great nation like the United States?" says one. "A mere drop in the bucket. What [are] one or two or five bond issues to us—the richest people on earth?"

Nothing, evidently, to us, the richest people. Nothing to the 500 millionaires who take the bonds and the 2000 semi-millionaires who find a profitable investment therein.

Nothing to this one, individually, or that one—scarcely a cent more taxes, yet there are those who cannot afford to pay the cent.

There ought to come some reflection shortly, some deep pondering, for we are careening along at a great rate, and our national ledger has not shown a balance sheet in years. Let it be remembered that, as in no other land, railroads, telegraph, telephone, express, lighting and water supply are in the hands of corporations, and it has come that a handful of millionaires can so stagnate business as to force the government to issue bonds to them for their safe investment. Let it dawn upon the masses that money invested in government bonds is safe so long as the govern-

"Reflections," *Ev'ry Month* 1 (March 1896): 2. Signed "The Prophet."

*See the headnote for "The Oligarchy of Wealth," p. 45.

ment stands, and that every energy of the government in times of peril is constrained to protect the investors in its financial stability. In other words, the government becomes "for and of" the possessor of her bonds. When it is figured out who the holders of bonds now are, it can be understood who are safe in the arms of our loving mother, Columbia.

Entrenched were the nobles of France in the grace and favor of their king, and unheard were the plaints of the poor, a century ago. The few who controlled the favors of the land did not know of the many who had absolutely nothing, until they rose from their misery in rage and were upon them like a pack of wolves. It never reaches the boudoirs of the wealthy that there are more rags than raiment in the land and more gloom than joy. It never sounds within halls of affluence that without are many with hate and unreason in their hearts who would have carnage rather than peace. It may sound foolish to phrase so gloomily, and yet there is vast social unrest at present, and never before has the world seen wealth gathering and entrenching itself so rapidly. If the government persists in selling its power to the wealthy in the form of bonds it will soon have need of the splendid militia it is so diligently fostering. The worm at the core is beginning to eat.

[The Culpability of American Newspapers]

The press of this country is a world in itself and as a world, quite unassailable, for there is no outer force capable of contending with its inner evil. People, as a rule, stand in fear of newspapers—that is, people whose affairs are sacred to themselves, and no one in private life can reasonably hope to cope with an organ of wealth and influence in a public one on its own ground, as it were. As a result of this condition newspapers have gone their way doing much as they pleased and people have continued to read them, glad to get the news at any price and putting up with much that is not news, nor even common sense, when it came printed on the same pages. They have observed newspapers grow and become vastly powerful, and they have beheld vanity, self-glorification and sensationalism creep in without being able to inveigh against them, because, as has been said, the press is a world to itself, and quite unassailable from without.*

In view of these evils and conditions, it is well that a reaction against sensationalism and vanity, against self-glorification and immorality has set in, not from without but from within the newspaper world itself. Certain papers have taken a decisive stand on [the] subject, and have begun to call their fellow-craftsmen vigorously to account. We hear much of "crime-sheets" and "sensation-mongers" and it is not novel to see a complete exposé of one journal's errors in another, and not always a rival journal's column at that. Newspapers in widely separated cities are beginning to take account of one another, and Chicago does not hesitate to arraign New York or St. Louis journals and *vice versa*.

This is good and to the interest of real news, as all must suspect, for there is an immense amount of sham about the newspapers of to-day, and a vast amount of wrong-doing. Some journals

"Reflections," *Ev'ry Month* 2 (May 1896): 2–3. Signed "The Prophet."

*Dreiser is no doubt alluding primarily to Pulitzer's New York *World* and Hearst's New York *American,* both of which had achieved large circulations and much power by means of sensational journalism.

work their way to prosperity by means of great parade of charity when really greed is the actuating influence. They make a great show of standing for the rights of the people, when they know that the majority of the battles which they begin are already won from the people and their outcry can work no harm. They make a great show of going into the police courts and justice shops to protect some helpless creature from arbitrary injustice, when as matter of fact, they know that they have selected their defendants with scrupulous business acumen, so as to entail the least amount of struggle while reflecting the largest amount of glory upon themselves. They espouse the cause of religion, not for religion's sake but to gain subscribers of a sanctimonious turn of mind. They challenge the cause of labor not with any especial desire to see it triumph, but from a desire to retain and gain labor readers. They stand for justice or injustice, truth or falsehood, wealth or the poor, according as the business office dictates and they aim to cater to as many elements as may be without conflicting them or injuring their own prestige and income.

Such is a portion of the newspaper world as we see it— exemplified in a hundred so-called bright, newsy journals. There are exceptions of course. Here and there are great men arrayed for this life's battle in editorial mail, who stand for right, charity, generosity and would not cater to a cause or an element though it brought them a mint of gold. Here and there are true men, just as they are in every cause, who are grand in their serene indifference to all save the true and pure as they see it, and to them the world stands indebted. But like poets and philosophers they are rare indeed while the temple of news is filled to overflowing with money changers of the most grasping, and rapacious kind.

[Genius and Matrimony]

More than one young man dreams of a brilliant future in these sharply contested days of business, and while there is no need to shower the cold water of experience upon him, some facts concerning life will prove entertaining if nothing more. There is many a brilliant young nobody, who at twenty-six years old imagines that he is dying unrecognized because he has not attained fame, nor the love of some bright, dashing, beautiful and wealthy girl. We all, more or less, dream that things are bound to come our way, because, in our heart we sincerely wish them. In fact a young man may be put down as rather tame who does not place himself, in dreams, upon a pedestal and weave crowns for his head, while he glories in the possession of the love of a young queen of fortune. In dreams it is easy to be a general, nay, an emperor, and many have been a Byron at one moment, only to realize that they were nobody, the next.

After such sport upon these pinnacles of human achievement it is usual that we become aware that all the real difficulties and steeps of life are yet to face. With some, exuberant self-esteem comes to their aid; they have that intense belief in *their destiny,* which perhaps amounts to genius in those who will not permit themselves to be distracted by contact with the world, as sheep that leave their wool on the briers of every thicket they pass by. They mean to cover themselves with glory, and to work in silence for the ideal sweet-heart whom they hope some day to possess. Women, for them, are resolved into a single type, and this woman they expect to meet, in the first that comes glancing into their eyes. In each and all they see a queen, and as queens must make the first advances to their lovers, they are expected by these innocents to draw near, to actually coax them, poor, unknown, oftentimes silly and shy, as they are. For her, who should take pity on genius, his heart holds in store such gratitude over and beyond love, as would insure her his sincere worship her whole life long. At least the youth possessed of genius, dreams this way of his future feelings for a delightful girl who should seek him out.

"Reflections," *Ev'ry Month* 2 (May 1896): 5–6. Signed "The Prophet."

But, it is this feeling that incurs the risk of them remaining companionless for good. The incomprehensible bent of women's minds appears to lead them to see nothing but the weak points in a clever man, and the strong points in a fool. They feel the liveliest sympathy with the fool's good qualities, which perpetually flatter their own defects; while they find the man of talent hardly agreeable enough to compensate for his shortcomings. All capacity is a sort of intermittent fever, and no woman is anxious to share in its discomforts only; they look to find in their lovers the wherewithal to gratify their own vanity. It is themselves that they love in men. But the artist, poor and proud, along with his endowment of creative power, is furnished with an aggressive egotism. Everything about him is involved in a whirlpool of ideas, and even the mistress of his heart must gyrate along them. How is a woman, high enough in the social scale to be spoiled with praise, to believe in the love of a man like that? Will she go to seek him out? That sort of lover has not the leisure to sit beside a sofa and give himself up to the sentimental simperings that women are [said] to be fond of, and on which the false and unfeeling pride themselves. He cannot spare the time from his work, and how can he afford to humble himself and go a-masquerading? He is ready to give up his life, once and for all, but he is not ready to degrade it in detail. Besides, there is something indescribably paltry in a stock broker's tactics, who runs on errands for some insipid, affected woman; all this disgusts an artist.

Love in the abstract is not enough for a great man in poverty; he has need of its utmost devotion. The frivolous creatures who spend their lives in trying on cashmeres, or making themselves into clothes pegs to hang the fashions from, exact the devotion which is not in them to repay. For them, love means the pleasure of ruling, not obeying. She who is really a wife, one in heart, flesh and bone, must follow wherever he leads, in whom her life, her strength, her pride and happiness are centered. Ambitious men need those oriental women whose whole thought is given to the study of their husband's requirements, yet ambitious men are usually the ones who are most hopelessly attracted by these other she-coxcombs. They wish to obtain a society belle, without money,—to scale the heavens without a ladder. Usually they are possessed of a wealth of knowledge, so imperfectly arranged in their youth (when they most dream of a gilded palace) that it stands a wealth which will not circulate. They are away in the city, without near relatives or friends, forging their way, and dreaming. They are in the midst of a lone and ghastly desert, one of paving stones, full of wealth, dignity, carriages; of animation, life and thought, wherein everyone is worse than inimical, is indifferent to genius. So there they must fight life's battle, there win, there lose—and if fortune, fame, a beautiful, sympathetic girl do not come to them, then, there suffer, repine and die.

[New York in May]

In the more crowded quarters of a city like New York, this particular period is deeply appreciated, one should judge, for now the narrow streets are neither gusty with bitter winds nor listless with suffocating heat. In the long summer to come, the hard paving stones will store up the heat so that night will bring no coolness, and morning no remembrance of delicious slumbers.

If there are poets living in some of these narrow, dreary confined little quarters they must find some sort of pleasure in observing the short-lived plant life of streets and gutters, where occasional weeds sprout between the stones, poor weeds that a storm soon washes away. They must find some charm in watching the street games of urchins, of hearing their songs and cries and now and then the melody from some distant organ. For them the dreary tinkle of the bells upon the street car-horses must become vaguely musical, as must the far off whistle of moving tugs and steamers, and of engines speeding through the night with their trains of cars.

The myriad shop lights, the patter of pedestrians upon the pavements below, the lolling creatures, talking from out the windows, the thin smoke curling from distant chimneys, the stars—these, blended, blurred, merged until none are distinct and all are softened, makes for them the city, such as it is, vast, sad, romantic, the city as it is, in May.

"Reflections," *Ev'ry Month* 2 (May 1896): 6. Signed "The Prophet."

[Stephen Crane's *The Red Badge of Courage*]

But if literary failures are always dreary and disagreeable to contemplate, all the more pleasant is it to chronicle true literary success.* There is no joy to be gained by pointing out the weak spots of writers who aspire to literary distinction. Sometimes, having been duped by some means or other into reading a miserable makeshift novel the spirit revolts, and one feels like saying[,] bitterly, truthful things, but that is only for the moment. None of the American critics are very severe, and it would surprise many to know how many really bad novels are allowed to pass with a sort of half praise, when in all justice they should have been left unnoticed or dismissed with crisp and concise contempt.

However, dismissing all this half-writing to the winds, it is pleasant to think of Stephen Crane and his splendid war story, *The Red Badge of Courage*. Here is a novelist for you, if you want an American; strong, incisive, bitter and brilliant, who has the genius which perceives and appreciates (without physical experience to any great extent) and which expresses sentiments that are nothing, if not the whisperings of an oversoul. He never could have witnessed personally what he writes of, and his heart is too young, too free and enthusiastic, to have ever raged with such wondrous fear and frantic terror as swells in the heart of his hero. This is not necessarily paradoxical for some hearts seem to grow out of graves of the anguished dead, and to throb with all the griefs and passions that went to the soil with the body when it ceased its toil and cares. It is not strange nor inconceivable, that in a land so torn by discord and battle as has been this union of ours; so haunted with memories of the many who went and never came back, who loved and fought, struggled and fell, and now lie in lone, uncared for graves, that there should rise a heart made up of the memories and bitterness of the past, and throbbing with a deep, innate sentiment for all

"Literary Notes," *Ev'ry Month* 2 (May 1896): 11–12. Signed "Edward Al."

*Crane's novel had been widely acclaimed both in America and England during the winter of 1895–96.

the old woes and old terrors. It is not strange, but rather to be expected, and Stephen Crane, the first, is not necessarily the greatest nor last, for the mighty woes of the rebellion have not yet dwindled into a song nor a story, either. Crane is brilliant, *The Red Badge of Courage,* a proud effort, but it is only *one* novel after all, and this earth has had its battles by scores and multi-scores, while the human heart has been wrung as only as the dead know or could tell, were they permitted to live again and speak.

[Balzac]

One of these [additional subjects requiring discussion] is the translation from French into English of all of the novels of Honoré de Balzac, the greatest of all French novelists, and at the sound of his splendid name, how the thought of our own little writers seems to pale. *There* was a novelist for you! There was a man who knew the human heart, proud, foolish, self-glorifying, self-abasing, and one who never ridiculed nor traduced it, but simply presented its trials and contentions, how it developed, loved, hated and died. Grand, gorgeous, self-conscious Balzac, the Alexander of literature, in whom romance and realism blend and become one! Oh, what a school are his novels to the well-balanced heart! What a revelation to the mind of its own vagaries! Here was a man who knew us, body and spirit; our every passion, our every whim. He it was who could make clear what men toil for; how pitifully they slave for fame, how weakly they struggle with it, when their efforts are crowned with success. He it was who pictured the young man's dream, the old man's skepticism, the fool, the cynic, the lover, the miser and the innate vagaries of a woman's heart. He knew what hunger means, what cold, and what shabby clothes to the proud heart. He knew how the lover worries, how the mother, and how the friend. The bed of sickness and the couch of luxury were alike familiar to him. Meetings, partings, the loss of the last penny at gaming tables, the gain of millions by one move; the pawning of a coat, a keepsake, a loved one's hair, for bread or medicine, were all familiar to that wondrous brain of his. Society, the poor, trades, professions, talents, were all well learned lessons with him, from which he drew his characters and his plots and upon which he based his moral reflections. Such was Balzac, of such his novels. Americans will do well to profit by them—but they will. His novels are the most remarkable of any in all the world.

"Literary Notes," *Ev'ry Month* 2 (May 1896): 12. Signed "Edward Al."

[Two Types of Men]

Dreiser's sketch of "a strong man" is a loose paraphrase of Walt Whitman's "I Sing the Body Electric," section 3. Whitman's lines begin, "I knew a farmer, the father of five sons."

Which is it better to be, a strong man with average knowledge or a weak man, with great knowledge—the latter as great mentally as the first is strong physically? This is not a question to decide by saying neither, or striking a golden mean and declaring that well balanced body and brain are best of all. Granting either proposition, as you choose, and retiring from the argument entirely, let us put the conditions to think about and suspend judgment.

Here is the strong man, say, the common farmer and father of five sons. Here he is, a man of wonderful vigor, calmness and beauty of person. The shape of his head, the richness and breadth of his manners, the pale yellow and white of his beard, the immeasurable meaning of his black eyes—these are all delightful. He is six feet tall, he is over eighty years of age, his sons are massive, clean, bearded, tan-faced and handsome. They, and his daughters love him, and all who see him love him, not by allowance but with a personal love. He drinks water only, and through the clear, brown skin of his face his pure blood shows scarlet.

He is a frequent gunner and fisher and loves his boat and fowling pieces. Going with his five sons and many grandsons to hunt and fish, you would pick him out as the most beautiful and vigorous of them all; you would wish long and long to be with him; that you might be near him and converse, touch his hand and enjoy the beam of his kindly eye. He would linger upon your fancy as a splendid man, until you met the other who is the intellectual man, physically weak.

He also is tall and wide of eye, but his shoulders are round and his head droops. His forehead is high, but sadly pale, and his eye large but dim, weak and downcast, as though the charms of

"Reflections," *Ev'ry Month* 2 (June 1896): 2–3. Signed "The Prophet."

nature were no longer apparent. He has no children of sturdy beauty, nor any appearance of commanding self-reliance. To him outdoor life is scarcely pleasurable, for he cares neither to hunt nor to fish, nor yet to stroll about, for his limbs fail him. While others move in real life, he dwells in the theoretical one, the life of fancy, memories, principles, which are beautiful but unfilled. Among his books he labors, reasoning away the false of life, establishing the principle of the true. To his fancy, the world once bright is now darkened by evils; to his taste the pleasures of life are dulled by the pain of others. He cares not for hunting, for the many cannot hunt; nor for fishing, for the many cannot fish, though they willed. Gold does not interest him; honors are as wearisome burdens; flattery, the piping voice of insects. While acknowledging pleasures as vanities, he still craves them for others. While spurning charity as such, or sympathy for his age and weakness, he still prays that charity and sympathy may become great factors in driving out the bitterness of life. Alone he walks, alone labors, alone dreams a great dream, working it out at the expense of his own body, his own life, for the pleasure of the many who are aweary and need rest.

Of the two, there being no happy medium, having no choice but one or the other, which would you be?

[The Struggle for Existence]

A western fruit grower has announced his belief that plants have certain senses, not strongly developed of course, but as much so as oysters and certain slugs and snails, and that they respond to kindness and attention as quickly as some animals of sluggish intelligence. Common as this knowledge has been for a long time to such scientists and philosophers as have made a study of the lower forms of creation in their endeavor to trace the growth and progress of the life principle from the beginning, it is a matter of much satisfaction to know this excellent intelligence is finally filtering through books, scientific periodicals, journals, and the daily press down into the minds of the common people where, like good seed, it is certain to take root and grow, and so bring the intelligence of the mass to a better comprehension of what life really means. If the knowledge that the life principle is the same in plants as in animals is once fully understood; if it becomes part of the commonest intelligence that plants are created, male and female, and come into existence the same as animals; that they have their courtship and love affairs in the mild form of attractions for one another, and that sometimes they will refuse to receive pollen from another plant of the same species, but will take it from another plant a greater distance away, for which it has an affinity, a greater reverence for all life forms will have come into the hearts of the people. When man works and gets himself food and clothing and a home, we call it intelligence. When a plant delves with its roots in the ground, or when it exudes a sweet, sticky substance that attracts and gathers bugs and flies, upon which it subsists, we call it instinct. If man is injured physically by another we call it crime, for he bleeds and moans and dies. If his intelligence is injured and he pines, or sorrows, we say he has been victimized or insulted, and we are moved to sympathy. Those who inflict wounds or insults upon their fellow men are to our eyes brutes and criminals. We forget, however, that when plants are injured that they show every evidence of pain. Cut them and they bleed. Wound

"Reflections," *Ev'ry Month* 2 (June 1896): 3–4. Signed "The Prophet."

their branches and they wilt. Disturb them and they fade and droop, and show every evidence of discouragement. Many plants are even sensitive to touch. Put your finger on them and they recoil like a frightened bird. Yet injuring them so is no crime in the sight of man, for with him nothing is wrong except where it affects an intelligence similar to his own. He acknowledges no sins except those which all his fellowmen acknowledge out of pure self-protection.

Nevertheless, if he will not acknowledge that his conduct towards the lower forms of life is wrong he will admit that he cannot progress through this world without injuring many things that lie in his path, from men to plants. In the first place he cannot be born without endangering a life, nor can he grow without wearying the patience and bringing the pain of labor to those who must have him in care. He cannot eat, but something must die, animals and plants, to make him food. He cannot keep warm but by robbing the cotton plant of its bloom, or the sheep of his wool. He cannot walk abroad but grasses and flowers must be ruthlessly crushed under his feet, and the humble stones worn to thinness. All must die that he may live—fruits, flowers, animals and vegetables. The very hills must be torn to give him homes of stone, and the forests destroyed that he may have the beauty of ornamental carving about him. He must step in where others have failed, crowd out the old and feeble, override the desires and hopes of others, who also wish for success, and so on, until death. This is the law, cold, hard immutable—the law of self-preservation, and upon it all must take their stand and press forward so or die. It is hard to think that such must be the condition of living, but nevertheless such it must be, and all honor to him who fights bravest but with as much charity and as many tears as the dread of failure will permit.

[Self-Preservation and Charity]

We hear much, each day, of men who are cruel, or tyrannical, or disagreeable, and so on, through the long catalogue of evils, and we pass judgment without much thought, condemnatory of course. We read much of the perverse independence of our fellow-citizens and anyone who spends much of his time outside, knocking up against all sorts and conditions of men, can usually testify as to what manner of treatment men and women serve one another in the rush of the day's affairs. "Every man for himself" has come to be a fond maxim with a majority, and he who is not either strong,—physically, or mentally, or financially—is pushed and jostled, shoved aside here and forgotten there, until timidity and despondence possess him and he is ready to weaken and flee, going, as the wounded animal goes, into some lone place to die.

It is quite true that to the victor belongs the spoils, and to the strong the race, but at the same time it is sad to think that to the weak and vanquished belong nothing. The law of preservation has been announced, and day by day we go about seeing it fulfilled in a thousand ways. Beggars are refused a penny because the possessor desires to preserve it, thinking to use it for some personal need. Work is withheld from anxious hands, because the one who has work to give feels the need of economy, preserving what he has to himself. Pleasures are withheld from the many, because pleasures can usually be sold in the form of admission, and so on.

In the face of this, one is inclined to exclaim that self-preservation has nothing to do with boorishness; that the need of struggling to preserve one's self from poverty is no excuse for inconsiderate conduct towards others, and yet, under existing circumstances, there is something to be said on this side also. We know that those who sprawl comfortably in a car, leaving others to stumble over their feet, are inconsiderate. We realize that women who obstruct the view of others at theatres by wearing huge headgear are self-engrossed to the extent of causing annoyance to others. We are fully aware that all who consult their own ease,

"Reflections," *Ev'ry Month* 2 (June 1896): 4–5. Signed "The Prophet."

leaving inferiors or those who have no particular claim upon them to wait or stand, or come after unnecessarily, are either vain or cruel, or dead to sentiment and decency in the true meaning of these terms.

The well balanced man, strong in body, sturdy in brain and of an equable temperament, is alive to the obligations so effectively implied in the Golden Rule. His dignity does not demand that others wait about his door while he amuses himself with some trifle. His ease is not disturbed by the things which may be trifling to him, but of considerable importance to others. His honor is never sullied by contact with the meanest of we things called men.

It follows that all men are not well balanced, and no wonder. How frail is man, veritably vermin upon the face of so great a globe, and in so boundless a universe. We find his race sickly and disturbed by a thousand ills. We have his weakness evidenced in the vast asylums and hospitals, the wondrous tribe of doctors, and the marvelous trade of drugs. We see more in the weaklings who line our thoroughfares, the maimed, the halt, the blind and the deformed. We gather it from the pale and wan about us, sometimes distant sometimes dear, and from death that lays its hand, ever and again, on some one close to our side, before our very eyes. As we grow, we realize and abjure vanities, knowing that all are frail and many are foolish, and that we, too, shall suffer the miseries of age—being pushed aside and half forgotten, for from this neither wealth nor fame can save us.

And when we realize once and quite fully how weak are men and how erring; when we understand that sorrow can upset their reason, and want turn their brain, we will be more impressed with that "Do unto others," which now seems trite but which will then come to be a great philosophy after all. We will learn to remember that most of us eat in a hurry and in disagreeable places, dwell in chill and bare rooms, slave in great shops and mills, and are debarred from books and pleasures. Then will we sometimes reflect that all may not have tasteful surroundings nor elegant companions, and so may not be always graceful, smiling and contented. We will come to realize that there are hard grim forces at work day after day, warping and moulding our brothers, and making them queer creatures, and in this realization our sneers will melt to sympathy. We will simply obey our code and commandments. Don't lie, don't steal, don't be wilfully cruel to any living creature. For all else a man is still a man however often he may fail.

65

[The Decadent School]

Public revulsion against Wilde, Beardsley, and the "school" of literature and art associated with the Yellow Book *reached a high point in May 1895, when Wilde was found guilty of homosexual offenses and sentenced to two years in prison. Beardsley had served as art editor of the* Yellow Book *and had also illustrated Wilde's* Salome.

One of the best illustrations of the truth that all shams are self-destructive and that make-believes cannot for long retain the interest of those who are true and right-hearted, is just now being consummated in the decadence of the recent school in art and literature, which for want of better names might well be called the "weird" and "obscure" schools. Last year every one was talking about the peculiar black and white drawings of Aubrey Beardsley, and praising their strength and effectiveness, and every one said what wonderful things they were and how talented Mr. Beardsley was, and how art in general was sure to be affected, changed and improved by his work. So great was this enthusiasm that it became a subject of sad wonder as to what was to become of Mr. C. D. Gibson and his beautifully natural drawings, and Mr. George du Maurier and his, and Chéret, and all the other natural French artists and their work. And while all this talking was going on and everybody was wondering, Mr. Beardsley was vigorously "drawing away" at a great rate, and Mr. Bradley was beginning to imitate Mr. Beardsley, and Mr. Hazenplug was beginning to imitate both of these, and a host of little artists everywhere were springing up and beginning to imitate everything and anything that looked crude and weird, until it seemed for awhile as though drawing had really been revolutionized, and that Mr. Aubrey Beardsley was a true prophet in the art world. The country was flooded with strange posters and pictures; the magazines were strong with descriptive chapters concerning the strange pictures, and a host of small fry periodicals sprang up with no other claim to distinction than that

"Reflections," *Ev'ry Month* 2 (June 1896): 5. Signed "The Prophet."

they were illustrated after this peculiar new art fashion and contained reading which no one could understand—and the art craze was "on" in the widest sense.

About this time the weird and obscure in literature reached its flood. Young persons in all parts of the country, who were anxious to succeed, and were ready to crawl through any cranny or loophole up into the sunlight of note and literary prosperity, began to write as strange and recklessly as they possibly could in the hope of being able to sign and sell their matter to the new school of periodicals. It looked for awhile as though these artists and strange writers were really brighter and better than others, and that those who could not understand them were inferior in intelligence. Not being able to understand them, people were awed, which is, primarily, the influence of all great truths and shams upon the intellect. Only time, bringing familiarity with them, can dissolve these first illusions and prove whether that which is so new and curious is really harmful or of value.

Time has worked on the new art and the new literature. What was strangely obscure has now become ridiculous affectation, and what was so peculiarly weird has become vain distortion. People are no longer wondering; they are no longer awed. From the wooden idols the gilt has worn off, disclosing the tawdry imitation. Beardsley is no longer a nine day's wonder. Wilde no longer a preacher of higher knowledge. New art drawings do not sell, and half of the peculiarly *fin de siècle* periodicals have passed away because no one bought them. Gibson is still great. So also is du Maurier. Hundreds have not imitated them. Their art has not become a fad. Neither have the writings of Kipling, or Caine, or Garland. Why?

[Suicide]

It may be well said that it is so common a thing to-day to read of suicides, that to speak of the reasons which compel men to it is to almost impose upon common intelligence with something that is as unimpressive as a tale that is told. Men die so numerously and under such widely different conditions that nothing concerning methods would be interesting. It is in the philosophy of it that we find the strangeness—the wonderful fact that the human brain can calmly contemplate its own annihilation. That men have not courage to face unfortunate conditions; that they dare not await naturally that death which they seek suddenly by poison or the pistol, is that which makes the contradiction in suicide—the strange paradox of reason which can say "I will be brave and end my misery now!" Surely nothing else in life is so remarkable and so inconceivable in the abstract as this.

And yet, from the suicide's standpoint, from the mental vantage ground of the weary, disheartened, and wounded creature who has no place to turn, no where to go; who walks miserable and unfriended as if he were in some desert, elbowed by men whom he cannot see, undone by conditions which he cannot control or avoid; who is tasting of the last dregs in the cup of life and feels the numbing influence of its poison—from his standpoint there is something to say. Vehement must be the storms which compel a soul to seek for peace from the trigger of a pistol—cruel the path of his progress that can lead him to see nothing but ineffable content at the bottom of some noiseless stream.

How much young power starves and pines away in the garrets of these great cities of ours for want of a friend, for lack of a woman's consolation, and that, too, amid millions of fellow creatures, in the very presence of a listless crowd quite burdened by its wealth! How many hearts are discontented, how many efforts made all vain by the hard, cold system that gathers all and gives nothing! Between the time when the voices of abundant hopes call a young man to the city, and his later desponding self-sought death,

"Reflections," *Ev'ry Month* 2 (June 1896): 5–6. Signed "The Prophet."

God only knows what may intervene. Great ideas have contended within that soul perhaps, poems have swelled the heart and been set sadly aside, moans and despair repressed, masterpieces proved abortive, endeavors vain! When one remembers all this, suicide looms large.

"Yesterday," says the papers, "at three o'clock, a young man threw himself in the East River from the pier at the foot of Thirty-fourth street," and where will you find a work of genius floating above the seas of literature that can compare with such a paragraph. Dramas and romances pale before this concise and common metropolitan phrase. Such a creature may have wandered about all day until that hour, hoping vainly against hope, only to fully realize at last that there was nothing, nothing more, except to go. Carriages may have jingled past impressively, and richly garbed creatures alighted here and there, bent upon expenditures as large and reckless as they are shallow and vain. He may have glanced through gorgeous shop windows, upon wealth of endless value; may have studied the gems in the jeweler's window, the laces in the cloth fanciers, the luxury of books here, the wealth of bric-a-brac there, all barred by polished glass, and at last sadly realized that all was as distant as paradise, as impossible to him as wings. He may have fixed upon the fortunate fair stranger a gaze as wistful and eager as man can give, only to receive in exchange an indifferent glance, such as lights by accident upon a passer by. For him, then, as for all such, would come the leave taking of love, and interest and life, and while he went slowly to his self-acknowledged doom, realizing that while his strenuous, questioning, despairing glances had been neither understood nor felt by the hundreds who had swept past, gayly content—he was actually perishing for want of aid.

But pshaw! what is it to the rich? what is it to anyone? these last despairing glances of the unfortunate poor. One more piece of adulation given, think they; one more sigh of envy caused by the sight of their glory; one more thought created, of how splendid they are, and then that night, while the suicide sleeps with his head upon the weeds beneath the stream, they sink to their splendid couch sighing "How well I looked this day; how splendid, indeed, am I."

[F. Hopkinson Smith's *Tom Grogan*]

Mr. F. Hopkinson Smith—painter, writer, contractor and connoisseur of art matters generally—possesses the pleasurable habit of writing from notes and close observation, for which reason his sketches and short stories are usually interesting. When he does water-colors he resorts to scenes that have long held his fancy, and faithfully copies them. When he thinks of a short story he thinks along the line of his contracting experience, which involves the grimy laboring man, the hard-working wives and daughters of the same, and the muddy-faced, often sickly, little children of laborers, who are blessed but little and suffer much. Like many another student of life, Mr. F. Hopkinson Smith does not clearly see what is to be done for the very poor whom he employs, and he does not agree with the methods employed by the leaders among the poor to improve themselves. Like all other scholars of this life he is mentally at sea, knows no scheme but the levelling process of time, and the ameliorating influence of education. Until the sentiments of men are so elevated and made tender by knowledge, until each one realizes unto himself what "unkind," "cruel," and "inhuman" mean, so long will the condition of the poor remain a bitter condition, and suffering the greater element in life. The remedy is in the improvement of their mental condition and the invention of processes that will do away with the brutalities of the meaner forms of labor.

In this spirit Mr. Smith has written a sentimental, effective little story called *Tom Grogan* (Houghton, Mifflin & Co.), which describes some conditions which competition among the laboring classes involves, without offering any suggestions as to how the conditions may be remedied. He pictures Tom Grogan as a woman who, having lost her husband and having two children and an aged father dependent on her, takes her husband's name and manages his hauling business as best she can. She contracts with sea-wall builders, breweries, and village contractors generally, about Staten Island, to do such stone, coal and dirt hauling as they have to do, and makes out her bids in the name of Tom Grogan, until everyone comes to know her by that appellation.

"The Literary Shower," *Ev'ry Month* 2 (June 1896): 21. Signed "Edward Al."

[*Smith's* Tom Grogan]

Of course, the effect upon her nature was marked. She became huge, rough, and brawny; her manner one of good-natured bravado, with which she ruled her men. She had a mighty fist and a powerful arm, and did not mind standing in sun or rain to superintend her portion of work, where anything was being constructed. Such a character naturally stirs interest in the tale.

However, she was hiring drivers at less than union rates, and taking contracts for hauling at eight and ten cents per load less than others. This cutting furnished the excuse for the hostility of Daniel McGaw, who wanted to crowd her out and secure her hauling trade. By the aid of the *union* he stirred up a general clamor against her, and, finding that unavailing, laid a veritable Clan-na-gael plot—*a la* Chicago and the sad fate of Dr. Cronin.* To head her off from securing a pending local hauling contract which McGaw wanted, the latter had her barn fired, and two horses were burned to death. Seeing this did not deter her, he even went so far as to have another horse of hers poisoned about dusk, and then, when she came to the barn to see about it, he was in the shadow with a hammer, ready to tap her on the head. Though she was supposedly left for dead, her heavy hood protected her, and she arrived before the contracting board just in time to receive her contract for the work.

Natural as this story runs, it winds up wrong. Tom Grogan comes out successful and McGaw, Quigg, Lathers and the union, which Mr. Smith mercilessly scores, are foiled. While the facts are evidently drawn from some experience of his as a contractor, still one cannot help but feel that poor Tom, being a woman, should have been outwitted and killed in her efforts to earn an honest living. It is the way of the world as per every day evidence. That the tale winds up pleasantly for Tom simply proves the tenderheartedness of Mr. Smith and not the rule of living.

As the characters are all Irish, Mr. Smith will have to answer personally for any seeming aspersions cast.

---

*The clan-na-gael was a secret Chicago society devoted to the cause of Irish freedom. Dr. R. H. Cronin of Chicago, who had denounced its leaders for misappropriating funds, was found murdered in May 1893.

71

[New York as a Literary Center]

Richard Harding Davis, of whom considerable is heard now, along with the younger writers, rather retains the habits that characterized his reportorial days upon the newspapers of the metropolis. He is one of the many literary men employed by one of the older publishing houses and very frequently is compelled to pack his grip and hie himself to some foreign shore. He was to have traveled to Greece during the early spring, there to witness the revival of the Hellenic games, but he did not go, and now contemplates remaining for the summer in New York. Despite its lack of sylvan charms and regardless of its hard, cramped, stony aspect, New York still grows in literary popularity, its latest acquisition being young Percival Pollard and his *Echo,* and Bliss Carman and his *Chap-Book*[,] both recently of Chicago.* Trade, the facilities for buying and selling paper that has been written on, is what draws, and this magnetism neither Richard Harding Davis nor any other literary aspirant can resist. In other words, if you have it in you to be great you must come to New York.

"The Literary Shower," *Ev'ry Month* 2 (June 1896): 21–22. Signed "Edward Al."

*Pollard did bring his little magazine *Echo* to New York in 1896, but Bliss Carman, though a contributor to the *Chap-Book,* was never an editor of it, and the magazine never moved from Chicago to New York.

[Journalism and the Writer]

Newspapers take a delight in pointing out, immediately some writer dies, as for instance the late H. C. Bunner, that he began life in a newspaper office, or was a bright reporter on such and such a journal, where his abilities first received encouragement.* It is all very well for the newspapers and does not detract from the truth in the least, but people should not draw from such instances that newspapers, particularly, foster genius. On the contrary the ability of a man to work and do something in this world receives such a cold shock by the great grind of a daily paper, his endeavors to aid himself here and there by an hour of application are so broken in upon and nullified by constant demands for his service by the paper, that he becomes usually disheartened and decides that either he must fail in his ambition or rise into something that will give him more leisure. Genius struggles up. Talent often lingers and wears itself out in journalism unheard of.

"The Literary Shower," *Ev'ry Month* 2 (June 1896): 22. Signed "Edward Al."

*Bunner, a popular short story writer, died on May 11, 1896.

[The Jury System]

Recently a man subpoenaed to serve on a jury in New York City was roughly ordered from the court-room by a judge called McAdam because he gave as his reason for not wanting to serve on a jury that he did not believe in the jury system. His plain, and to him reasonable view, was taken as an insult to the Republic generally, and the matter was hailed in the papers as something wonderful. Judge McAdam, it is true, was moderately censured; but the odium of the incident was cast entirely upon the citizen, who could so sin against heaven and nature as to live in a country with whose jury system he did not agree.

The incident re-emphasizes the fact that many are truly dissatisfied with the entire legal arrangement of this country, and particularly with the time-honored plan of calling twelve men to pass upon the evidence for and against an accused citizen. They are constantly working to reform and improve the jury system, when, as a matter of fact, the system cannot be improved. It is old and established, and has reached the limit of its usefulness, so that the only thing to do in the matter is not to reform but abolish. Never was there another relic of the feudal ages so fortunate in retaining the blind, unreasoning support of the people, nor was there ever anything so utterly subversive of the rights it was invoked to maintain.

The jury system, as exemplified in actual daily practice throughout the United States, in courts of every degree of decorum, is a rank and outrageous mockery. It is the most expensive appendage of our judicial system, and its results are the most worthless. It is above all things a breeder of bribes, a refuge of ignoramuses, a castle from which to work in safety any sort of injury—a useless, idiotic, malice-infested, and ghost-supported pest. There has not been a litigant in the past fifty years who was profited the weight of an honest penny by the intervention of a jury, whereas the litigants who have suffered are named legion. Through it all the public has sat by, patient and suffering beyond all

"Reflections," *Ev'ry Month* 2 (July 1896): 2–4. Signed "The Prophet."

bounds of reason, while paying the larger portion of the expense of the iniquity.

Not without reason are these charges made. Absolutely a jury is helpless, except to work injury. It is more powerful than armies to do wrong, and at the same time the most contradictory and anomalous thing civilized man ever contemplated soberly. A jury is the judge of evidence, yet the court can order a certain verdict, and may set a verdict aside if it is not in accordance with the evidence! The jury is a co-ordinate branch of the court, yet the judge may send a juryman to jail—or all of them, if he likes, because they refuse to recognize him as a superior! Jurymen are the "bulwark of American liberties," the "safeguard of freemen," the chosen "peers," and yet they may be bullied and brow-beaten and insulted and ordered about by every little scrap of a lawyer who can borrow his way to a diploma.

As a matter of fact, few men are tried by their peers, and few cases see a jury of qualified or competent men in the box. Imagine the average jury trying the case between Hetty Green on the one side, and the numerous skilled claimants to some of her property on the other—a suit involving the closest mathematical calculations, an acquaintance with big affairs, a knowledge of men and laws in various parts of the country—a case, in short, involving millions.* And yet this sort of thing goes on every day. Lawyers invariably choose the weakest, nonopinionated, most imbecile creatures that can be had of a special venire of ten thousand, and the rag-tag and bob-tail get into the jury box by a system that, like the peace of God, passeth all understanding. It is paid a price which wouldn't begin to hire competent men. Evidence which not a man of the twelve is capable of understanding is douched upon the jury for days and weeks at a stretch. Matters of the nicest balancing are given for this indifferent body to determine. No wonder the old lawyer said if there was anything God Almighty didn't know, it was what verdict an American jury would bring in. The situation is really stupendously ridiculous, or something else to that effect, and reason fails to follow the idiocy in all its wondrous ramifications.

But it is in criminal trials that the gravest injustice is done. Now, as in civil trials the rights of each party are equally sacred, so in criminal trials the public is as much entitled to consideration as

*During 1895 Hetty Green, who had inherited a large estate, successfully fought off a number of law suits attacking her inheritance.

is the man accused. Absolutely, if guilty, the man should be punished, and the measure of his guilt should be the measure of his punishment. There should be no guesswork about it. But the jury after being selected in a dark, mysterious way, is placed in the box, and the lawyers whet their wits upon the twelve. Everybody knows it is going to be a show, and consequently the court is filled to overflowing with people troubled by an undue craving for sarcasm. All the papers send their "funny-men" and caricaturists, while the public generally gaps agog and passes the good news around that the lawyers are going to have some fun out of the matter. When it does begin, the jurors are immediately accused, covertly, of using undue influence to get on the jury, of being there for a sinister purpose, of desiring to do anything rather than be fair minded and honest. A talesman cannot get up and knock a lawyer down. He would be put in jail for contempt instead of being liberated for manliness. And yet, what can the lawyer do? He knows that only by treating every juror as a scoundrel can he hope to get the services of an honest man. Isn't it the height of all things ridiculous?

There are unnumbered cases of perjury and bribe-taking by jury-men. Jury corrupters have been chased to Canada so often that the thought of it gives rise to jokes in the comic weeklies. One man was chased to Canada several years ago because everyone knew he was corrupting juries and had made a living at it for forty years. There are half-a-dozen men in every city in the country who can get a jury to acquit or save (by disagreement) any man who has money to pay them for their services. The friends of these men are beyond the reach of punishment. Many cities *boast* lawyers, who will to an absolute certainty secure an acquittal or disagreement if they can come into the case before the jury is drawn. Some of them can come into a case the day the panel is called, and guarantee a disagreement at least. Scandals without number illustrate a far worse condition than is here described.

Of what good is the jury? How does it help the ends of justice? Where can it, even if it were ideal, do a single thing better than can the judge? Is there an objection to trusting your life, your liberty, or your fortune to any single human intelligence? Very well; but one man decides it anyway. All twelve must agree or there is no verdict. It were too much to describe how they arrive at a verdict sometimes; but that golden calf, a verdict, there must be or the whole work must be done over. Any *one man* of the twelve may *prevent it!*

There was a reason for juries when they came. When Magna

Charta was signed a jury really stood for something. It did protect the freeman. It did represent the average intelligence. It was not subject to brow-beating, money-purchased, legal sharps. Again, the judges are different now. They are far more intelligent, far more cultured, far better informed, certainly as unprejudiced, and surely as honest as any average jury ever seen in a box. If the rule should fail when the reason fails, why should the jury system outlive all apology, and survive every attribute save that of ill-fame[?] Why, moreover, should a citizen be driven from a court because he does not believe in such a system? Surely the learned judge has sinned against liberty and reason if he never sinned before.

[Problem Novels]

Problem novels may be defined as novels in which a lot of difficulties are propounded, which the author cannot explain himself. They are very recent affairs and go hand-in-hand with problem plays, only the latter have been driven by insufficient patronage on the part of the public from the stage. Similar treatment will soon rid us of the problem novel, for which all may offer devout thanks.

The latest freak of this kind is known as *The XIth Commandment,* by Halliwell Sutcliffe, and its boom was started in England, where it was commended as a powerful study and one destined to cause a stir. This commendation in England produced its invariable complement commendation in America, and the American publishers (New Amsterdam Book Company) are consequently expecting a goodly sale of copies. In the novel a number of girl sweethearts are pictured as very superior and commendable in their ideas of loving, and in their conduct towards their respective lovers. They are described as loving in a calm, powerful way (very suggestive of girls with brows bulging with infinite knowledge and wisdom) and of ignoring conventional bonds such as those of shy simplicity, and due trepidation in the presence of their fiancees. They are shown in the light of personal rights philosophy, especially the principal young lady character who is used to point the moral and adorn the tale. This particular young lady, Beatrice Doneholme, has a father whose record is quite unsavory, and of this record she knows something; she therefore figures out that his opinions and advice generally deserve to be disregarded. When in the course of several long drawn chapters she meets an ultra-respectable young collegian, and in several other long drawn chapters falls in love with him, she calmly decides to disregard all parental objections, and even goes so far as to burn a letter from her father in which he takes occasion to object and to point out that a marriage with a poor young man is not desirable. Furthermore, she carries herself in a smart, "I am above common clay" kind of

"The Literary Shower," *Ev'ry Month* 2 (July 1896): 24. Signed "Edward Al."

way, doesn't think anything of secret meetings or the opinions of others, and is, in fact, entirely strong and self-sufficient, after the fashion of the new women we hear so much about.

It is my opinion that a good many honest, well meaning and thoroughly experienced people are thoroughly sick of this idea which is being harped upon so much in novels of late. They are weary of the idiocy of writers who are always trying to cover up the human element in human beings and showing love as a high, thoroughly reasonable and philosophical affair. They are not enthused by descriptions of girls who are invariably reasoning about everything, when they have met only women who are sweet in their unreasonableness. They are inclined to believe that a little dabbling in half-understood philosophy is hopelessly mixing the ideas common to average minds and that neither authors nor women know very much about human nature, when they write novels to show that love is a discussable, and a matter to be calmly reasoned about.

Most people who know anything of women know that the more staid and trustful they are the more lovable they are, and that only a man of weak intellect can endure a woman of the philosophical, determined, Mary Ellen Lease kind.* Most men love a dainty, affable, common-sense little woman, with some vanity and some foibles, who believes trustingly in the promises of her lover and would be heart broken if he were untrue to her, and who further believes in fulfilling the natural capacities of women and not in running after a lot of schemes of reorganizing the world and putting love on a higher basis.

As for Mr. Halliwell Sutcliffe, he is away off on a good many things, one of which is his diction and another his philosophy. In his book there is too much babbling of time worn odds and ends of philosophy, not well-enough put together to make a system and not short and decisive enough to adorn a tale. He has badly mixed his plot, and his suggestions for human guidance, so that we realize that they are not artfully blended—an excellent way of making a novel dull and disagreeable. He has evidently secured his thoughts of spirituality in love from poets and mystics like Goethe and Carlyle, where it can be found in a very confused and unstable state. If he had gathered love's meaning from hard [merciless] teachers like Spencer, Huxley and Hume, his story would not sound so unnatural and meaningless—or better still he would not have written it at

*Mrs. Lease was a famous Populist orator.

all. Like all other authors who write problem stories he seems beset with a wearisome desire to do things that no one else has done, to change human nature (when it won't change) instead of depicting it as it is. Like "Ideala," "Heavenly Twins," "Yellow Aster," and a hundred others the book's chapters are filled with bright chatter, but no detail—no action.* Life is action and actions point their own morals better than any reasoning about them can do. If the actions are wrong they will bring their own dramatic bitterness, if right their own joy—better all plot and no philosophy or vice versa, than an irrational arrangement of the two, without combining and blending them nicely. Lastly the moral aspect of courtship and marriage is as old as heat itself and will not change any faster than heat is changing and the earth is cooling. In other words Mr. Halliwell Sutcliffe's reasonings upon the subject is so much wasted energy, as are the reasonings of the hundred other very progressive people who are worrying about it.

Ideala (1888) and *The Heavenly Twins* (1893) by Sarah Grand (pseudonym of Mrs. Frances McFall) and *A Yellow Aster* (1894) by Kathleen M. Caffyn were all mildly feminist novels.

[A New York City Tragedy]

In this world of struggle and discontent nothing so tends to alleviate one's digust with one's own condition as the honest contemplation of the condition of others. It is not by reading that this can be done, for reading begets a false sentiment, nor by retiring within one's self, as it were, and there brooding; but by going out among the people and into the places where misery gathers. Every city has its countless dramas and tragedies of suffering, as has every town and village—yes, and every home. One need not go far, in fact cannot, for the things which are fit to soften the heart and make tender the hardened spirit are at every turn and by every path and while sentiment may be a bad thing generally, sympathy is not, and no heart can do itself or the world harm by being in constant beat with all others, no matter how low or how high. Therefore it would be well if each sought out the by-places and shadow spots in life, and in them studied the conditions and the aspirations of their occupants, and endeavored to do something for them.

It is curious that more misery does not show itself upon the pages of the daily newspapers, when one realizes that no day is without its shadow somewhere. It is curious and yet explainable because it requires talent to perceive true suffering and talent, also, to write of and describe it, and when the newspaper world is sifted so very much talent is not discoverable after all. Usually the more spirited writers on papers are assigned to the more fanciful matters of daily life, while the care of small courts and police-stations, where the largest amount of suffering bubbles up and subsides again, are left to the less talented reporters, or beginners, in the journalistic school. These, when a fitful tale shows itself, either have not the heart to appreciate, or lack the ability to describe, or they are lazy or indifferent, or hardened by long labor in the same field. Once in a while a young beginner gets hold of a "good, sad story," as the journalistic phraseology will have it, and then a tale sees the light, fresh from the haunts of misery and woe, and people

"Reflections," Ev'ry Month 2 (August 1896): 6. Signed "The Prophet."

wonder that such sorrow can exist, and even doubt, laying it all to newspaper enthusiasm, which is synonymous to-day with newspaper untruth.

One such story appeared during the past month in one of the New York papers, and it concerned a woman who was very poor, whose husband was a wandering vagabond, and whose dwelling-place was a cell of [a] room, bare, unodorous, and dark. This creature was sick and weak, and while she was physically unfit to support herself she had a child to care for and that was enough to fire her strength, though it could not increase nor preserve it. And this woman, when hunger threatened, left her pallet and hunted for work, finding it, after a time, in a rag shop, where by sorting fourteen long hours out of twenty-four, she could earn a few cents, not more than forty, a day, and so managed to live. But after a time even strength to earn this much failed her, and one night she crept homeward—weak, fevered, blind with pain and unable to climb the long flights of steps that led to her tenement lodging. There she lingered, sick and helpless, before her own doorstep, and there they found her, prone and dying, after a time, with a great, wealthy city lying all about her, and the roll of carriages and the laughter of the idle within an arrow's flight away.

All day the body of the dead woman lay there on its mattress in the heat, and the little, grimy, half naked children of the tenants came and played about the doorway, not thinking of the pitiful thing within. The others in the house who had known her stepped in to look at the body and express in crude fashion their sympathy and sadness, and to question how it happened. But there was no one to feel deep sorrow for the dead. And then late in the afternoon the coroner's wagon came and took the body away.

Such at least is the story and such the woe which now and then sees day; but, of course, this is only one case, and our human hearts are small, so we need not worry.

[Strength and the Struggle for Existence]

In a number of his minor poems Walt Whitman beautifully emphasizes the need of being strong, of entering the race with sturdy, fleet limbs, and flesh fair and sweet, and now a younger bard, Ernest McGaffey, is singing the praises of the mighty and urging the weak to retire from the thronged highway of life, and seek the gloom where a single shadow shall suffice them. It is eminently needful that men should cultivate their muscles these days; that they should grow tall and solid, and that the bloom of health should be upon their cheeks. As industries become more and more confining, the strain upon bodies become more and more wearing, until, but for wondrously well preserved physiques, the many would sink to early graves and be entirely forgot. As the arts, sciences, inventions and systems become more and more complex, it is patent that much tried brains should have fine muscles and nerves, fed by leaping blood, to sustain their weariness.

All know that in a crowd it is the athlete with steady step and masterful eye who attracts attention; and in love, the weak are ever despised. Fair women turn their bewitching glances softly upon the physical princes of men, leaving the weak, pale and sentimental to go their way unnoticed.

Fair women! Ah? that is the gall and wormwood in the life-cup of those who by birth or folly find themselves handicapped in the great life struggle. It is the knowledge that ravishing dreams of beauty—women—turn ever to the rich, the strong, the beautiful, and that those who fail in any form of development are left to fight the battle of life unloved and unfriended, alone, that stabs.

And yet, admitting all—that the weaklings are disagreeable, uninteresting, wearisome, and that the strong in their manifest independence to charity and sympathy are deserving of admiration—the failures in this world are not to blame for their condition. They did not make the environment in which they were born; they could not regulate the early influences which prevailed over them.

"Reflections," *Ev'ry Month* 2 (August 1896): 6–7. Signed "The Prophet."

Poverty: it was not of their making. Ignorance: it was there to thwart their earliest aims. Good companionship: it was denied them. The pleasures of respectability in clothes, pocket-money, home decorations—how sadly they were lacking! The help of tenderness, sympathy, advice—how remarkable were they for their absence.

Can we complain because men, coming up from such drear, lack-lustre childhoods are hard? Can we complain because they are bitter, cynical, sad spirited? Can we decry them for their mad anxiety to obtain the luxuries of life, though we realize that their dwarfed, broken, perverted intelligence will never be able to comprehend the right use of luxuries, nor enjoy them properly? Can we do anything but pity and endeavor to stay them in their own ruthless course, doing more injury than they received?

Admire the strong we must. Before youth and health and strength make way—upon the victor's brow place the laurel; but to these human results of early miseries and deprivations we can extend a charitably regulating hand, while we go down into the childhood of to-day and do what we can. Neglect the infants much longer we dare not, else we imperil the ultimate life of the race itself.

[Man's Insignificance]

What a world this is of ours, anyhow. What a ball of earth, indeed, and how we grovel from birth to death. We wonder at the almost countless numbers of men, and yet we have only to stoop to see the countless grass at our feet. We wonder at the variety of our emotions and sentiments, where sometimes we take the variety of colors and odors in plants and flowers as a matter of course. We wonder at the boundless, limitless desire within our hearts to be omnipotent in everything, of everything, when we utterly fail to take cognition of the constant lap of the sea on the shore. It, too, is bounded like us; beats mournfully and ceaselessly, as though it would cover all the land, be all in all. We walk misunderstood, each to himself a world; immeasurably deep, immeasurably potent, unknown in his fullness and capacity to all save his maker.

How vain is man; how useless; how mean. He will not recognize his brother because, almost unknown to himself, it is a law that he cannot. One says, "Ah, I am not hard. I love, I do not hate, I give freely and without thought;" but he does not say, "How do I live?" If he would ask, "Am I poor? Am I ill-clothed[?] Am I hungry? Am I lacking in strength, insight, personal beauty?" he would ask some things that would modify his goodness and make his charity look mean. Men do not give except from the fullness of their coffers; they do not love but from the fullness of their passions; they do not so much as hate except from greed of their own peace. And yet, these are they among whom we dwell; they whom we love, hate, aspire to, and imitate. This is the world—great, round, non-conjecturable, non-explainable—a world of beauty or deformity according as we are beautiful or deformed, in flesh and spirit. This is the world of which we are as nothing—so small that we cannot even conjecture our position in it, the meaning of our life, the trend of our efforts. This is it—at once great and small, and we are born, struggle and die in it, leaving no trace, taking hence no knowledge. Surely the lever that moves the Universe is pain.

"Reflections," *Ev'ry Month* 2 (August 1896): 7. Signed "The Prophet."

[Reading for Self-Improvement]

Let this not be taken as an attack upon novel reading, but suppose you are reading novels. The natural inference is that you read to become wiser, although there is the exception of those who read for pleasure only, but they are few, and life was not arranged for pleasure seekers. If you read to grow wise any sort of reading is commendable because you cannot read long in any direction without encountering some truths that are just as well for you to know, and better. It is commendable, this reading, but only from a general standpoint. From the dogmatic one, namely that this life needs to be improved, and that you are a part of life and therefore need to improve yourself as much as possible so as to keep in touch with the trend of the universe, any sort of reading is not commendable. From this point only the highest form of literature is commendable—the kind of literature from which you can draw a moderate inference as to what the privilege of living imposes upon you.

Do not imagine that hereupon follows a call for you to read the classics of Greece and Rome, or the old masters of Europe; not at all. Do not think for an instant that Shakespeare, Milton, and the lesser poets are to be here fervently commended to you—not in the least. You need not read any of them unless you choose, forever and ever, and in fact it would be wise for you not to try, unless you have given some thought to more specific forms of knowledge.

Supposing, for instance, that instead of spending a few hours every little while over the "Dolly Dialogues" or "A Yellow Aster,"* or any of a hundred such bright and clever works that have attracted attention, you hunted up some light, readable works on astronomy, botany, chemistry, physics, and so forth, of which there are many now-a-days, and that you gathered from them a little knowledge of the flowers and plants, the rocks and minerals and their qualities, and the position of the earth, which is a compo-

"Reflections," *Ev'ry Month* 2 (September 1896): 4. Signed "The Prophet."

*Anthony Hope, *The Dolly Dialogues* (1894), and Kathleen M. Caffyn, *A Yellow Aster* (1894).

86

site of all these, in its relations to the sun and the other worlds which make the night beautiful. After learning a little about these, don't you imagine it would be pleasurable to begin with the earliest history of men, as Rawlinson tells of them in his "Seven Great Monarchies," and learn a little about how they made use of this world and its contents as you, after reading, now know them?* And, furthermore, don't you imagine that once you saw how these early men of this earth were getting along, you would like to trace their progress—the progress of the best and strongest and fittest of them, through Greece, as Grote tells of them; through Rome, as Gibbon brilliantly relates of them; through the Middle Ages, as Hallam has pictured them, and up to our times as you can learn from Guizot and Froude, and one or two others.

And then, having a foundation for some opinions of this life of to-day, don't you think it would be worth your while to strenghten them and clear your judgment by reading what Cuvier has to tell of the rocks and the stratas of slate, lime and coal that are beneath us, and what Darwin, Huxley and Tyndall have to tell of their efforts in tracing the growth of all life since the time when the earth was fire and the sky a shimmering arc of bronze, studded with stars of a brighter gleam than we can now well conceive. And when you had read of these do you not think that it would be agreeable to have the whole universe passed in review before you, as Spencer marshals it, showing you how certain beautiful laws exist, and how, by these laws, all animate and inanimate things have developed and arranged themselves; how life has gradually become more and more complicated, more and more beautiful, and how architecture, sculpture, painting and music have gradually developed, along with a thousand other features of our life of to-day.

If you did all this, following this very simple and readable order, don't you imagine that then, if you wanted to read a poem like "Paradise Lost," or "Childe Harold's Pilgrimage," you would find it not only easy but delightful, and that you would get a world of meaning out of it? Don't you realize that then, if you wanted to read a novel, whatever was spoken of in it would be familiar to you and that there would be some pleasure in having a judgment of your own in the matter, so that you could say this is true or not true, according to life as I know it? Don't you believe that all literature would then have a greater charm, and that the opinions of

*George Rawlinson, *The Seven Great Monarchies of the Ancient Eastern World* (1885).

this one or that, in poetry or prose, would then bring pleasure to you, according as they agreed or disagreed, learnedly, with you. Certainly there are a lot of beautiful and wonderful things which you do not know much about, which would interest you if you did. Why not think of them. The novels will wait, you know, and when you come to them after awhile, wise and able yourself, they will seem even better than they do now, if they are good novels, whereas, if they are bad ones, you will know too much to trouble yourself about them. Why not begin now?

[Man's Place in Nature]

If there is one thing more than another that is calculated to throw one into a serious mood, and discourage by convincing that man is the sport of the elements; the necessary, but worthless dust of changing conditions, and that all the fourteen hundred million beings who swarm the earth after the manner of contentious vermin, are but one form which the heat of the sun takes in its protean journey towards dissipation, it is to stand by helpless in the face of great atmospheric disturbances, and see men swept to death by those irresistible forces of nature over which man exercises no control. The storm comes and drives all before it; the lightning gathers and hurls its deadly bolts, and men and animals, like rocks and trees, are struck down and destroyed, just as though they were not reckoned for in the great arrangement of nature. At St. Louis the wind rises, rain and hail sweep onward, and a few hundred are lacerated beneath the ruins of their habitations, whereon the sun rises on the morrow and shines, and in life there is no difference. A great emperor crowns himself at Moscow, and a hundred thousand gather upon a plain to do him honor, when in offering a few gifts, a great greed is stirred in the mass, and five thousand are crushed as a result of their rushing forward. In earth some slight convulsion takes place and immediately the sea recedes from a portion of the coast of Japan, rushing to its place again at the expense of thirty thousand lives. Sometimes we see nature's disregard of life working out through individual men, as where careless employes plunge a train into [a] great wreck, and destroy lives and property, one iota of which they could not reproduce and replace, though they could live a thousand years. In short, man seems not only the sport of nature, but of his fellowmen, and although nothing may be set against him, yet he does not seem to be considered in the great economy of nature, and any moment may see him completely destroyed, in order that some element or force may complete its mission unimpeded.

"Reflections," *Ev'ry Month* 2 (September 1896): 4–7. Signed "The Prophet."

There is another phase of this earthly condition of ours which is even less comprehensible, and that is that everything tends to equalize and seek a common level. There is something that pulls down, and makes dust of the things which are in evidence about us. There is in nature a corroding breath, which causes marble and men to peel off and waste away, film by film, until nothing remains. Tyndall for years stood in awe of the Alps, so vast and rugged, upon which time seemed to have no effect, until from its summit he viewed the Matterhorn and saw how torn and dismantled it was, and how great were the wounds time had inflicted upon it. To him it seemed old and decrepit, its sides so scarred and splintered, its whole appearance denoting certain decay, and that eventual time when it should be humbled to the earth, crumbled and made dust of. Its quondam grandeur in his eyes, forsook it, and a new solemnity of woe spread about, so that although he was thrilled, his sentiment was not unmixed with sorrow for such great and proud monuments, whose bases cover the earth, and whose peaks look into very eternity. Sorrow was awakened in him, mite that he was, for all that splendid pile, for it was old, decrepit and worn: the sport of relentless elements and the victim of age and death. Where once it commanded his awe because of the thought that it was for all time, it now aroused his pity when he found that after all, like himself, it was for a time only.

Similar situations have appealed to minds in all ages, the power of disintegration in nature being the source of all tears. Poets have sung in funereal measures, orators taken account of, in periods of resonant beauty, the pity of the hopeless helplessness of men in this earthly condition. It has been the desire of men that there should be no crumbling and no decay. There has grown a desire that things should be accounted for, and that one thing should not be the hopeless sport of another. Men in their might and pride have protested against the thought that they were not especially considered in the scheme of nature, and have felt that such power as theirs must assuredly be watched over and especially guarded by a higher power. The idea that they could be swept to nothingness by wind or water, could be crushed by a stone, obliterated by eruptions or destroyed by disease has ever proved repugnant to them, and they have built up a faith that takes account of them and their deeds, and makes of them agents instead of mere clods in the scheme of the universe. That,—

90

Many a flower is born to blush unseen,
And waste its sweetness on the desert air*

is one of the bitter possibilities which they are sadly unwilling to
admit, and therefore the philosophy of the "eternal fitness" of
things appeals to them, and to it they willingly subscribe. Nothing
is lost, say they, nothing disordered. The great path of progress is
being unerringly followed, the great flow of life is onward to the sea
of peace. No sparrow falls unheeded, no flower fades unseen. Justice reigns and these dread calamities which sweep you and me
away, giving us over to dust and oblivion, are little elementary
dissensions which work good, and our souls are accounted for.
Nothing is lost.

Yet in the face of all this stand the facts, hard, cruel, appalling and here they remain. Poetry: it is the song of those who
seem to be uncared for in the order of life. Literature: its greatest
records are of lives that were hopeful, but came to naught. Art: its
masterpieces picture the helpless who are destroyed for naught
(seemingly) and forgotten. There is no song in life like a sad song,
no seduction like that of tears. Over it all, like a pall, hangs condemnation, the law of death. Like Dante's inscription, it is above
life's entrance, "prepare to die, ye who would seek to live," while
to say whether or no we choose to come into this life is denied us.
These are the things that hang upon the spirit like weights and
fetters, the things from whose insistent presence there is no escape
except through the doorway of that unquestioning faith which
Newman accepted, and of which he sung;

Lead kindly light, amid the encircling gloom;
Lead thou me on.

On the other hand certain evidences tend to establish a reasonable faith in the heart, and to solace it for its inability to know.
Man is not exactly the sport of the elements in the same sense with
rocks, trees and the countless creatures of the air and forest. It is
true the latter make some shift to protect themselves, and do, in
many instances, preserve themselves from continuous and contig-
uous evils, but in nothing like the brilliant manner of man. Like
man they are blessed by the protecting influence of the law of

---

*Thomas Gray, "Elegy Written in a Country Church Yard," ll. 55–56, slightly
misquoted.

instinct, which preserves and heals, but with them instinct is all, where with man, it is only the beginning. In him is the wondrous faith that things are in his favor and that he is born to rule. Unawed by the vastities of force about him, he endeavors not only to shield himself, but schemes to bring nature to his aid in the struggle. Unterrified by the possibility and even probability of annihilation he presumes upon the weakness, inaction or indifference of all things, great and small, about him, and at a signal claps the iron of his reason upon them and harnesses them to the car of his progress. Not only has he seized upon inanimate, but upon animate nature. Vegetation has been enslaved by his culture and made to serve him although his life means its destruction. Animals, once his equal, and of whom he stood in awe and terror, have been either subjected or obliterated, and such as remain either aid his progress by mutely yielding their lives in toil, or die that he may eat. He has driven before him hostile creatures of every sort, has slaughtered his enemies, and even seized upon his own kind, branding them as slaves and endeavoring to supply needed force by making brutes of them, and has at last asserted his right and desire to live in peace among the creatures of earth, in order that he may have time and leisure to attack those greater forces about him, which from time to time sweep him to death. There is no fear in his attacks upon the forces that rule the universe, although, as ever in the face of all his battles he is uncertain of the result. Where in the past he sent warriors with axes to hew the contending force of enemies from his path, he now sends powerful specialists in science, officered by financiers and philanthropists, and generaled by philosophers, who see to it that all conquered provinces are immediately harmonized with the conditions of the present great empire of thought. From earthly material and with the aid of immediate forces, he has fashioned and equipped himself with instruments that make of his eyes, great, penetrating organs, wherewith he is now engaged in scanning the uttermost bounds of the material universe. Similarly he has improved his ears, hearing with the telephone the sounds of most distant earth. Electricity has made all the earth responsive to his touch, has increased his speed to marvelous degree and opened the air to the flight of his mechanisms, with which, and by the aid of as yet unsubjected forces, he bids fair to explore the outer darkness and traverse the spaces which now seem so immeasureable. Endowed with divine desire to know and a power to analyze, he has proceeded to sift the materials of the earth and to compel each in turn to explain its right to exist, and its meaning and relation to other materials. The law of integration has instilled in him a sense of the effectiveness of combining, whereby he has aided iron to be stronger. In unity there is strength, and this truth he has uniformly applied, bringing likes together and accumulating stores of each, by the aid of which he is now conducting his Herculean labors. By combining iron he has succeeded in building Babel towers; by separating gold and silver from dross, supplied himself with a medium of exchange. All minerals and vegetables have been freed, each unto itself, and the possibilities of each as a factor in earthly progress examined. As a result of his labors, his inheritance of implements with which to further his universal supremacy, has been multiplied a thousandfold.

In the presence of such a creature pity has no mission. More likely is the thought to rise, that, after all, he is self-sufficient, a veritable God, slowly forging the chains that are to bind a universe. Forces may sway inconsiderate of him now, but in time they will bend to his will. He may not now be a king, but nevertheless he is heir to a throne, and will some day rule. Nothing can withstand him, for he is working in harmony with great laws which place splendid powers in his hand and assist him to rise. A great maker of stars above is his master, and these, His laws, though cruel in their precision, will do an obedient follower no harm. To-day they sweep the heedless and unthinking from their path, but to-morrow they will aid students and disciples to rise to the highest point of physical and mental power. As a student and disciple of such masterful laws man needs no pity; as a victim of error and misunderstanding regarding them, he deserves none. This is the order of the universe, the plan of irresistible progress, and as an earnest part of it man is safe.

At any rate, a system which involves the regulation of countless sidereal systems and which shapes at the same time the material form of a mustard seed is to be trusted. Where countless forms are everywhere evident, each organized after a fashion wondrously adapted to surrounding conditions and each so admirable in the details of its economy, an over-ruling and kindly direction is implied. If the evident force in everything is not so directed, then why should it assume such multifarious forms, and why should each form resolve itself into such admirably arranged details? Force is but force, and if not regulated for a purpose, why need it bloom as a rose yonder, drift as a cloud there, flow as a brook through the grassy meadows or walk as a human in all the charm and radiance of manhood.

If no superior intelligence guides and fosters, then surely these beauties of nature are enormities and man an inexplicable oddity, no better than the least of these. Mind cannot follow so devious a path to nothingness, and before it reason would quickly abdicate. Therefore, in the face of the countless calamities that assail mankind without let or hindrance, it must reasonably be contended, that while some men[,] like some mustard seeds and some stars, may not be especially preserved from the destroying onslaught of superior forces, yet all such contending forms, both great and small, must conform to the laws of growth, form and duration, and this, if nothing more, would indicate that over all rules a Being, and that in His wondrous superiority, He is not unmindful of the least of his creatures.

[The City]

To those who are infatuated with the thought of living in a city and of enjoying the so called delights of metropolitan life, the recent strikes in the sweater shops of New York may furnish a little food for reflection.* Usually the thought of miles of streets, lined with glimmering lamps; of great, brilliant thoroughfares, thronged with hurrying pedestrians and lined with glittering shop windows; of rumbling vehicles rolling to and fro in noisy counter procession, fascinates and hypnotizes the mind, so that reason fades to an all-possessing desire to rush forward and join with the countless throng. Usually, to the mass of humans, the vision of a great metropolis, throbbing with ceaseless life, pulsating after the fashion of a great heart and extending its influence by means of tracks to all parts of the world, is one of the most inspiring and impressive visions imaginable. To go to the city is the changeless desire of the mind. To join in the great, hurrying throng; to see the endless lights, the great shops and stores, the towering structures and palatial mansions, becomes a desire which the mind can scarcely resist. Mansions and palaces, libraries, museums, the many theatres and resorts of wealth and pleasure all attract, just as a great cataract attracts. There is a magnetism in nature that gives more to the many, and this you will see in the constant augmentation of population in the great cities, the constant rushing of wealth to those who have wealth, the great hurrying of all waters to where there are endless waters and of stars to where there are myriads of stars already gathered, until the heavens are white with them. It is a magnetism which no one understands, which philosophers call the law of segregation, and which simply means that there is something in nature to make the many wish to be where the many are. From that law there is no escape and both men and planets obey it. It makes towns, cities, nations and worlds, and does nothing per-

"Reflections," *Ev'ry Month* 3 (October 1896): 6–7. Signed "The Prophet."

*The bitterly contested strike of New York sweat-shop workers began in late July and lasted through August.

haps, except show what mites we are in the stream and current of nature.*

This desire to attend and be part of the great current of city life is one that seldom bases itself upon well mastered reasons. It is simply a desire, and as such, seldom begs for explanation. Men do not ask themselves whether once in the great city its wonders will profit them any. They do not stop to consider whether the great flood will catch them up and whirl them on helpless and unheeded. They never consider that the life, and dash and fire of metropolitan life is based on something and not a mere exotic sprung from nothing and living on air. They seldom reflect that all here is a mere picture of wondrous, living detail, but as cold and helpless as any vision, and as far from their grasp as the gems of a wintry sky. If they did it would appall them and make them cautious of the magnetic charm that draws them on, for they would perhaps come to realize that men may starve at the base of cold, ornate columns of marble, the cost of which would support them and many like them for the remainder of their earthly days. All is not gold that glitters, nor will anything that delights your fancy give you food. Certainly the city glitters, but it is not always your gold.

Perceive first, that what delights you is only the outer semblance, the bloom of the plant. These streets and boulevards, these splendid mansions and gorgeous hotels, these vast structures about which thousands surge and toward which luxurious carriages roll, are the fair flowers of a rugged stalk. Not of color and softness and rare odor are the masses upon which as a stalk these bloom; not for fresh air and sunshine are they. Down in the dark earth are the roots, drawing life and strength and sending them coursing up the veins; and down in alleys and byways, in the shop and small dark chambers are the roots of this luxurious high life, starving and toiling the long year through, that carriages may roll and great palaces stand brilliant with ornaments. These endless streets which only present their fascinating surface are the living semblance of the hands and hearts that lie unseen within them. They are the gay covering which conceals the sorrow and want and ceaseless toil upon which all this is built. They hide the hands and hearts, the groups of ill-clad workers, the chambers stifling with the fumes of midnight oil consumed over ceaseless tasks, the pallets of the poor

---

*Herbert Spencer had discussed the "law of segregation" in his *First Principles*. The law deals with the tendency in evolution for like physical or social units to organize themselves into like groups.

and sick, the bare tables of the hopeless slaves who work for bread. Endless are these rows of shadowy chambers, countless the miseries which these great walls hide. If they could be swept away, or dissolved, and only the individuals left in view, there would be a new story to tell. Like a sinful Magdalen the city decks herself gayly, fascinating all by her garments of scarlet and silk, awing by her jewels and perfumes, when in truth there lies hid beneath these a torn and miserable heart, and a soiled and unhappy conscience that will not be still but is forever moaning and crying "for shame."

The striking tailors, coat makers, pressers, bushelmen, they are of this vast substrata on which the city stands; a part of the roots that are down in the ground, delving, that the vast flowerlike institutions may bloom over head. They belong to that part of the city which is never seen and seldom heard. Strange tales could be told of their miseries, strange pictures drawn of their haunts and habitations, but that is not for here nor now. When they issued their queer circular it was published as a curiosity because it told a strange and peculiar story, and to those who are fascinated by dreams of the great metropolis it may prove a lesson. All is not gold that glitters. Neither is the city a place of luxurious abode despite the brilliancy of its surging streets. Here is the circular:

Extra.

To the Pressers:

Brethren—The last hour of need, misery and hunger has come. We are now on the lowest step of the ladder of human life. We can do nothing more than starve. Take pity on your wives. Are not your children for whom you have struggled so hard with your sweat and blood, dear to you? Do you think you have a right to live? Do you think you ought to get pay for your work? We only strive for a miserable piece of bread.

Signed,   Coat Pressers Union, No. 17.

There is surely no need for comment here, certainly no call for explanation. They are down there in narrow rooms working away again. The great thoroughfares are just as bright as ever. Thousands are lounging idly in cafes, thousands thronging the places of amusements, thousands rolling in gaily caparisoned equipages, and so it will continue. Some imagine this condition can be done away with but it cannot. As well imagine that men can be made equal in brain, intelligence and perception, by law. As well imagine that this law of segregation which brings thousands together can be reversed, or that men can be made to desire complete isolation and solitude. Oppression can be avoided, that is true, but the vine must have roots else how are its leaves to grow high into the world of sunlight and air. Some must enact the role of leaves, others the role of roots, and as no one has the making of his brain in embryo he must take the result as it comes.

For those who are inclined to believe that the above is mere rhetorical sentiment, unwarranted by any facts, the fruit, as it were, of a morbid imagination, let an incident in point suffice. It would seem as though one who enters a stranger into a city, enters as into the gorgeous storehouse of that eastern king whose jewels were heaped in glittering masses, and upon which he was left chained and helpless, to stare and starve. Endless jewels can this city show; treasures so vast as to seem improbable; glories so numerous that in their very number they rob each other of their individual charm; pleasure so elaborate and costly as to pall upon the pursuing imagination; yet, amid all, men starve. It strikes one as the acme of the paradoxical, but nevertheless court records do not lie. Of one such case the papers have spoken only recently and the singular description is here presented as evidence. It says:

"A wretched, dwarfed specimen of masculine humanity picked up by the police late Monday night was brought into Jefferson Market Court yesterday charged with vagrancy. The creature had been seen lurking in back alleyways in the neighborhood of Minetta Street, and persons whose curiosity had been aroused noticed that he spent his time rummaging in garbage cans under back stoops. Those who observed more closely declare that the man was devouring parts of the refuse. The man ate this because he was starving. Policeman McCarthy, of the Mercer Street Station, approached the wild-eyed, bushy-haired and shrunken outcast, whose clothes fell from him in rags, and he slunk away like a hunted animal. He had not gone far when he staggered and fell against a lamppost and cut his head. He then started to crawl into a hallway. The policeman found him and took him to the station house. The man, who was about 4 feet 3 inches high, was dreadfully emaciated. His hair was 18 inches long. His beard had been uncut and untrained for so long that little of his face could be seen. He wore no shirt, and was clad in a ragged coat and a pair of tattered trousers. A pair of soles which had once belonged to shoes were tied to his feet. At the station house he devoured soup and bread with an eagerness which showed his pitiable condition. When led before Magistrate Cornell yesterday he was still so weak he could scarcely stand. He is a native of the West Indies, and gave the name of William Wilson. He could not obtain work nor aid and was obliged to go to the garbage cans in trying to stave off starvation. Wilson was committed to the workhouse."

Thus runs the dry description of one creature. Thus could be written the story of many another. And between this one and that topmost type, whose clothes are costly and delicate of texture; whose linen is ever immaculate; whose chambers are soft with comforts and ever resplendent in detail; how many graduations are there? How many of the half hungry? the half weary? the half clothed? the half happy, are there? How many who endure severe privations uncomplaining, and how many who endure moderate wants with a trusting heart? Ah! this is a wonderfully conglomerate world, filled with a million grades, and still a million, and the one cares not for the wants of another. There are shades of suffering innumerable as the countless tints of a roseate sky; grades of poverty as various as the hues of a changeful sea. No type so faint but what there is one fainter still, and none so marked but that another more impressive rises. Indeed, they are as the sands of the desert, as the stars of the trackless night, and he who enters among them does so as one who ventures his frail craft amid the massive ships of a crowded sea; the idle rocking of which may insure his watery doom. But this is trite, perhaps; very wearisome, no doubt; very much like the threshing of straw upon a forsaken field.

[The Decline of the American Theatre]

Have you observed that which has come over the theatrical world in recent years? It seems to have gone all to pieces. It was strong and vigorous once. Like a rock it was firmly based on such dramatic Atlases as Booth, Barrett, McCullough, Wallack, Raymond, and Salvini. There were such men as Jefferson, Florence, Sothern, Stoddart, and Campbell, who were young and vigorous and whose very name lent prestige and lustre to the stage. Drama was in high favor, the very best of drama, and its exponents were not only honored, but financially supported and otherwise made much of. There were excellent stock companies and many plays of fine, enduring quality, and not only were they brought forth, but they were retained and supported. Now, however, all that has changed.

Instead of a vigorous and progressive dramatic element in our national life we have a disordered and disintegrated stage world, the better element of which has hard strife to make a living. There is no respect nor any evident desire for high-class drama as it has heretofore been conceived of. There is no great halo for the more vigorous and exemplary individuals who present it. Even straight-out temples of dramatic art are no longer endured, and musical comedies are now resorted to to make them pay. In short, the drama has gone to pieces. In its place we see a world of cheaper mimicry, the very buffoonery of royal art crowding the stage to its utmost capacity. There is a rush for that which is light and trivial. The people seem to want vaudeville. They are after something that is meaningless and showy. Nonsensical humor, paltry music, the most flippant of jesters—these are the desired and the financially befriended. There is no love for anything serious—that is, no great popular love. It is all variety—variety, variety, variety—until one wishes that the "spice of life" phrase had never been thought of or promulgated. It is no wonder that the stage is tabooed by a large and respectable element—more wonder, if any, that the element is not larger than it is; for certainly, if any one thing has deteriorated and disintegrated, that one thing is the stage. The most scornful

"Reflections," *Ev'ry Month* 3 (January 1897): 5–6. Signed "The Prophet."

100

opinions concerning it are much more than half justified by the exact condition of the elements which comprise it, and one is tempted to allow that they are safest who come in contact with it least.

And yet, seriously attended to, there is something wrong about this attitude toward the stage, just as there is something wrong about the stage itself. As a means of moral and intellectual benefit it is admitted the stage has run to seed, and at the same time the utter disregard and bad opinion sustained by the better element toward the legitimate drama has, in its argument, run also to seed. There is good drama, there are great actors, and from these combined there are great and uplifting moral lessons to be drawn, let him gainsay it who may. If this is not true, what are we to say of such men as Irving and Mansfield, and wherein are Jefferson, Willard, Tree, and Whiteside lacking in the divine artistic fervor?

The fact is, they are not. There is no more question as to the high aspiration and ideal fervor of these men than there is as to the aspiration of Dr. Parkhurst and Mr. Spurgeon,* or such poets as the late Tennyson and the present Johanna Ambrosius. These are to the drama what Talmage and Thomas are, and Swing was, to religion; what Sherman, Reed, and Carlisle are to politics, or Chase, MacMonnies, and Whistler are to art. They are great, massive men, strong of intellect, high in ideals, who have worked and slaved for their art, who have sacrificed upon the altar of truth and perfection their comforts and pleasures, their sorrows and joys, and have slowly and by toilsome efforts fitted themselves to correctly and ideally represent the passions, trials, and deeds of earth as they are and should be. They are great, powerful, magnificent representatives of the ideal in earthly life, and that which they are they have attained to by ways no less thorn-bestrewn than that followed by every other who attains to greatness. They have toiled and perhaps wept, and have come up into the favor of the wide universal heart fully conscious of the truth of the lines of Cowper, which assert that—

The path of sorrow, and that path alone,
Leads to the land where sorrow is unknown.†

*Charles H. Parkhurst and Charles H. Spurgeon were popular clergymen.

†William Cowper, "Epistle to an Afflicted Lady in France," ll. 9–10.

101

They stand for the best in art just as much as does Canova or Browning or Wagner, and whoso frowns upon them and refuses to recognize the stage (their field) because of the rag-tag element that hangs on to it, in other senses, refuses to extend his favor to one of the most helpful elements in life, and by so refusing commits a grave wrong. There is no explanation to be offered, nor valid excuse to be put forward. If pretension is made to sanction and support art, then these men, who are equally with others art's most dignified ambassadors, deserve also to be supported and their work sanctioned. There is no sense in withholding such support. There is no reason in closing the eyes to the value of their work because they are of the stage. There is no justice in the charge that condemns all the stage and does not except their labor. Such condemnation is on a par with the religious fervor that gives all to savages in Africa and ignores the unfortunates at one's door, and smacks strongly of the pharisaism that crowds a metropolitan opera house with diamond-begirded matrons, because it is fashionable, and leaves the young and ambitious among the talented strugglers in the same field to walk threadbare and hungry without, unable to earn so much as the price of admission.

There is no question that the stage has deteriorated. There is no longer a doubt that almost all of its once pretentious art has run to vaudeville seed, but there is little additional doubt that the same is in part, and even largely, due to that very class who are so very good and so very righteous that they are unable to distinguish anything after the word stage is mentioned; who leave genius in this form to struggle alone and ineffectually against the very evils of the stage which they in their pompous righteousness decry, and yet who affect to appreciate art in other forms and to further by their purse and social consent the works of genius in other fields. Certainly the stage has deteriorated, but it would not have done so if the so-called better element had but opened their eyes and ears and attended to the all but divine voices that are preaching a message no less important to the race than those emanating from the rostrum and the pulpit. They are important along with all else that is important, and the fact that the drama has deteriorated and been pushed aside is not so much a commentary upon the quality of the dramatic profession as upon the stubborn, blind, selfish, and vain pharisaism of those who pretend to be something, and to do something, and while promoting art in one field ignore this other important factor because some one has said that it is not proper. They are not fools half so much as they are hypocrites, and they are not either of these in near so deadly proportion as they are dupes and dawdlers, the followers after anything that is supposed to lead to exalted condition without involving any danger of anything which would reflect upon their very mediocre mentality.

[The Role of the
"Reflections" Column]

A western and rather optimistic journal takes exception to the tone of this reflective matter, and does not hesitate to stigmatize it as pessimistic. "The world is not going downward to ruin, as the writer would have us believe. Everything in this splendid country has an upward trend, despite the wail of the cynics."

No cynicism will you find in this steady contemplation of the trend of events; no assertion that the world or the Union is trending irretrievably toward ruin; on the contrary, a firm and undisturbed faith in nature, and in men true to nature, despite the decay of a few of the species, or schools, or tribes, of which there are so many. The trend of all life is upward, and when goodness and truth have withered in this land, sweeter and fairer elements are causing them to wax and flourish on other shores.

Elements in our life may decay, but life does not. We see a stage deteriorating from splendid, uplifting dramatic power and becoming a miserable, crumbled, and discolored variety mass, but the drama is not passing so in other lands. We see an evident decay so far as political honor is concerned, but political honor in other countries is trending rather upward than otherwise. Some of our literature is decadent, and our newspapers are assuredly drifting into a flash and sensational channel, but literature and journalism, taken the world over, are improving in character. We look upon our cities and find that great wealth is certainly robbing a certain number of some of the qualities that are necessary to complete manhood, but the wide and bountiful soil of a splendid land is rather adding to than subtracting from the strength and serenity that make for justice and truth in men.

Pride, avarice, hauteur, and indifference may arouse anxiety as we look upon these qualities strongly displayed by American "gentlemen of leisure," but a turn to the many whose humble position and pleasant homes assure the strength and prosperity of the nation is rather reassuring. The few are surely decaying, but the nation is not, nor ever will be, let us hope.

"Reflections," *Ev'ry Month* 3 (January 1897): 7. Signed "The Prophet."

[*The Role of the "Reflections" Column*]

Nevertheless, since the decaying few will soon affect the many, it is not for any one to sit idly by. Such poison and decay should be excoriated with a rod of fire. Evil of every description should be assaulted, and without thought of compromise. There should be no decaying drama. Our literature and our art should, unchangingly, be pure. Flash journalism and dishonest politics should not for an hour be endured. Although literature, religion, law, medicine, and even science and philosophy, are apt, in some countries and at various times, to develop fallacies and quackeries, such deception needs to be none the less fiercely combated in order to be overcome and annihilated.

It is, then, not general decay that need be bemoaned, but the decay of some few of the more prominent features of our life.

False prophets arise and false doctrines gain credence, and these, like disease, seize upon some tribe or nation and kill it. He is a wise man who at such times can logically distinguish the good from the evil—and a true savior is he who can marshal the nobler sentiments of the people and array them for successful combat. There are many false schemes and doctrines in evidence today, and against these there must be no end of war. But the nation is sound, and when that cannot longer be said, then other lands and other climes will nourish the virtuous and the patriotic, and other nations will bear aloft the torch of light and truth which must ever blaze the path that leads onward and upward.

[Herbert Spencer]

In England there is one man whose life is serenely drawing to a close, in whom human interest will centre absorbingly for ages to come.* This man in his greatness does not at all fulfill the French definition of fame—one at whom the average pedestrian points a finger with a "That is he!" He is not known to the pedestrian, average or below the average, although the fame of his name is gradually spreading. He would not be recognized in a crowd, and yet all beings and all ages to come will owe him a debt of gratitude. Like a refreshing spring he lies midway in a boundless life-desert, and all who would be refreshed or strenghthened must either journey to him, or ask of those who have been, and so share in the knowledge which they have brought away. Thus far, the spring is known only to a few who are making themselves carriers. The many are still ignorant of the fact that it exists at all.

It does not matter though, in the life of Herbert Spencer, whether he is personally known or not. It would not avail him the slightest if all men could point him out among a vast number. Neither their interest nor their plaudits would affect him, for he has labored well and completed his work, and has wrought so efficaciously that all ages will be his debtors and all men his pupils. He is a great father of knowledge, and his word is to be spread before all; but at present many are too young to understand him, and many more too idle to heed. But the young and the truants will all gather about his teachings after a while, and then the world will be vastly better.

It is not necessary here to expatiate as to his life and teachings. The fact that he is a philosopher will not redound to his credit with the many. If it were said he is a mighty general; if a hundred battles and a million slain attested his valor; if a vast kingdom and a panoplied throne marked his sovereignty, no one would doubt his greatness, none would question the value of his deeds. It would be Spencer the warrior, Spencer the general, Spencer the glorious;

"Reflections," Ev'ry Month 3 (February 1897): 2–4. Signed "The Prophet."

*Spencer was in ill-health at this time but he did not die until December 8, 1903.

and comprehension of the meaning of his efforts would be within the range of all. Blessedly enough, he was not born militant.

His is generalship of the mind—the great captaincy of learning and literature, the field-marshalship of the forces of reason. As Napoleon studied the military map of Europe, so Spencer studied the intellectual map of the world. He learned where the sands are, and where the stars, and where the types and tribes and races. By long and patient study he learned of the nations, their lives and deeds, and of the men of nations, and of the deeds and accomplishments of men. Through the long ages he traced the progress of this circular earth of ours, and found where it came from and to where it is going, and all that which sunlight has done and is doing for it. He ransacked with his army of learned subordinates the cities and valleys of dead-and-forgotten ages, and caused them to yield up their story of life and labor and the treasure of its meaning. At the approach of his victorious mentality all living things bowed in vassalage, and he exacted the tribute of their reason and meaning from all. "Wherefore are you?" and "what do you accomplish?" were his great field-pieces, and with these he thundered at the walls of ignorance and the city of darkness until they cracked and tottered, and finally yielded. From point of knowledge to point of knowledge he victoriously proceeded, here annexing this domain of truth, there laying waste that fortress of untruth, putting all lies to the sword, adding all facts to his army, until the whole visible universe had submitted to him, and, like Alexander of physical war, he could sigh for more worlds to conquer. Everything submitted to him; each province of knowledge took its subordinate place in his empire of the mind; everything fell into his order and scheme, and he has now proceeded to rule in peace.

Our minds belong to the universe which Spencer has united; our thoughts upon its meaning are subject to the laws which he has laid down. A new-comer arises to dispute him, and he is forthwith marched against and defeated. Spencer has pointed the history of the past—it is he who has defined our puny place in the world and the universe; it is he who has bound our minds together into one empire, and pointed the path along which progress is easiest and best. All life has been comprehended best by him. He has explained the value of the things that are, and the purposes for which they are intended. Rain, sunlight, the seasons; charity, generosity, virtue,—all these are set down in their true order, and having established the empire of mind, he invites you, as subjects, to acquaint yourselves with its laws. They are unalterable laws, these

107

of the empire. Rebellion neither affects them nor saves you from punishment. Familiarity proves to you how beneficent they are, how much good they will do you if submissively observed, how vast and glorious is the kingdom of life, and how admirable its philosopher and vice-regent Spencer. He has given forth his teachings after years of mental conquest, and now all are called upon to take note and obey.

Centuries ago, when the great Cyrus united Persia, it was years before all knew of the union, or before all observed and prospered under the laws. They did not know of Cyrus until his satraps arrived and, taking charge, promulgated his fame and power. Even so is it with the great Spencer and his system. He has bound the world of knowledge in one, and his student emissaries are going forth into the most distant provinces proclaiming his laws and his greatness. Years must elapse before all hear of him, more years before that which he has accomplished is understood; but time will elapse, and with each recurring year the meaning of life according to him will become more clear and more efficacious until the most lowly beings will be affected and benefited thereby, and all mankind will conform to the laws which he has written down, as they were given to him by the One whose work is creation, and whose all-covering generosity has given the world a mind so philosophic as that of Herbert Spencer.

[The Survival of the Fittest]

This winter, so far, has been more than ordinarily productive of instances of suffering and want, it seems. There has been in the large cities, where such incidents form interesting newspaper paragraphs on a cold morning, no end of freezing and starving cases recorded, and some of them have been most vividly presented—a fact largely due, no doubt, to the actual sternness of the reality. There have been many who perished from hunger in the streets, and many more who suffered through the cold and by lack of proper raiment. Thousands succumbed under these severe conditions to sickness and death, and the returning sunshine will, no doubt, cause the grass to grow upon many a mound which under other conditions would not have been made. Nature has by storm, sleet, and hunger weeded out the weaklings and the incompetents before offering the gentle springtime and the luxuriant summer to those fit ones who by strength and good fortune have withstood the inclemencies, and have thus managed to survive. All the others— the thousands who fell and could not rise—were, in just so much, unfit to enjoy the coming season as they were unfit to survive the harshness of the passing one, and were, therefore, properly cut off—a very unchristian conclusion let us say, but a just one.

There were the large charitable organizations distributing aid right and left for the asking, and there were the police courts consigning all sufferers to the workhouse and the hospital, and there were the general public giving here and there without any pharisaical discrimination, and yet these unfit ones were found by Nature and weeded out, and their graves are already white with snow and will be indifferently green when all is gay and lightsome again. They were found out in many places, however carefully concealed their want, and claimed. The fit creature survives the most trying conditions. He is either fit to make money or to beg it, or to steal, but he is fit, and therefore gets it and keeps himself intact. His fitness consists either in the ability to avoid the necessity of seeking sustenance by any other than the most select methods, or when

"Reflections," *Ev'ry Month* 3 (February 1897): 4–5. Signed "The Prophet."

not that, then in being hardened enough to employ any method for self-preservation. It is the fit creature who manipulates bank, mining, or general market stock, and puts the acquired wealth between himself and possible destitution, and equally is it the fit creature who steals when hunger threatens, and who employs weapons and becomes a noiseless footpad when anything is to be gained and the discomfort of poverty is to be set aside. Both classes are not "fit" in the same degree, but in the theory of their fitness to survive there is no flaw. They get enough to keep body and soul together— they do not hesitate and retreat, when hesitancy and retreating work to their bodily injury. On the contrary, they arise and do, whether it be good or evil, and by doing good or evil they survive, which proves their fitness.

It is only the unfit who fail—who suffer and die. They slink their way, weak in their inability to see or to grasp, and utterly unable to gather the firmness that will enable them to seize and hold, either honestly or dishonestly, that which might preserve their lives. They are weak-bodied and weak-hearted, lack the nerve to endure rebuff, and are short of the unblushing effrontery that permits others to either overawe weaker ones or to cringe and whimper before strong ones. They are unfit because, unlike the fit ones, they lack these peculiarities which invariably aid one to survive. They are too shy to complain openly, too thin-skinned to endure pity, too fearful of public opinion to seek refuge in a workhouse, and too timid and weak-bodied to risk seizing what is not their own.

As a consequence of all this earthly unfitness, their suffering is concealed and unheeded. That they are cold is by them not made evident; that they are hungry is mentally impossible for them to own; that they are weak and failing they are too vain to admit,— and so in all their weakness, unaided and unsheltered, they are less and less able to resist the onslaught of time and the bitter natural elements, and gradually become not at all able, and so fall a prey to the many elements. Unequipped, with dull moral faculties and but ill-provided with the nerveless indifference to opinion and opposition, they are weaklings, and decidedly unfit to compete with the many, and therefore fail. In this world generally failure opens wide the gates to mortal onslaught, and the invariable result is death.

That, then, is what the paragraphs mean when they describe pathetically how the victims were discovered suffering. In each case it was unfitness. Each recurring snowstorm found those who could not endure one more such, and who therefore died. Each recurring day broke upon those whose fitness had all but vanished, and whom death then claimed. Each hour of combined wintry severity was but an hour too much for some who had been long gradually failing—and so they came to their end, day after day, examples of what men ought not be.

Peculiar, a lesson like this, taught all through the long and tedious winter, but it still fails to prove that the fit are the righteous, or the unfit the evil ones. He who tempers the wind to the shorn lambs, and takes note of the tiniest sparrow's fall, perhaps distinguishes between these vast classes and marks where the just have been stricken down and the unjust raised up, but to the earthly eye it is all but indistinguishable. Often it appears that every noble quality is but a poor match for every base one, but that may be only in appearance—a thing of the eye, and not of reality. It may be that justice has been done those who have thus fallen before the winter; it may be that only the good have been preserved. Anyhow, the weak, the helpless, the unfit have been destroyed, and we, the fit, have been preserved and retained to do, let us hope, what good we can.

[The Trust]

In these latter days of social unrest and discontent, it has come to pass that we are beginning to worry over trusts. That simple word, once so agreeable before being pluralized and anathematized, now represents a so-called great evil in which the people rightfully take a deep interest. It is known that officered combinations of huge aggregations of capital exist, the object of which is to secure the monopoly of some particular branch of trade, industry, or commerce, and so stifle wholesome competition. It is known that certain companies or individuals in the same line combine and protect themselves. They do it, perhaps, to protect themselves against the necessity of keeping two mills running at a small profit, where one could do the work at a large profit. They do it to protect themselves against paying any more for labor than labor will actually take and subsist on. They do it to protect themselves against sudden unprofitable low prices, and because it gives them the grasp which can compel high prices. They unite because there is strength and power in unity, and because it is their nature to desire strength and power in order that they may live. They desire greatness in control.

Of course those who make a trust know what they do. They realize what power is theirs, how they can crush the rival and humiliate the foe. They are fully aware that whereas their little individual lives come to a brief and unfortunate end, that of the trust lives through many of the lives, reassuring their heirs and assigns of comfort after its death. They are well aware that while they have souls, this huge combination has none, and must always abide by a majority decision of its component individuals, however wrong the decision. They know that it lives and lives, and its debtors are never forgotten, and that down to the last sou, just or unjust, are all its obligations collected. They realize that this trust which they create can have no heart. Fully aware are they that they cannot endow so huge a corporation with pity. They only know that they can create it, that it can aid them to crush opposi-

"Reflections," *Ev'ry Month* 3 (March 1897): 2–3. Signed "The Prophet."

tion, and that it can make return opulently, and with so much are they content.

Now the people, seeing these things, also desire to form a trust defensive, which shall overawe and destroy these other trusts,—strong and often oppressive, and thereupon comes the argument. The trusts are called to the bar to make answer. They are asked to make plain why they are not satisfied with a moderate profit, and why they allow greed to stifle competition and raise prices. They are questioned as to the wisdom and kindness of their motives, why tradesmen are harassed and lobbyists employed, and why they are so sharp in their dealings generally. They are arraigned before commissions and judges, are rebuked and reviled, are condemned as wrong in spirit and action, are outlawed by legislation, and yet they flourish and remain uninjured, while constantly crying aloud to one and all that they do good.

As a matter of fact they are in accord with the very law and spirit of commerce. If two or four men unite their faculties and capital in one business, why should not four businesses, incorporated, unite their capital and strength in one trust? The object in each case is the same. The motive on either hand is not different, except in degree. The desire is not one shade less in either instance. All desire money; all desire power; all desire superiority over opponents and competitors—and combination makes for these things. Where in operation harm is done, where pity and the kindly virtues are set aside, where oppression is schemed—well, that is mournful and wrong. The principle of life, however, is that the higher form shall live by the death of the lower, and the trust is laying claim to be the higher. If it is not, there are the oppressed free to defend themselves; and if they do not, they merely admit their degradation. If they do, the trust, and those who stand sponsor for it, must be crushed in the struggle. Such a culmination will prove how wrong is the trust, and how right are the many in advocating kindness, generosity, love and mercy.

[The Struggle for Existence]

The characteristic of the time is that men can shut themselves in or apart from the general life, and with some little feature selected from nature labor assiduously to accomplish distinction. It is called *specialization* now. They can either take a line of business or a line of art, or something equally specific and withdraw into themselves, giving all their energy and thought to the labor of attaining distinction. There is no fault to be found with this from the point of earthly progress, nor from belief that all mankind should work and accomplish something. It is the selfishness in it that ignores the efforts of others to accomplish something also, that is the forbidding feature. One would think that each might work and at the same time assist every other to work, as much as possible. Specialization, coupled with selfishness and an extreme desire to succeed speedily, is the very element that makes life difficult. Speed is well, but it leaves no time to look about when others cry for assistance, nor will it permit a halt when someone has been trampled on. It leaves suffering and supplication, the drip of tears and moan of prayers to die on the wind behind, while it rides rapidly on. That is the way men go forward these days. And they go singly in feeling, though to the eyes of the onlooker there are thousands in the same company.

Well, it may be best for the progress of the world that there should be such a wide gap between the very rich and the very poor, between the highly educated and wholly uneducated; but the difference, coupled with the number of people, makes life a very fierce struggle. It may be necessary that some should drudge and slave, and others walk in elegance and conduct the more honored affairs of life, but it certainly makes a grind of things. The drudges are so numerous. It looks so often as though they were held down by lack of advantages and that men might do more for them. They have to struggle so hard for bread. They have to wear such wretched clothes. Their days are all toil, and their nights weariness. They are hounded by their desire to taste a few of life's

Ev'ry Month 4 (May 1897): 21. Unsigned.

pleasures, and by those who wish to sell them the mockery of these exorbitantly. They live in close, stifling quarters and sleep vilely. They are subject to results of droughts and panics, go hungry when crops fail, die when plagues come, and are tortured by sickness and suffering in its endless forms. One sees the city packed with them. The mills are filled by them, who are not half so valuable as the machines. They toil under the summer sun in grain fields, and suffer cold before the mast over all the wide seas as sailors. They are so numerous and there are no schools. They are so willing and there are no machines. They work hard and the product of their labor is stored up, and then they are turned out, because they have manufactured enough to last those who buy a long time.

With all this they are cursed with minds and hearts. They reason some, and think of their position. They have laughter and tears and those horrible things called nerves, and all the conditions play upon them. You can find dozens of them with full minds, fine-looking hands, graceful bodies, in every way equal to some of those who ride by outside in jingling equipages, crowded into one small, ill-smelling room, working unceasingly from morning till night. Their fingers fly, their eyes linger on their labor, they stoop, they never speak, and all day long they work, work, work, until they are yellow and faded and limp—and they are humans.

Who put them there? An eternal law. What makes them stay? Hunger, fear of death. Why don't they do something else? They don't know how. Why don't they? They were never taught, never had the time, were made to work by parents whom they have been taught that they owe something to for being grown into such a condition. That is the great mass of creatures. They are nothing at all, a mere mass, worms hidden at the roots of the tree of life.

And this is the life they are expected to rise in. If they try they may succeed, but no one is going to help them. They are going to encounter enmity, that foremost characteristic of the ambitions, the moment they try. Everyone is trying. Everyone is pushing the other for place—is training that he may crowd the other out of the way, shove him back, put him below—that he may be first and free to go farther. If one of these strugglers tries for a higher place he may starve. Certainly he will be buffeted, as certainly hated, and persistently undermined. That is the character of ambition. It throttles its competitors.

Why should men struggle? Well, because they want to be somebody. They want nice clothes, nice hands, their bodies kept from showing wear and painful usage. They have inherited pride, and would like people to speak well of them. They would like to laugh, to feel merry, to have plenty to eat, a fine place to sleep, and to be healthy and admired. They would like a nice home, soft lights and shades in it, beautiful views in it, and the smiles of love. They would like to be favored of Providence and to have the things which they understand contribute to and make happiness, and why shouldn't they? This understanding has never been educated out of them. Other people seek such. Why not they? With this feeling, inculcated by everything in their life and about them, they are tempted to try. They see how others set about it. They learn that one must save; furthermore, that one must seize upon all that possibly can be seized upon and hold it. They must not give anything from their store. They must hold, seize more; hold, and seize still more; and so on to riches. Pleasure will come afterward. Love will come afterward, the ability to admire, to enjoy, to understand—oh! that will all come. First, get the money, that will buy the things to admire.

So it goes through all grades of life, from men to microbes, and the change is not visible. Virtue doesn't seem to flourish exotically. Charity is not growing stronger or more pronounced, pity isn't any more in evidence. At least it seems so at times, and although this strange, agonizing turmoil seems more and more deadly, pity may be growing, human sympathy widening, charity coming more and more in evidence. If so, blessed be these qualities. May they thrive! A world agonized and despairing awaits its redemption, prostrate, at their hands.

2

1898–1910

A Talk with America's Leading
Lawyer: Or, What Success Means

Joseph Choate was from a prominent Massachusetts family. He was graduated from Harvard in 1852 and from Harvard Law School in 1854 and soon became one of the most successful lawyers of his day. In 1897 Choate lost the New York Republican senatorial primary to the incumbent, Thomas C. Platt. He later served as ambassador to Great Britain from 1899 to 1905. For the background of Dreiser's work for Success *magazine, see his "O. S. Marden and* Success Magazine*," pp. 272–81.*

* * * * * *

I called one evening at the residence of Mr. Choate. Previous inquiry at the law office of Evarts, Choate, and Beaman, on Wall Street, elicited the information that Mr. Choate's days were filled to overflowing with legal affairs of great importance. Consequently it was surprising to find him so ready to see a stranger at his home.

It was into a long room on the ground floor that I was introduced, three of its walls lined with tall, dark walnut book-laden cases, lighted by a bright grate fire and by a student's lamp on the table by night, and by two heavily-shaded windows by day. As I entered, the great lawyer was busy prodding the fire, and voiced a resonant "good evening" without turning. In a moment or two he had evoked a blaze, and assumed a standing attitude before the fire, his hands behind him.

"Well, sir," he began, "what do you wish?"

"A few minutes of your time," I answered.

"Why?" he questioned succinctly.

"I wish to discover whether you believe special advantages at the beginning of a youth's career are necessary to success?"

"Why my opinion?"

I was rather floored for an instant, but endeavored to make

Success 1 (January 1898): 40–41. *Little Visits with Great Americans*, ed. O. S. Marden (New York, 1905).

plain the natural interest of the public in the subject and his opinion, but he interrupted me with the query:—

"Why don't you ask a man who never had any advantages," at the same time fixing upon me one of his famous "what's in thy heart?" glances.

"Then you have had them?" I said, grasping wildly at the straw that might keep the interview afloat.

"A few, not many," he replied.

"Are advantages necessary to success to-day?"

"Define advantages and success," he said abruptly, evidently questioning whether it was worth while to talk. A distinguished looking figure he made, looking on, as I collected my defining ability. The room seemed full of his atmosphere. He is a tall man, oaken in strength, with broad, intelligent face, high forehead, alert, wide-set eyes, and firm, even lips expressive of great self-control. His fluency, his wit and humor, his sound knowledge, his strength and perfect self-possession, were all suggested by his face and expression, and by the firmness of his squarely set head and massive shoulders.

"Let us," I said, "say money, opportunity, friends, good advice, and personal popularity for early advantages."

"The first isn't necessary," said the jurist, leisurely adjusting his hands in his pockets. "Opportunity comes to everyone, but all have not a mind to see; friends you can do without for a time; good advice we take too late, and popularity usually comes too early or too tardy to be appreciated. Define success."

"I might mention fame, position, income, as examples of what the world deems success."

"Foolish world!" said Mr. Choate. "The most successful men sometimes have not one of all these. All I can say is that early advantages won't bring a man a knowledge of the law, nor enable him to convince a jury. What he needs is years of close application, the ability to stick until he has mastered the necessary knowledge."

"Where did you obtain your wide knowledge of the law?" I asked.

"Reading at home and fighting in the courts,—principally, fighting in the courts."

"And was there any good luck about obtaining your first case? Was it secured by special effort?"

"None, unless it was the good luck of having a sign out, large enough for people to see. The rest of it was hard work, getting the evidence and the law fixed in my mind."

120

"You believe, of course," I ventured, "that advantageous opportunities do come to all?"

"Yes," said he, drawing up a chair and resignedly seating himself. "I believe that opportunities come to all,—not the same opportunities, nor the same kind of opportunities, nor opportunities half so valuable in some cases as in others, but they do come, and if seen and grasped will work a vast improvement in the life and character of an individual. Every boy cannot be President, but my word for it, if he is industrious, he can improve his position in the world."

* * * * * *

"If equally valuable opportunities do not come to all," I went on, "hasn't an individual a right to complain and justify his failure?"

"We have passed the period when we believe that all men are equal," said Mr. Choate. "We know they're free, but some men are born less powerful than others. But if an individual does not admit to himself that he is deficient in strength or reasoning powers, if he claims all the rights and privileges given others because he is 'as good as they,' then his success or failure is upon his own head. He should prove that he is what he thinks he is, and be what he aspires to be."

"You believe, of course, that an individual may overestimate his abilities."

"Believe it," he answered, with a deprecatory wave of the hand, "trust the law to teach that. But if a man does overestimate himself, he still owes it to himself to endeavor to prove that his estimate of himself is correct. We all need to. If he fails, he will be learning his limitations, which is better than never finding them out. No man can justify inaction."

"What do you consider to be the genuine battle of a youth to-day?—the struggle to bear poverty while working to conquer?"

"Not at all," came the quick answer. "Poor clothes and poor food and a poor place to dwell in are disagreeable things and must be made to give place to better, of course, but one can be partially indifferent to them. The real struggle is to hang on to every advantage, and strengthen the mind at every step. There are persons who have learned to endure poverty so well that they don't mind it any longer. The struggle comes in maintaining a purpose through pov-

121

erty to the end. It is just as difficult to maintain a purpose through riches."

"Money is not an end, then, in your estimation."

"Never, and need is only an incentive. Erskine made his greatest speech with his hungry children tugging at his coat-tails. That intense feeling that something has got to be done is the thing that works the doing. I never met a great man who was born rich."

This remark seemed rather striking in a way, because of the fact that Mr. Choate's parents were not poor in the accepted sense. The family is rather distinguished in New England annals. His father was a cousin of the famous Rufus Choate, and the latter, at the date of Joseph's birth, January 24, 1832, was just entering his second term in Congress to distinguish himself by a great speech on the tariff. Mr. Choate was the youngest of four brothers, and, after receiving a [high] school education in Salem, was sent to Harvard, where he was graduated in 1852, and later from its law school in 1854. Influence procured him a position in a Boston law office. After a year of practical study, he was admitted to the Bar of Massachusetts. In October of that year he made a tour of observation in the Western states, in company with his brother William, and on his return determined to settle in New York.

"Isn't it possible, Mr. Choate," I ventured, "that your having had little or no worrying over poverty in your youth might cause you to underestimate the effect of it on another, and overestimate the importance of sticking with determination to an idea through wealth or deprivation?"

"No," he replied, after a few moments' delay, in which he picked up one of the volumes near by as if to consult it; "no, the end to be attained makes important the need of hanging on. I am sure it is quite often more difficult to rise with money than without."

"You have had long years of distinction and comfort; do you find that success brings content and happiness?"

"Well," he answered, contracting his brows with legal severity, "constant labor is happiness, and success simply means ability to do more labor,—more deeds far-reaching in their power and effect. Such success brings about as much happiness as the world provides."

"I mean," I explained, "the fruits of that which is conventionally accepted as success; few hours of toil, a luxuriously furnished home, hosts of friends, the applause of the people, sumptuous repasts, and content in idleness, knowing that enough has been done."

"We never know that enough has been done," said the lawyer. "All this sounds pleasant, but the truth is that the men whose great efforts have made such things possible for themselves are the very last to desire them. You have described what appeals to the idler, the energyless dreamer, the fashionable dawdler, and the listless voluptuary. Enjoyment of such things would sap the strength and deaden the ambition of a Lincoln. The man who has attained to the position where these things are possible is the one whose life has been a constant refutation of the need of these things. He is the one who has abstained, who has conserved his mental and physical strength by living a simple and frugal life. He has not taken more than he needed, and never, if possible, less. His enjoyment has been in working, and I guarantee that you will find successful men ever to be plain-mannered persons of simple tastes, to whom sumptuous repasts are a bore, and luxury a thing apart. They may live surrounded by these things, but personally take little interest in them, knowing them to be mere trappings, which neither add to nor detract from character."

"Is there no pleasure then in luxury and ease without toil?" I questioned.

"None," said the speaker, emphatically. "There is pleasure in rest after labors. It is gratifying to relax when you really need relaxation, to be weary and be able to rest. But to enjoy anything you must first feel the need of it. But no more," he said, putting up his hand conclusively. "Surely you have enough to make clear what you wish to know."

* * * * * *

The Real Zangwill

Israel Zangwill was well-known for his novels and short stories of London ghetto life. He arrived in America in late August 1898. The dinner commemorating Tolstoy's 70th birthday occurred on September 8, 1898.

In this our day of quickly-made reputations and rapid declines, when the world, so anxious to seize upon a doer of deeds, examine him, estimate his worth and classify him, we see strange things. All our promising youths of the time have scarce a season in which to mature before they are plucked green, as one might say, and sunned, lauded, idolized, until what with their achievement of this public recognition, so often the only or chief incentive to great endeavor and labor, they become perverted from silent but glorious tasks and for want of other aspiration or inspiration, decay. That it is true that you cannot eat your cake and have it, too, meets daily its exposition in the literary world. You cannot be lauded as a genius, a world wonder, see all your dreams of distinction realized and still dream of distinction. Once you have had it the haunting desire to obtain it, the great desire *to do,* and be honored therefore passes, and genius too quickly hailed, withers and decays, a victim of the overestimate.

I shall not say this with any particular emphasis on its relation to the present subject, but merely as a general truth, which borne in mind, makes for a clearer and more honestly critical atmosphere, and helps each to decide with the aid of the evidence presented, what the value of a man may be.

The readers of many magazines and reviews have heard of Mr. Zangwill—I. Zangwill—and of late in our own country the general public has caught the name from the daily papers, and bandied it, without further knowledge, from mouth to mouth, as the general public is very often wont to do. We have asserted, as accepted, that he has talent; fine critical ability, wit, good nature and even sympathy. Accepted as of great value in the critical

Ainslee's 2 (November 1898): 351–57.

world, he is also read as a novelist, admired as a contributor and
railed at for what is so common a failing to-day, excessive egotism.
You will find him, said a writer of the *Critic* to me, "a most self-
assured individual. Heaven save young men from modesty, but
there are limits. This man is as peculiar as he is able, and you will
find him possessed of most extraordinary conceit."

This I knew before was a characteristic of his books, but
never having met him, I did not know it extended to his person. In
"Without Prejudice" we find, "I know I am cleverer than the man
in the street," and not said in way that can be modified or softened
by the context. Whatever we may think of this and other sen-
tences, men usually halt before saying so disputable a thing. To
write smartly is but a peculiarity, some maintain—a thing apart
from greatness, and the humblest may meditate such heights of
truth perennial that no reviewer great or small could say "I am
cleverer," without convicting himself of smallness in being so. The
very ignorant sympathies of the poorest of the unwashed are often
more holy in tendency than the finer analyses of the egotist, devoid
of sympathies, small or large.

However, this is of the book, not the man, and there endeth
the charge. Consensus of opinion has not rendered to Mr. Zangwill's literature the highest, though a high, place. The critics of the
world have said "The Ghetto Tragedies" were well done, "Flutter-
duck," too, was excellent work. We have laughed at the "King of
the Schnorrers," and there have been one or two other short
stories since, and what else is there? Nothing save some witty,
precise and keenly analytical essays, in which we cannot expect to
find great heart or soul! because these qualities are not usually put
there, forsooth.

Good fortune blessed me with a happy day. I saw him fresh
from the boat, a slow, peculiar man. He looked tired, he was in
tow, there was neither wish nor intention on my part to speak with
him, but there he was. Readily came the thought, he ignores
smooth dressing. As striking as a celebrity with long hair, he still
did not wear his hair long. With trousers loose and baggy, a commonplace frock coat, hat indifferent, loose flowing tie, he glanced
as with a heavy head, and shuffled with his feet at times, peculiarly. Nothing strange about this, if a man so chooses, but it is not
common to all literary men and therefore mentionable. It would be
impossible to say *affected,* for he looked too serious, his head is
too large, his features too marked, there is a stillness in the eye,
and an altogether physical ugliness, so modified by intellect as to

become wholly interesting and strange. If he were poor, ignorant, divested of that critical light of reason and forward self-assertiveness of wisdom, you would turn him out of doors for his looks. As it is, you draw near and listen.

Next he appeared at the Tolstoi dinner. Seated at the right hand of the spokesman of the evening, a guest of honor but little changed in dress. A sea of white shirt-fronts danced before his eyes. The gentlemen were in black, solemn and in perfect order, but not so the young English Jew, so peculiar unto himself. Everything was quite conventional, but there he sat, loose tie, a sort of short coat of many wrinkles indicating long and comfortable adjustment to his person, a plain vest and trousers of some light check, which might have been faint green in color, or some other shade belied by the lamps. Others ate comfortably while he listened and talked; others eulogized Tolstoi most unaffectedly and some gushingly. When he arose, however, tall, thin, his shoulders stooping, his large near-sighted brown eyes looking through and around a pair of drooping noseglasses, and his mop of kinkiest black hair standing out about his head in a surprised manner, it was to say in a thin, unoratorical voice that he disagreed somewhat with what had been said.

He spoke facetiously, with a shaft of plain wit ever and anon, and a tendency to pun a little, as Englishmen do. Tolstoi was not wholly glorified. Not altogether were the white shirts, he said, honoring the Russian author, for if great honor were done him his admirers would abandon white shirts and wear blouses. So fine a repast was no honor, since Tolstoi believes in plain living, and he continued, showing wittily the incongruity of a feast in honor of the opponent of feasts, as well as pointing the limitations and failings of the Great Peasant, while admitting his sincerity. He divorced the man from his art, and admitted partial good in him, sitting down, only to hear the next speaker eulogize where he had but analyzed.

Great is the art of analysis, for it sits in judgment upon the heart. I was prepared for this facility of adopting and twisting facts in droll and unconvincing manner, but not for the conviction that he sees truth clearly, until he said: "Nature is a great effort to express truth. The constant changing, shifting, appearing and disappearing material is the effort of the spirit to express itself more and more clearly—more and more perfectly—that is beautifully." Afterward I decided that he sees truth as one sees an appearing man or bird or other moving object in the distance. You can easily imagine him saying: "Ho! there goes truth. See it. Do you follow quickly, it is good," and then calmly sitting still himself and looking for some other interesting object. That is the way his Tolstoi address affected me.

The last time I saw him we came straight up against each other, he self-absorbed, careless, indifferent, ready to get rid of another dull thing quickly, and I careful, curious and quite humble.

"Well," he said, brusquely, in a manner soon to change, "what will you have—what do you want to know."

I explained a moment, and then we strolled roomward, his feet shuffling occasionally. Evidently he expected the machinery of thought to begin at once, and there was something of condescension and a "I will assist the nervous and bashful" in the way in which he said, "Well, begin. Why—um, you are as bashful as a young girl with her first sweetheart," whereupon I laughed.

"Not wholly—considerate, let us say."

He fumbled for a key, but being near-sighted could not find the keyhole, so I took the matter in hand and opened the door.

"Now, then," he said, when the lamps were turned up.

But not to be hastened, I let him work off the interest he manifested in an open portmanteau, loaded with a confusion of letters and papers, out of the jumble of which he sought something. When deepest in his search I said:

"I want to know about your critical point of view."

He stopped and straightened up out of the depths of letters, holding many in his hand and surveying the walls blankly.

"My point of view. Well, I have certain literary canons, certain canons of art, by which I measure things. It is one of my rules that you must never blame a book for not being some other book, a work of art for not being like something else. If you criticize it at all, that should be a warrant that the thing is worth criticizing. All that remains is to classify it. It is of such and such a period, such and such a school, such and such merit."

I wish every one who admires Zangwill sincerely could hear his voice. I wish they could feel how pleasant it is, how measured, how cadenced. It is but justice to offer praise here, when so little can be said for his oratorical ability. His "Well" is something fine, and the "I have my" is soft and not exasperating, however often repeated. The head is so solid, the bones so marked, the chin receding and therefore should be the augur of sensitiveness and a readiness to weep genuinely. It is the grace of learning he has with him, the music of refinement in motion, in voice, in glance. He appeals as grotesque old porcelain appeals, after a little while, but, ah! it is not always the artistic, the intellectual, that satisfies. We accept all these things as fine premonitions and then seek and seek. But if we find not the heart, if we find not the heart!

"You find many good things that way," I said.

"All that I criticize has its place," he answered.

"Under such a system as that it seems to me you should find a place for everything and quite a respectable word for everything if you chose."

He turned on me a quizzical glance, which did not rest long. The truth is, he sees so poorly through glasses that it does not repay him to stare.

"No. A work once classified must be judged in relation to its value to the world in its particular field. There are still ample grounds for praise or condemnation."

"You have noted, of course, the tendency of the literati to grow more and more mournful, more pessimistic? One of your Englishmen, Hardy, strikes a peculiarly despairing note."

"Yes, every age has its pessimism. Pessimism is not a sign of despair but discontent. Now we know, of course, that discontent is the lever that moves the world, and the greater the pessimism the surer is the approach of change, for pessimism means that one order is bad and most give way to something else. Therefore it is a hopeful sign."

"What do you admire most in literature—what spirit or attitude?"

"The hopeful defiant one, of course. Such a note as we find in Shakespeare."

"And you consider great literature to be always hopeful literature?"

"Well, if a poem is inspiring, if it lifts you up and makes you strong, it is certainly the best thing."

"That may be, but we have still to say whether the great literature is hopeful. Take the world novels, the world poems—are not the masterpieces sad, the most thrilling passages those of agony undergone?"

"Well," he said, pausing with a critical air and extending one hand with that argumentative grace common to lawyers, "of course the note of bitterness, the wail is always the most moving. We cannot deny that the grand things are spoken of human sorrow and human suffering. It is so in all nations and all literatures."

"Yet you count this general acclaim of the works which are

The Real Zangwill

most sorrowful, which drag down the spirit and often compel tears, a hopeful sign?"

"Yes, in the main, the grand passions which move the heart, uplift and strengthen and broaden."

"And still the hopeful defiant note which sees only good in life is best?"

"I think so."

"We are confronted at this day and date by what I choose to call Omarism—the vast and growing delight of the many in the pathetic and despairing verses of the Persian Poet. You have noted it, of course?"

"Poor poem it is—poor in philosophy, I mean. That is a kind of weakling view to take of life to say, 'I cannot understand it, we are victims of fate, therefore I will drown the memory of it in drink'. Quite a poor view I should say."

"And what of the many who read it with delight, take it to heart, and call it a true exponent of the real conditions?"

"They share a poor view."

"Then you would call it anything but a hopeful sign?"

"I must."

The conversation languished at this time, owing to the arrival of a bellboy, who lorded the situation for a moment and patronized us both.

"I believe," said the eminent critic, "I shall have a stimulant of some kind," and therewith glanced at me.

"Thanks, I never do," I smiled.

"How curious, and an American journalist, too; how curious!" he drawled. "I thought you all did."

"You were saying in your Tolstoi address," I went on when the boy had departed, "that the relationship between a man and his work means nothing either for the merit of the man or the merit of the work."

"Exactly. You would not call a good pair of shoes bad because they were made by a drunken, swearing shoemaker, nor a poor pair good, though they were by one who devoutly practices the Christian code of morals. Neither can you condemn a book for any failing of its author."

"How," said I, "about the works of Paul Verlaine, Oscar Wilde, or the historical Villon?—would you accept their work as valuable, and preserve it as a part of the world's treasure?"

"Um-assuredly. What would we say of their work, if nothing were known of their personality—as is the case with Shakespeare?"

129

"Then a man may degrade himself as he pleases and still be accepted on his literary side."

The critic halted, looking upward with one eye, his mental machinery fully at work.

"Pray do not misinterpret me. Understand I speak from the purely critical point of view. I speak of the works as divorced from the man, you know. They could be accepted where the man could not. What the moralist would say of the man, how his personality might or should be treated by the religionist, the lover of pure society and so on, need not concern the critic. It is the work he deals with."

"True at least to your philosophy," I answered, and not without discretion, for I spoke from knowledge of Mr. Zangwill's writings.

He is a man who sees all that is to be done, the politics that are to be purified, the religions revised or swept away, the art to be renovated, the social inequalities to be adjusted, and yet, who seeing the need in each particular field for a man to lay hold and help improve—who hearing the call for enthusiasts, prophets, reformers—men to put their shoulder to the separate wheels, prefers where there are so many things that need attention, to sit critically at the centre and observe them, judging of the efforts of those who come with separate convictions, to toil with various aims. One can imagine this man saying to the reformer: "Ah! you have only one portion of the question. You ignore all the other things done, you are narrow," and so going the rounds, while doing absolutely nothing himself but criticizing. It is the great analytical spirit, useful no doubt, but the world loves an enthusiast better, who criticizes not at all, but seizes upon the first thing to his hands and toils kindly, if blindly, in the thought that his is the great and necessary labor. Certainly such a life bespeaks a greater soul, if keen sympathies make soul, than does that of the man who can sit off and eternally pass judgment, unmoved forever to ally himself heart and hand with any one great effort for the uplifting of humanity. If no cause ever appeals to him sufficiently to enlist all his effort, he has not the wealth of sympathy, which the other man has who can be moved to so ally himself—is in other words the pure critic.

* * * * * *

Curious Shifts of the Poor

At the hour when Broadway assumes its most interesting aspect, a peculiar individual takes his stand at the corner of Twenty-sixth Street. It is the hour when the theatres are just beginning to receive their patrons. Fire signs, announcing the night's amusements, blaze on every hand. Cabs and carriages, their lamps gleaming like yellow eyes, patter by. Couples and parties of three and four are freely mingled in the common crowd which passes by in a thick stream, laughing and jesting. On Fifth Avenue are loungers, a few wealthy strollers, a gentleman in evening dress with a lady at his side, some clubmen, passing from one smoking room to another. Across the way the great hotels, the Hoffman House and the Fifth Avenue, show a hundred gleaming windows, their cafés and billiard rooms filled with a pleasure-loving throng. All about, the night has a feeling of pleasure and exhilaration, the curious enthusiasm of a great city, bent upon finding joy in a thousand different ways.

In the midst of this lightsome atmosphere a short, stocky-built soldier, in a great cape-overcoat and soft felt hat, takes his stand at the corner. For a while he is alone, gazing like any idler upon an ever-fascinating scene. A policeman passes, saluting him as Captain, in a friendly way. An urchin, who has seen him there before, stops and gazes. To all others he is nothing out of the ordinary save in dress, a stranger, whistling for his own amusement.

As the first half hour wanes, certain characters appear. Here and there in the passing crowd one may see now and then a loiterer, edging interestedly near. A slouchy figure crosses the opposite corner and glances furtively in his direction. Another comes down Fifth avenue to the corner of Twenty-sixth street, takes a general survey and hobbles off again. Two or three noticeable Bowery types edge along the Fifth avenue side of Madison Square, but do not venture over. The soldier in his cape-overcoat walks a line of ten feet at his corner, to and fro, whistling.

Demorest's 36 (November 1899): 22–26. *Sister Carrie* (New York, 1900), chaps. 45–47.

As nine o'clock approaches, some of the hub-hub of the earlier hour passes. On Broadway the crowd is neither so thick nor so gay. There are fewer cabs passing. The atmosphere of the hotels is not so youthful. The air, too, is colder. On every hand move curious figures, watchers and peepers without an imaginary circle, which they are afraid to enter—dozens in all. Presently, with the arrival of a keener sense of cold, one figure comes forward. It crosses Broadway from out the shadow of Twenty-sixth street, and, in a halting, circuitous way, arrives close to the waiting figure. There is something shamefaced, a diffident air about the movement, as if the intention were to conceal any idea of stopping until the very last moment. Then, suddenly, close to the soldier comes the halt. The Captain looks in recognition, but there is no especial greeting. The newcomer nods slightly, and murmurs something, like one who waits for gifts. The other simply motions toward the edge of the walk.

"Stand over there."

The spell is broken. Even while the soldier resumes his short, solemn walk, other figures shuffle forward. They do not so much as greet the leader, but join the one, shuffling and hitching and scraping their feet.

"Cold, isn't it?"

"I don't like winter."

"Looks as though it might snow."

The motley company has increased to ten. One or two know each other and converse. Others stand off a few feet, not wishing to be in the crowd, and yet not counted out. They are peevish, crusty, silent, eying nothing in particular, and moving their feet. The soldier, counting sufficient to begin, comes forward.

"Beds, eh, all of you?"

There is a general shuffle and murmur of approval.

"Well, line up here. I'll see what I can do. I haven't a cent myself."

They fall into a sort of broken, ragged line. One sees now some of the chief characteristics by contrast. There is a wooden leg in the line. Hats are all drooping, a collection that would ill become a second-hand Hester street basement collection. Trousers are all warped and frayed at the bottom, and coats worn and faded. In the glare of the street lights, some of the faces look dry and chalky. Others are red with blotches, and puffed in the cheeks and under the eyes. One or two are raw-boned and remind one of railroad hands. A few spectators come near, drawn by the seemingly

132

conferring group, then more and more, and quickly there is a pushing, gaping crowd. Someone in the line begins to talk.

"Silence!" exclaims the Captain. "Now, then, gentlemen, these men are without beds. They have got to have some place to sleep to-night. They can't lie out in the street. I need twelve cents to put one to bed. Who will give it to me?"

No reply.

"Well we'll have to wait here, boys, until someone does. Twelve cents isn't so very much for one man."

"Here is fifteen," exclaims a young man, who is peering forward with strained eyes. "It's all I can afford."

"All right; now I have fifteen. Step out of the line," and seizing the one at the end of the line nearest him by the shoulder, the Captain marches him off a little ways and stands him up alone.

Coming back, he resumes his place before the little line and begins again.

"I have three cents here. These men must be put to bed somehow. There are," counting, "one, two, three, four, five, six, seven, eight, nine, ten, eleven, twelve men. Nine cents more will put the next man to bed, give him a good, comfortable bed for the night. I go right along and look after that myself. Who will give me nine cents?"

One of the watchers, this time a middle-aged man, hands in a five-cent piece.

"Good. Now I have eight cents. Four more will give this man a bed. Come, gentlemen, we are going very slow this evening. You all have good beds. How about these?"

"Here you are," remarked a bystander, putting a coin into his hand.

"That," says the Captain, looking at the coin, "pays for two beds for two men and leaves five for the next one. Who will give seven cents more?"

On the one hand the little line of those whose beds are secure is growing, but on the other the bedless waxes long. Silently the queer drift of poverty washes in, and they take their places at the foot of the line unnoticed. Ever and anon the Captain counts and announces the number remaining. Its growth neither dismays nor interests him. He does not even speak of it. His concern is wholly over the next man, and the securing of twelve cents. Strangers, gazing out of mere curiosity, find their sympathies enlisted, and pay into the hands of the Captain dimes and quarters, as he states in a short, brusque, unaffected way, the predicament of the men.

133

Part 2: 1898–1910

In the line of men whose beds are secure, a relaxed air is apparent. The strain of uncertainty being removed, there is moderate good feeling, and some leaning toward sociability. Those nearest one another begin to talk. Politics, religion, the state of the government, some newspaper sensations, and the more notorious facts of the world find mouth-pieces and auditors here. Vague and rambling are the discussions. Cracked and husky voices pronounce forcibly on odd things. There are squints and leers and dull ox-like stares from those who are too dull or too weary to converse.

Standing tells. In the course of time the earliest arrivals become weary and uneasy. There is a constant shifting from one foot to the other, a leaning out and looking back to see how many more must be provided for before the company can march away. Comments are made and crude wishes for the urging forward of things.

"Huh! There's a lot back there yet."

"Yes, must be over a hundred to-night."

"Captain's a great fellow, ain't he?"

A cab had stopped. Some gentleman in evening dress reaches out a bill to the Captain, who takes it with simple thanks, and turns away to his line. There is a general craning of necks as the jewel in the broad white shirt-front sparkles and the cab moves off. Even the crowd gapes in awe.

"That fixes up nine men for the night," says the Captain, counting out as many of the line near him. "Line up over there. Now, then, there are only seven. I need twelve cents."

Money comes slow. In the course of time the crowd thins out to a meagre handful. Fifth avenue, save for an occasional cab or foot-passenger, is bare. Broadway is thinly peopled with pedestrians. Only now and then a stranger passing notices the small group, hands out a coin and goes away, unheeding.

The Captain is stolid and determined. He talks on, very slowly uttering the fewest words, and with a certain assurance, as though he could not fail.

"Come, I can't stay out here all night. These men are getting tired and cold. Someone give me four cents."

There comes a time when he says nothing at all. Money is handed him, and for each twelve cents he singles out a man and puts him in the other line. Then he walks up and down as before, looking at the ground.

The theatres let out. Fire signs disappear. A clock strikes eleven. Another half hour, and he is down to the last two men.

A lady in opera cape and rustling silk skirt comes down Fifth

134

avenue, supported by her escort. The latter glances at the line and comes over. There is a bill in his fingers.

"Here you are," he says.

"Thanks," says the Captain. "Now we have some for tomorrow night."

The last two are lined up. The soldier walks along, studying his line and counting.

"One hundred and thirty-seven," he exclaims, when he reaches the head.

"Now, boys, line up there. Steady now, we'll be off in a minute."

He places himself at the head and calls out, "Forward, march!" and away they go.

Across Fifth avenue, through Madison Square, by the winding path, east on Twenty-third street, and down Third avenue trudges the long, serpentine company.

Below Tenth street is a lodging house, and here the queer, ragamuffin line brings up, while the Captain enters in to arrange. In a few minutes the deal is consummated, and the line marches slowly in, each being provided with a key as the Captain looks on. When the last one has disappeared up the dingy stairway, he comes out, muffles his great coat closer in the cold air, pulls down his slouch brim, and tramps, a solitary, silent figure, into the night.

Such is the Captain's idea of his duty to his fellow man. He is a strange man, with a strange bias. Utter confidence in Providence, perfectly sure that he deals direct with God, he takes this means of fulfilling his own destiny.*

Outside the door of what was once a row of red brick family dwellings, in Fifteenth street, but what is now a mission or convent house of the Sisters of Mercy, hangs a plain wooden contribution box, on which is painted the statement that every noon a meal is given free to all those who apply and ask for aid. This simple announcement is modest in the extreme, covering, as it does, a charity so broad. Unless one were looking up this matter in particular, he could stand at Sixth avenue and Fifteenth street for days, around the noon hour, and never notice that, out of the vast crowd that surges along that busy thoroughfare, there turned out, every few seconds, some weather-beaten, heavy-footed specimen of humanity, gaunt in

*Dreiser later wrote an additional sketch of the Captain, "A Touch of Human Brotherhood," *Success* 5 (March 1902): 140–41, 176.

countenance, and dilapidated in the matter of clothes. The fact is true, however, and the colder the day the more apparent it becomes. Space and lack of culinary room compels an arrangement which permits of only twenty-five or thirty eating at one time, so that a line has to be formed outside, and an orderly entrance effected.

One such line formed on a January day last year. It was peculiarly cold. Already, at eleven in the morning, several shambled forward out of Sixth avenue, their thin clothes flapping and fluttering in the wind, and leaned up against the iron fence. One came up from the west out of Seventh avenue and stopped close to the door, nearer than all the others. Those who had been waiting before him, but farther away, now drew near, and by a certain stolidity of demeanor, no words being spoken, indicated that they were first. The newcomer looked sullenly along the line and then moved out, taking his place at the foot. When order had been restored, the animal feeling of opposition relaxed.

"Must be pretty near noon," ventured one.

"It is," said another; "I've been waitin' nearly an hour."

"Gee, but it's cold."

The line was growing rapidly. Those at the head evidently congratulated themselves upon not having long to wait. There was much jerking of heads and looking down the line.

"It don't matter much how near you get to the front, as long as you're in the first twenty-five. You all go in together," commented one of the first twenty-five.

"This here Single Tax is the thing. There ain't goin' to be no order till it comes," said another, discussing that broader topic.*

At last the door opened and the motherly Sister looked out. Slowly the line moved up, and one by one thirty men passed in. Then she interposed a stout arm and the line halted with six men on the steps. In this position they waited. After a while one of the earliest to go in came out, and then another. Every time one came out the line moved up. And this continued until two o'clock, when the last hungry dependent crossed the threshold, and the door was closed.

It was a winter evening.† Already, at four o'clock, the sombre hue of night was thickening the air. A heavy snow was

*Henry George, the founder of the single tax movement, almost won the mayoralty of New York in 1897.

†Several recent critics have noted the similarity of this sketch to Stephen Crane's "The Men in the Storm," published originally in the *Arena* in October 1894, and republished in the *Philistine* in January 1897.

falling—a fine, picking, whipping snow, borne forward by a swift wind in long, thin lines. The street was bedded with it, six inches of cold, soft carpet, churned brown by the crush of teams and the feet of men. Along the Bowery, men slouched through it with collars up and hats pulled over their ears.

Before a dirty four-story building gathered a crowd of men. It began with the approach of two or three, who hung about the closed wooden doors, and beat their feet to keep them warm. They made no effort to go in, but shifted ruefully about, digging their hands deep in their pockets, and leering at the crowd and the increasing lamps. There were old men with grizzled beards and sunken eyes; men who were comparatively young, but shrunken by disease; men who were middle-aged.

With the growth of the crowd about the door came a murmur. It was not conversation, but a running comment directed at anyone in general. It contained oaths and slang phrase.

"I wisht they'd hurry up."

"Look at the copper watchin'."

"Maybe it ain't winter, nuther."

"I wisht I was with Otis."*

Now a sharper lash of wind cut down, and they huddled closer. There was no anger, no threatening words. It was all sullen endurance, unlightened by either wit or good fellowship.

A carriage went jingling by with some reclining figure in it. One of the members nearest the door saw it.

"Look at the bloke ridin'."

"He ain't so cold."

"Eh! Eh! Eh!" yelled another, the carriage having long since passed out of hearing.

Little by little the night crept on. Along the walk a crowd turned out on its way home. Still the men hung around the door, unwavering.

"Ain't they ever goin' to open up?" queried a hoarse voice suggestively.

This seemed to renew general interest in the closed door, and many gazed in that direction. They looked at it as dumb brutes look, as dogs paw and whine and study the knob. They shifted and blinked and muttered, now a curse, now a comment. Still they waited, and still the snow whirled and cut them.

*Harrison G. Otis was one of the generals leading American troops against Philippine insurgents during the winter of 1898–99.

Part 2: 1898–1910

A glimmer appeared through the transom overhead, where someone was lighting the gas. It sent a thrill of possibility through the watcher. On the old hats and peaked shoulders snow was piling. It gathered in little heaps and curves, and no one brushed it off. In the center of the crowd the warmth and steam melted it, and water trickled off hat-rims and down noses which the owners could not reach to scratch. On the outer rim the piles remained unmelted. Those who could not get in the center lowered their heads to the weather and bent their forms.

At last the bars grated inside and the crowd pricked up its ear. There was someone who called, "Slow up there now!" and then the door opened. It was push and jam for a minute, with grim, beast silence to prove its quality, and then the crowd lessened. It melted inward like logs floating, and disappeared. There were wet hats and shoulders, a cold, shrunken, disgruntled mass, pouring in between bleak walls. It was just six o'clock, and there was supper in every hurrying pedestrian's face.

"Do you sell anything to eat here?" questioned one of the grizzled old carpet-slippers who opened the door.

"No; nothin' but beds."

The waiting throng had been housed.

For nearly a quarter of a century Fleischman, the caterer, has given a loaf of bread to anyone who will come for it to the rear door of his restaurant, on the corner of Broadway and Ninth street, at midnight. Every night, during twenty-three years, about three hundred men have formed in line, and, at the appointed time, marched past the doorway, picked their loaf from a great box placed just outside, and vanished into the night. From the beginning to the present time there has been little change in the character or number of these men. There are two or three figures that have grown familiar to those who have seen this little procession pass year after year. Two of them have missed scarcely a night in fifteen years. There are about forty, more or less, regular callers. The remainder of the line is formed of strangers every night.

The line is not allowed to form before eleven o'clock. At this hour, perhaps a single figure shambles around the corner and halts on the edge of the sidewalk. Other figures appear and fall in behind. They come almost entirely one at a time. Haste is seldom manifest in their approach. Figures appear from every direction, limping slowly, slouching stupidly, or standing with assumed or

138

real indifference, until the end of the line is reached, when they take their places and wait.

Most of those men in the line are over thirty. There is seldom one under twenty. A low murmur of conversation is heard, but for the most part the men stand in stupid, unbroken silence. Here and there are two or three talkative ones, and if you pass close enough you will hear every topic of the times discussed or referred to, except those which are supposed to interest the poor. Wretchedness, poverty, hunger and distress are never mentioned. The possibilities of a match between prize-ring favorites, the day's evidence in the latest murder trial, the chance of war in Africa, the latest improvements in automobiles, the prosperity or depression of some other portion of the world, or the mistakes of the Government, from Washington to the campaign in Manila. These, or others like them, are the topics of whatever conversation is held. It is for the most part a rambling, disconnected conversation.

"Wait until Dreyfus gets out of prison," said one to his little black-eyed neighbor one night, "and you'll see them guys fallin' on his neck."*

"Maybe they will and maybe they won't," the other muttered. "You needn't think, just because you see dagoes selling violets on Broadway, that the spring is here."

The passing of a Broadway car awakens a vague idea of progress, and some one remarks: "They'll have them things running by liquid air before we know it."

"I've driv mule cars by here myself," replies another.

A few moments before twelve a great box of bread is pushed outside the door, and exactly on the hour a portly round-faced German takes his position by it, and calls "Ready." The whole line at once, like a well-drilled company of regulars, moves swiftly, in good marching time, diagonally across the sidewalk to the inner edge and pushes, with only the noise of tramping feet, past the box. Each man reaches for a loaf, and, breaking line, wanders off by himself. Most of them do not even glance at their bread, but put it indifferently under their coats or in their pockets.

In the great sea of men here are these little eddies of driftwood, a hundred nightly in Madison Square, 300 outside a bakery at midnight, crowds without the lodging-houses in stormy weather, and all this day after day. These are the poor in body and in spirit.

---

*Zola's *J'Accuse,* published January 13, 1898, had created world-wide interest in the Dreyfus case.

The lack of houses and lands and fine clothing is nothing. Many have these and are equally wretched. The cause of misery lies elsewhere. The attitude of pity which the world thinks proper to hold toward poverty is misplaced—a result of the failure to see and to realize. Poverty of worldly goods is not in itself pitiful. A sickly body, an ignorant mind, a narrow spirit, brutal impulses and perverted appetites are the pitiful things. The adding of material riches to one thus afflicted would not remove him from out the pitiful. On the other hand, there are so-called poor people in every community among its ornaments. There is no pity for them, but rather love and honor. They are rich in wisdom and influence.

The individuals composing this driftwood are no more miserable than others. Most of them would be far more uncomfortable if compelled to lead respectable lives. They cannot be benefited by money. There may be a class of poor for whom a little money judiciously expended would result in good, but these are the lifeless flotsam and jetsam of society without vitality to ever revive. Few among them would survive a month if they should come suddenly into the possession of a fortune.

Their parade before us should not appeal to our pity, but should awaken us to what we are—for society is no better than its poorest type. They expose what is present, though better concealed, everywhere. They are the few skeletons of the sunlight—types of these with which society's closets are full. Civilization, in spite of its rapid progress, is still in profound ignorance of the things essential to a healthy, happy and prosperous life. Ignorance and error are everywhere manifest in the miseries and sufferings of men. Wealth may create an illusion, or modify a ghastly appearance of ignorance and error, but it cannot change the effect. The result is as real in the mansions of Fifth avenue as in the midnight throng outside a baker's door.

The livid-faced dyspeptic who rides from his club to his apartments and pauses on the way to hand his dollar to the Captain should awaken the same pity as the shivering applicant for a free bed whom his dollar aids—pity for the ignorance and error that cause the distress of the world.

The Real Howells

Howells, it can be truly said, is greater than his literary volumes make him out to be. If this be considered little enough, then let us say he is even greater than his reputation. Since it is contended that his reputation far outweighs his achievements, let this tribute be taken in full, for he is all that it implies—one of the noblemen of literature.

A striking characteristic of the man is that he understands himself better than any one else, and that he has the courage to write himself down without color or favor. Prof. Boyesen found, when he interviewed him in 1893, that he could "portray himself unconsciously (in conversation) better than I or anybody else could do it for him."* His manner is so simple, his wonder at life so fresh and unsatisfied that he appeals to the student and observer as something truly rare—a wholly honest man. He is evidently so honest at heart that he is everywhere at home with himself, and will contribute that quiet, homelike atmosphere to everything and everybody around. He will compel sincerity in you, when you talk with him, not by any suggestion from him but by the wholesome atmosphere which he exhales, and which steals over all, and makes plain that forms and slight conventionalities are not necessary.

We will not say that he was always thus. One can easily imagine the ideality of his youth when the world seemed young and green. Never insincere, we can believe, but enthusiastic and imaginative. But youth slipped away, the days waned in weariness of work, the mystery of life did not become clearer, and duty came to look more stern. I think that the thought of the final hour is too much with him; that the "watch, for ye know not," rings too much in his ears. He appeals to me as possessing a deeply religious nature unanchored to any religious belief.

My first sight of him was on a January day in Fifth Avenue. Some one who knew him said, "Here comes Howells," and I saw

Ainslee's 5 (March 1900): 137–42. *Americana* 36 (April 1943): 275–82.

*H. H. Boyesen, "Real Conversations. I. A Dialogue between William Dean Howells and Hjalmar Hjorth Boyesen," *McClure's* 1 (June 1893): 3–11.

a stout, thick-set, middle-aged man trudging solemnly forward. He was enveloped in a great fur ulster, and peered, rather ferociously upon the odds and ends of street life that passed. He turned out again and again for this person and that, and I wondered why a stout man with so fierce a mien did not proceed resolutely forward, unswerving for the least or the greatest.

The next time I saw him was for a favor. Some magazine wanted his opinion.* A total stranger, I knocked at his door in the apartments overlooking Central Park, and gave no card—only my name. "If he is in he will see you," said the servant, and, sure enough, see me he did, after a few moments. It was with a quiet trudge that he entered the room, and in a glance everything was put at ease. Anybody could talk to him providing the errand was an honest one.

There was none of that "I am a busy man" air. The wrinkles about the eyes were plainly not evidences of natural ferocity, but of kindly age. He even smiled before hearing all my request, motioned me to a chair, and sat down himself. When I had done I arose and suggested that I would not intrude upon his time, but he only shook his head and sat still. Then he propounded some question, for all the world like a kindly bid to conversation, and we were off on an argument in a moment.

How it came around to speculation concerning life and death is almost beyond recall. Andrew Lang had newly re-issued his translations of Greek odes.† They deal with the passions and pains of individuals dead thousands of years ago, and I expressed wonder at the long, inexplicable procession of life.

Mr. Howells folded his hands calmly and sat quite silent. Then he said, "Yes, we never know wherefrom or whereto. It seems as if all these ruddy crowds of people are little more than plants wakened by the sun and rain."

"Do you find," I said, "that it is painful to feel life wearing on, slipping away, and change overtaking us all."

"It is truly. Life is fine. The morning air is good. When I stroll out of a sunny day it seems too much that it should not stay and endure. It is wistfulness that overtakes us, all the more bitter because so hopeless. Every one suffers from it more or less."

*Apparently the meeting on which Dreiser based his earlier article on Howells, "How He Climbed Fame's Ladder," *Success* 1 (April 1898): 5–6.

†Dreiser is probably coalescing his two meetings with Howells, since Lang's *Homeric Hymns* did not appear until November 1899.

The Real Howells

From the flight of time and ever imminent death, the conversation drifted to the crush of modern life and the struggle for existence.

"It is my belief," he said, "that the struggle really does grow more bitter. The great city surprises me. It seems so much a to-do over so little—millions crowding into to obtain subsistence in a region where subsistence is least."

"Where would you have them go?"

"There are more fertile parts of the world. This little island is cold and bleak a great many months of the year. Nothing is grown here. When you come to think, there is no reason why the people of the world should not live in the tropics. The means of subsistence there are greater. Yet here they are scheming and planning, and sometimes dying of starvation."

"You have had no direct experience of this great misery."

"No; but I have observed it. All my experiences have been literary, yet in this field I have seen enough."

"Is it so hard to rise in the literary world?"

"About as difficult as in any other field. There seems to be almost invariably a period of neglect and suffering. Every beginner feels or really finds that the doors are more or less closed against him."

"Your view is rather dispiriting."

"Life seems at times a hopeless tangle. You can only face the conditions bravely and take what befalls."

Other things were talked of, but this struck me at the time as peculiarly characteristic of the work of the man. His sympathies are right, but he is not primarily a deep reasoner. He would not, for instance, choose to follow up his speculations concerning life and attempt to offer some modest theory of improvement. He watches the changeful scene, rejoices or laments over the various and separate instances, but goes no further. He has reached the conclusion that life is difficult and inexplicable without really tracing the various theories by which it is synthetically proved. He is inclined to let the great analysis of things go by the board, sure that it is a mystery and not caring much for the proof.

And yet this attitude which looks so much like pessimism is anything but characteristic of his nature. For all that life with him is a riddle, approaching death a bane, he works and lives gladly. His heart is warm. Since he cannot explain the earthly struggle he chooses to help others make the best of it. Is it a young poet longing, verses in hand, for recognition, Howells will help him. He

143

is not a rich man and must work for his living, yet he will take of his time to read the struggler's material and recommend him according to his merit. The country knows how often he has appeared in print with a liberal commendation of a quite unknown author. He it was who first read Stephen Crane's books and assisted him in New York. It was he who publicly applauded the ghetto story of Abraham Cahan when that beginner was yet unrecognized.* He has, time after time, praised so liberally that paragraphers love to speak of him as the "lookout on the watch tower," straining for a first glimpse of approaching genius.

On my first visit, and when we were discussing the difficulties beginners experience, I happened to mention what I considered to be an appropriate instance of a young man in the West who had a fine novel which no publisher seemed to want.

"You consider it good, do you?" he asked.

"Very," I said.

"You might ask him to send it on to me. I should like to read it."

I was rather astonished at the liberal offer, and thanked him for the absent one. It was no idle favor of conversation, either. The book was forwarded, and, true to his word, he read it, doing what he could to make the merit of the work a source of reward for the author. There were several similar instances within a comparatively short period, and I heard of others from time to time until it all became impressively plain—how truly generous and humane is the Dean of American Letters. The great literary philanthropist, I call him.

* * * * * *

The most likable trait of this able writer, is his honest, open delight in being appreciated. The driving force of his youth was this desire to do fine things and get credit for them. The applause of the world—what an important thing it seemed. To-day he is wiser, but the heart is the same.

I said to him: "Have you found that satisfaction in the appreciation of your fellowmen, which in your youth you dreamed it would give you?"

*Howells had praised both Crane's *Maggie* and Cahan's *Yekyl* in "New York Low Life in Fiction," New York *World,* July 26, 1896, pt. 2, p. 18.

"Yes," he answered, "truly. It is all that the heart imagines—sweet."

"Worth the toil?"

"Yes. I know of nothing more exquisite than to have labored long and doubtingly and then to find, for all your fears, your labor commended, your name on many tongues. It is reward enough."

* * * * * *

Some may think that such open expression of sentiment and pleasure is like hanging one's heart upon one's sleeve for daws to peck at, but more will feel that it is but the creditable exuberance of a heart full of good feelings. He is thus frank in his books, his letters, his conversation. His family get no nearer in many things than those in the world outside who admire his charming qualities. He is the same constantly, a person whose thoughts issue untinged by any corroding wash of show or formality.

What more can be said of a man? He is not rich, and can therefore provide no evidence of his character by his individual disposition of money. His field of endeavor is of that peculiar nature which permits of much and effective masquerading. Many an evil heart is effectively cloaked and hidden from the world by a show of literary talent. We can look only at his individual expression of himself, the hold his nature has taken upon those who know him and the extent and use of his reputation. Fame is a very good collateral in the hands of an able man, and Howells has made good use of his fame.

If Howells, by reason of greater advantages in his youth, had been able to go farther intellectually, if he had had direction along the lines of sociology and philosophy, he might have given the world something most important in that direction. The man has the speculative, philosophic make-up. His sympathies are of a kind that produce able theories for the betterment of mankind. As it is, what he has written, smacks of the social-prophetic.

How true this is the readers of "A Traveler from Altruria" can witness. Therein he sets forth his dream of universal peace and good-will. He sketches a state of utter degradation from which the brutalized poor rise to the purest altruism.

In a further sense, the socialistic-philosophic turn of his nature is evidenced by his confession of the hold the works of Tolstoi have taken upon him. "He charms me," he said, "by his humanity, his goodness of heart." And in the "Literary Passions" that

145

fine opening to the last chapter confirms this statement, "I came now, though not quite in the order of time, to the noblest of all these enthusiasms, namely, my devotion for the writings of Lyof Tolstoi. I should wish to speak of him with his own incomparable truth, yet I do not know how to give a notion of his influence without the effect of exaggeration. As much as one merely human being can help another, I believe that he has helped me; he has not influenced me in aesthetics only, but in ethics, too, so that I can never again see life in the way I saw it before I knew him."

Tolstoi's influence has led him back, as he puts it, "to the only true ideal, away from that false standard of the gentleman to the Man who sought not to be distinguished from other men, but identified with them, to that *Presence* in which the finest gentleman shows his alloy of vanity, and the greatest genius shrinks to the measure of his miserable egotism."*

It does not matter whether Howells is the greatest novelist in the world or not, he is a great character. There are many, who find sentiments and feelings so rich, so fair, so delicately drawn, in his work, that it seems as if he had gathered the very moonbeams out of the night to weave a wistfull spell over the heart, and it is certain that these perfect parts of his work will live. About the other it does not matter, for the larger part of the work of all authors is more or less bad, anyhow. What is more important is that he has been an influence for good in American letters—that he has used his strength and popularity in the direction of what he took to be the right. He has helped thousands in more ways than one, and is a sweet and wholesome presence in the world of art. By the side of the egotists in his field, the chasers after fame and the hagglers over money, this man is a towering figure. His greatness is his goodness, his charm his sincerity.

My Literary Passions (New York, 1895), pp. 250–51.

Author of *Sister Carrie*

This interview appears to contain the first references in print to two of the principal "facts" in the Sister Carrie *suppression legend— that Mrs. Doubleday played a major role in the suppression, and that a contract for publication was signed before Doubleday objected to publication. Mrs. Doubleday's part in the dispute has never been clarified, and it is now known that the contract was signed when Doubleday, despite his objection, agreed to honor the word of the members of his firm.*

Theodore Dreiser, a former St. Louisan, who has newly gained fame as a novelist, was in the city last week on his way to Montgomery City, Mo., to visit the relatives of his wife, whom he married in that city.

Mr. Dreiser was employed in newspaper work in St. Louis from 1891 to 1894.* He went East and engaged in magazine work, publishing many short stories.

It is his first novel, "Sister Carrie," which has brought him into prominence. The British literary reviews, in particular, give it high praise, ranking it with "The Octopus," by Frank Norris, at the top of the list of novels for the last year.

It is interesting to note that Frank Norris, as senior reader for a publishing firm, first saw the merit of "Sister Carrie," and recommended its acceptance.

To the Post-Dispatch Mr. Dreiser told the history of his novel, which is extraordinary in some features.

The novel was written in six months, from October, 1899, to March, 1900. It was rejected by one publishing firm because it was not considered an all-around interesting story.

He took the manuscript to Doubleday, Page & Co.[,] April 1, 1900, where Frank Norris, author of "The Octopus," in his capacity as senior reader, read it. He sent for Mr. Dreiser and congratulated him.

St. Louis *Post-Dispatch,* January 26, 1902, pt. 1, p. 4. Unsigned.

*Dreiser began working as a newspaperman in St. Louis in 1892, not 1891.

Mr. Norris passed it on to Mr. Lanier, one of the members of the firm, who read it and thought it was a good story. He, in turn, handed it to Mr. Page, and that gentleman said he considered it the best book brought into the house that year.

When Mr. Doubleday, the senior partner, returned from Europe, he heard so much about the manuscript that he took it home. Mrs. Doubleday read "Sister Carrie" and took a violent dislike to it. Mr. Doubleday read it and agreed with her. Before Mr. Doubleday had come home a contract had been drawn up and signed by which the work was to be published in the fall, and upon this Mr. Dreiser stood.

A friendly member of the firm sent a number of copies to newspapers and critical journals. They attracted much attention.

The newspapers, in fact, hailed Mr. Dreiser as the producer of a masterpiece of naturalism, and the critical journals acquiesced. "Sister Carrie" became famous.

"A copy of the book," said Mr. Dreiser, "was sent to Mr. William Heinemann, a London publisher. That gentleman read it and entered into a contract with me and brought out the novel in England. It appeared in London in May, 1901."

At this point Mr. Dreiser's triumph really began. There was a unanimous critical uprising in favor of "Sister Carrie." The Spectator called it "a work of the utmost power, exact as life itself." The Academy passed upon it as the first important novel out of America.

The Atheneum, England's leading critical journal, used the phrase, "great, with all the greatness of the country which gave it birth," and declared that it introduced a new method of telling a story.

Other critical journals, such as the Times, the Literary World, the Chronicle and the Mail, devoted space to analyzing and declaring the power of this American novel.

This created a boom for the book in England, where it began to sell at once.

The American firm of J. F. Taylor & Co., hearing of its success abroad, sought the author and entered into a contract whereby the book was transferred to that firm, by which it is to be released the coming spring.

"Sister Carrie" has been attacked, in America (not in England) upon the score of morality. Concerning these attacks Mr. Dreiser said:

"In 'Sister Carrie' all the phases of life touched upon are

handled truthfully. I have not tried to gloss over any evil any more than I have stopped to dwell upon it. Life is too short; its phases are too numerous.

"What I desired to do was to show two little human beings, or more, playing in and out among the giant legs of circumstance.

"Personally I see nothing immoral in discussing with a clean purpose any phase of life. I have never been able to understand the objection to considering every phase of life from a philosophical standpoint.

"If life is to be made better or more interesting, its condition must be understood. No situation can be solved, no improvement can be effected, no evil remedied, unless the conditions which surround it are appreciated."

Mr. Dreiser is well remembered by St. Louis newspaper men and other citizens. He is still a young man.

Christmas in the Tenements

Dreiser later republished the opening portion of this article—a portion which I have omitted—in The Color of a Great City. *The material here republished does not appear in* The Color of a Great City.

The evening wanes, and now after the army of toilers in the shops is thus safely housed, another and more enthusiastic atmosphere begins to make itself felt in various quarters of this region—a transferring of the centres of interest, as it were—as though the realm of the heart desire were now outside rather than in.

Over in the Bowery, that great thoroughfare which caters to the vanity and desire for amusement of all this submerged tenth, may be found a whirl of illusion, the glory of which, to these sweaters in the earthly treadmill, may not be eclipsed by anything that Broadway or Fifth Avenue can show. Sawdust and tinsel, the long rope of hemlock and the wreath of holly, lights, music, dancing, voices singing, all these have here combined to produce a splendid night flower and glittering show piece, the beauty of which is as a magnet to the hearts of the weary.

It is the interior of a Bowery dancing-hall, and this glorious Christmas-eve dance of the Diamond Pleasure Circle is about to begin. Three or four "gents" of the chipper East Side "cadet" variety are gathered about the main entrance of the ball-room, where, beneath a few yards of hemlock rope, and between two flaring but unglobed gas jets, the participants of this excellent function are already pouring in.

"Tickets, tickets," is the cricketlike reiteration of the dapper but rather pugnacious-looking youth who is engaged in collecting these pasteboard cards of admission, and in the glow of the flaring gas jets some very interesting characteristics are coming to light. It is noticeable, for instance, that all of the youths who are participating in this very excellent function are of a self-assured and rather

Harper's Weekly 46 (December 6, 1902): 53.

insistent type. Manners as well as actions betray a significant love of the subtle and secretive. Silk mufflers of the kind that grace the glass Christmas gift-box of the cheaper dry-goods store are folded artistically about necks whose redness and tough, goose-fleshy thickness of skin are but ill consorting with the soft and rather delicate nature of their folds. Dog-skin gloves of the kind that are frequently retailed here at seventy-five cents a pair are pulled over hands that, in some instances, are rough and broadened by the handling of garbage-cans or heavy merchandise about the stores and docks of the city, in others, delicate and white from long loafing and "kicking their heels" about the doorways of some of the principal political saloons. Some are slender and anaemic-looking, chill, blasé individuals from whom the blossom of youth has been sapped by a too early acquaintanceship with the follies of life—others are strong, vigorous, animal creatures, with an idea of greatness which reaches to the glory of Terry McGovern as a pugilist, or Timothy D. Sullivan as a politician.* All are ambitious; all designing: the highest conception of life being not marriage, but a vain cavalierlike success with women—a vanity which would seize upon any one of the maidens within their reach, and make of her what too many of them unfortunately already are, sad tragic examples of the degradation of which the human body is capable.

And the maidens—the "goils" or "rags" as they are variably called—the long procession of ignorant, unsophisticated, richly illusioned maidenhood that is here tripping at the heels of pleasure, and seeking, Heaven knows how, the realization of their pathetic dreams. Wonderful combinations of material charms are they— pale, waxy forms and faces; smooth, plump, and yet bloodless hands; hair dark as the night or light as the autumn corn; and eyes that are alive with a sad lustre, as if they knew, or the soul back of them knew, the hopelessness of their fate.

Pretty girls, some with thin, scarlet lips and pallid, waxen cheeks, some with heavy Austrian chins and short unsympathetic noses. Store girls, shop girls, girls who serve as servants the year through, and who nightly return to homes so cheerless and blank as to cause even their small, thoughtless minds to grasp the wretchedness of the contrast, and to make them restless with a mad desire to obtain something of that which they see. Life, life—not a bit of that which they are accustomed to endure, and which, to them,

---

*McGovern at that time was featherweight boxing champion of the world; Sullivan was a New York City alderman.

seems of all things the most wearisome, but something of that other world of show and beauty which is ever flashing before their straining eyes.

And so to-night, and on many nights like this, when the world throws off its oppressive realization of drudgery and feigns to believe that joy is a tangible, obtainable thing, they have come out and will dance away the hours.

"Partners, take your places."

A young, smooth-shaven, thin-lipped Irish youth with a most determined and aggressive under-jaw has stepped to the centre of the brightly lighted floor, and is calling the company to order.

"Partners, choose your places now. Hey, Eddie, get your rag, will you? Say, Jimmie, come on. All of youse, now come on."

A shuffling and turning ensues—butterflylike passing and repassing, until, gathered about the polished floor and exchanging bits of roughly couched, but pleasantly meant, badinage, the whole company in its commonplace show of finery stands expectant, "Salute your partners" being a signal which will set them bowing.

"All ready now. Let her go, Jimmie," the latter to the pianist, and with a pyrotechnic flourish of curious "rag-time" melody the whole company is off—"first couple to the right and second to the left"—a gay pleasure-loving, sorrow-forgetting throng, dancing out the pleasure of a season that has no significance except as a respite.

In yet another section of the Bowery, where stands the row of second-class theatres, the performances of which are especially designed for the amusement of the tenement patronage, the relaxation of the occasion is especially emphasized. Here, also, the balsam and the holly have been involved to give that air of Christmas festivity, the appearance of which is always far greater than the reality. Balsam has been wound about the pillars of the entrances and tacked within the arches of the foyers. Holly has been hung within the windows of the box-offices, and at either side of the entranceway two small cedar-trees are growing, as they grow in their original beds of earth in the groves from which they were extracted. Lights are blazing—a whole section of the Bowery aglow with a brilliant light in the glare of which a motley company is assembling—a vast unpersuaded horde of the East Side, its lovers of the drama.

"Tickets, tickets," here again the monotonous appeal to pay as you go, and, pouring in between the green oil-cloth doors[,] which conceal so much of all that is idealistic to them, is an eager-faced throng of men and boys, whose half-combed hair, hanging down in straight lines beneath their hats, and shabby, tightly buttoned and collar-upturned coats bespeak a nature not too nice in its physical distinction, but animally eager in its passions.

"Tickets, tickets."

The gallery and balcony are already full and toppling over with a strong, odorous, hardly washed company, whose swarthy countenances and bright vivid eyes glow like the faces of animals in the dim half-light of the theatre. Heads are hanging over railings, eyes bulging with interest, thin lips distorted with grimacing or whistling, and still they are packing in, a hot close theatreful, at ten, twenty, and thirty cents the head.

"Tickets, tickets."

"Gee, will youse get on to de bloke in de box," murmurs one, as a very ordinary individual, admitted on a complimentary, perhaps, is permitted to go forward and take a seat in one of the seldom-used boxes.

"Get on to de rag wit' de orstich feathers," exclaims another, as a flashy Bowery girl is escorted by her male companion to one of the five rows of reserved seats.

"And de bloke wit' de goggles. Lookit de eyes on 'im."

"Speech, speech."

The rare crowd of gamins are having it all their own way tonight, and it is only with the closing of the doors for want of even standing-room any longer, and the significant rapping and its accompanying "Hats off!" that this steaming representative body of the East Side settles down to three hours of solid enjoyment. Enjoyment because that the drag of the hall-boy servitude, and the labor of running an elevator, and the weariness of driving a wagon, and the ache of sewing up purses, and the ennui of running a greasy machine, are all laid aside, and in their places the real beauty of life secured.

Elsewhere throughout the crowded region other joys and other tragedies are manifesting themselves. In one section it is a small collection of newsboys in the Newsboys' Home, preparing to play some boyish prank upon a few of their homeless fellow-companions; in another section a bizarre and rather Oriental celebration of a Jewish wedding. Czechs, Poles, Bohemians, Suabians, each in their love of and devotion to the fatherland has in some way contrived a reunion or dance for this night, where now in the waning hours of the evening they may be found singing, dancing, holding forth in excited and high-flown periods; and all because of

153

the injunction given so long ago that man should be at peace and of good cheer.

O tenements! tenements! O vast army of our nameless and helpless kin! Brothers of a thousand grievances, sisters of a thousand ills. Dance, if dancing be yet your privilege. Sing, if the song be sweetness to your lips. Outside are darkness and the sorrow. Outside the fixedness, the regularity, the sameness. Yet another day, and ye, who so urgently struggle to loose the bonds of weariness for one short hour, will be, as in the long time gone, harnessed to the wheel of duty. Yet another day, and the sorrow ye so gayly mock will be dogging at your heels. Unloose, then, the chains of your misery. Fling hence the habiliments of your woes. Eat, drink, and be merry, for to-morrow you must die.

True Art Speaks Plainly

The sum and substance of literary as well as social morality may be expressed in three words—tell the truth. It matters not how the tongues of the critics may wag, or the voices of a partially developed and highly conventionalized society may complain, the business of the author, as well as of other workers upon this earth, is to say what he knows to be true, and, having said as much, to abide the result with patience.

Truth is what is; and the seeing of what is, the realization of truth. To express what we see honestly and without subterfuge: this is morality as well as art.

What the so-called judges of the truth or morality are really inveighing against most of the time is not the discussion of mere sexual lewdness, for no work with that as a basis could possibly succeed, but the disturbing and destroying of their own little theories concerning life, which in some cases may be nothing more than a quiet acceptance of things as they are without any regard to the well-being of the future. Life for them is made up of a variety of interesting but immutable forms and any attempt either to picture any of the wretched results of modern social conditions or to assail the critical defenders of the same is naturally looked upon with contempt or aversion.

It is true that the rallying cry of the critics against so-called immoral literature is that the mental virtue of the reader must be preserved; but this has become a house of refuge to which every form of social injustice hurries for protection. The influence of intellectual ignorance and physical and moral greed upon personal virtue produces the chief tragedies of the age, and yet the objection to the discussion of the sex question is so great as to almost prevent the handling of the theme entirely.

Immoral! Immoral! Under this cloak hide the vices of wealth as well as the vast unspoken blackness of poverty and ignorance; and between them must walk the little novelist, choosing neither truth nor beauty, but some half-conceived phase of life that bears no honest relationship to either the whole of nature or to man.

Booklovers Magazine 1 (February 1903): 129. *Modernist* 1 (November 1919): 21.

The impossibility of any such theory of literature having weight with the true artist must be apparent to every clear reasoning mind. Life is not made up of any one phase or condition of being, nor can man's interest possibly be so confined.

The extent of all reality is the realm of the author's pen, and a true picture of life, honestly and reverentially set down, is both moral and artistic whether it offends the conventions or not.

The Loneliness of the City

One of the most painful results of modern congestion in cities, with the accompanying stress of labor to live, is the utter isolation and loneliness of heart forced upon the average individual. So exacting are the conditions under which we are compelled to work, so disturbing the show of pleasures and diversions we cannot obtain, that the normal satisfaction in normal wants is almost entirely destroyed.

Not only is the whole energy of our lives turned into a miserable struggle for the unattainable, namely, the uninterrupted and complete gratification of our desires, but our hearts are soured and our natures warped by the grimness of the struggle. Life is made bitter. The natural hunger of the heart for righteous relationship is stifled. We become harsh, cold, indifferent.

The effect of such an unnatural order of existence is the almost complete disappearance of the social amenities. We do not interest ourselves in the hardships, discomforts and toil of our fellow-citizens, or rather, neighbors. We fail even in the superficial cordiality that might pass for friendship and which, for want of something better, will sometimes fill the void of despair. Men do not really interest us. The humor and tragedy of their social impulses do not attract, save as a spectacle. We have no time and no patience for anything but what are considered the larger interests— music, the drama, society in its most blatant and impossible phase, and life as a whole.

I live in a neighborhood which is an excellent illustration of this. There are perhaps a hundred people in our apartment house, a thousand, or it may be two or three thousand, in our block.* They live in small, comfortably furnished and very convenient apartments, but they live alone. No one ever sees any exchange of courtesies between them. They are not interested in the progress of the lives of the people about them. You might live there a year, or

Tom Watson's Magazine 2 (October 1905): 474–75.

*Dreiser and his wife were living in an apartment at Mott Avenue and 144th Street in the Bronx.

ten years, and I doubt if your next-door neighbor would even so much as know of your existence. He is too busy. Your business might fail, your children perish. You might suffer every calamity from heartache to literal physical destruction, and I doubt whether he would ever hear of it. Marriage, birth, death, any and all of the other homely and really essential happenings of life are all trivial under the new dispensation. Neither you nor your wife nor children nor your children's children have any interest for him. It is all as if you really did not exist.

The pathos of all this is that these people never quite realize, until some of the real calamities of life overtake them, what they have been ignoring and casting aside. Until they are old, until they are stricken with illness, until they stand bereft of fortune, or until they are visited by death—then, and then only, do they become aware of the importance of the individual relationship. It matters not in such an hour what the prime importance of the world may be. It will not avail them to know that the world still goes on and that the principal thoroughfares of the great cities are alive with a spectacle forever fascinating and forever new. Life in the abstract cannot aid them then. They are alone, left longing for a personal relationship, with an aching and, too often, a breaking heart. Friendship, affection, tenderness, how they loom large in the hour of despair!

I do not think the world quite realizes what an essential element the affections and the tenderness really are. We are disturbed for the time by the clamor of the hours. We are deluded by the seeming importances. Life cannot go on without affection and tenderness—be sure of that. We cannot forever crowd into cities and forget man for mammon. There will come a day, and an hour, in each and every individual life when the need of despised and neglected relationships will weigh heavy on the soul. We cannot do without them. After all is said and done, we must truly love one another or we must die—alone, neglected, despised and forgotten, as too many of us die.

A Lesson from the Aquarium

The New York Aquarium, which had been built in 1890 and rebuilt in 1902, was located in Battery Park.

When you are at the Aquarium if you will watch the glass swimming tanks containing the stort minnows, the hermit crabs or the shark suckers, you will be able to gather a few interesting facts concerning life, which may help to illuminate your daily career for you. In the first of these cases are small, brilliantly colored fishes whose lines show a striking pattern of purple and blue, with here and there a touch of salmon, as they turn swiftly in the light. They look as if they were only swimming about and enjoying themselves, nosing each other in hide-and-seek. In fact, they are engaged in a very serious business of life and death. If you examine closely you will see four or more on guard over nests in the bottom of the tank. The others are trying to rob them of their possessions. The watchmen do not have a moment's rest. Hundreds of their brethren are hovering and crowding round them, constantly slipping into their domain. As they dart open-mouthed at one offender, another, and many others, will shoot in from the side, where the weeds are, or from the top, where no one is watching, and begin to rummage among the pebbles for the eggs. If the guards do not immediately descend on them they will rob the nests. If they do, the invaders will go away peaceably. The desire to fight is less than that to dine.

These fish band together in a kind of offensive and defensive alliance. Each guard has but one side from which attack can come. The other sides are protected by the operations of his three companions. The other guards, since they are in the same peril, can be trusted implicitly. You will never see one guard attack another, though they sometimes collide in the pursuit of interlopers, and always overreach into each other's territory. They never molest or violate one another's nests, and in the excitement of the struggle, when scores of marauders are swooping down at once, and they

Tom Watson's Magazine 3 (January 1906): 306–8.

are dashing in all directions among them, nipping to the right and the left, they never mistake an ally for an enemy.

Their duty is to guard the development of the new life intrusted to them, and in the prosecution of this labor they even drive the mothers away, which would hint that the latter may eat their own eggs. Needless to say, they are in no great personal danger from the intruding crowd, for the latter have been, or may expect to be, guards themselves some day. They wish only to eat, and in the gratification of the desire they exhibit a degree of good nature, or cavalier indifference, which is amusing. If a guard is on the lookout, they will not disturb him. If not, they will eat his eggs. Even the guards themselves share this desire, for once they are off duty—that is, when the eggs are hatched—they give a defiant flip of their tails and look about for their neighbors' nests. Their roles as guardians of public morality are for the time discontinued.

The case of the hermit crab offers an even more interesting example of how the game of life is fought. These soft, spidery creatures, not having been furnished by nature with any protection of their own, are forced by the craving other creatures have to eat them to find some protection for themselves. As soon as he is hatched he hustles around on the bottom of the sea, and finding a very small snail, weaker than himself, pounces on it and drags it summarily forth. Then he crawls into its shell and is protected.

However, this is not for long. He grows, the shell becomes too small for him. It is then necessary for him to make another sortie; and you may frequently see in this tank the operation of the law of the survival of the fittest, that makes our world so grim. One will come scrambling along the bottom of the tank, carrying his ill-fitting house on his back, in quest of food and a more suitable shell. If he cannot find a snail to oust, he will sometimes seize a fellow-crab, whose shell is of suitable size, and him he will worry and torment until, by a process of poking and scratching, he finally succeeds in causing the crab to put his head and shoulders out in self-defense. He clutches the weaker brother and the struggle causes him to drop his shell. The victor drops his own shell, grabs that of his defeated kindred and scuttles off. The brandishing of claws and the grimaces that accompany the contest are sometimes very amusing.

Now the vanquished hermit must get a new home. He takes hold of the shell which the other has abandoned. Finding it too small he hurries on, peeping frantically into this shell, poking eagerly at that, hoping to find one untenanted or with an occupant too feeble to

160

defend himself. In the latter event he practices the same annoying tactics that were used on him. If he succeeds, his trouble is passed to the next one. If he loses, heaven defend him. Even now a monster has spied him, or, it may be, he has poked his claw into the wrong shell. It closes. He is grasped by a strong arm. A short, furious struggle ensues. He is pulled irresistibly in and devoured, a victim of what is sometimes called benevolent assimilation.

In the last tank, that of the shark-sucker, you find an example of the true parasite—the child of fortune who knows just enough to realize that he is weak, and who is willing to attach himself to anyone more powerful than he, in order that he may have some of the good things left after his master has eaten. This curious creature fastens itself to the belly of a shark, and lives on the morsels that fall from its mouth. It is about a foot long, and remotely resembles a three-pound pickerel on its back. Its belly is slightly curved upward, and comes to an edge like the keel of a boat. Its back is flat and on it is an oblong, saucer-like sucker, which enables it to fasten itself to the shark. When it is quite young its habitat is fixed by the location of its parents. It is born in the company of sharks and it dies in the company of them. The fact that it might be able to do something for itself never seems to occur to it.

As might be expected, it never does well when loose from its master or held in captivity. The one in the tank lies in the sand, exactly in the same position it would have if it were fastened to a shark. It protrudes its ugly point of a nose, with its slit of a mouth just behind, and waits for food to be dropped down. It will not skirmish and seek anything for itself. Rather it lies here, and if not fed, starves, a fine example of the parasite the world over.

Do not these examples furnish excellent illustrations of our own physical and social condition? What set of capitalists, or captains of industry, think you, controlling a fine privilege or franchise, which they wish to hatch into a large fortune would not envy the stort minnows their skill in driving enemies away? What sharper prowling about and viewing another's comfortable home, or his excellent business, or the beauty of his wife, if the desire seized him, would not seize upon one or all of these, and by a process of mental gymnastics, or physical force, not unlike that of the hermit crab, endeavor to secure for himself the desirable shell? What weakling, seeing the world was against him, and that he was not fitted to cope with it, would not attach himself, sucker-wise, to any magnate, trust, political or social (we will not call them sharks), and content himself with what fell from his table?

Bless us, how closely these lesser creatures do imitate us in action—or how curiously we copy them! The very air we breathe seems to correspond to their sea, and as for the tragedy of it—but we will not talk of the tragedy of it. Let us leave the Aquarium.

Talks with Four Novelists:
Mr. Dreiser

"The mere living of your daily life," says Theodore Dreiser, "is drastic drama. To-day there may be some disease lurking in your veins that will end your life to-morrow. You may have a firm grasp on the opportunity that in a moment more will slip through your fingers. The banquet of to-night may crumble to the crust of the morning. Life is a tragedy."

"But isn't that a rather tragic view to take?" I asked. "Hasn't each man something in himself that makes life worth living? If, as you say, you want to write more than anything else, isn't that power or ability to write something that would make life worth while under all circumstances?"

"No, not under all circumstances, because you can't use ability except under certain favorable conditions. The very power of which you speak may, thwarted, only serve to make a man more miserable. I have had my share of the difficulties and discouragements that fall to the lot of most men. I know something of the handicap of ill health and the necessary diffusion of energy. A man with something imperative to say and no time or strength for the saying of it is as unfortunate as he is unhappy. I look into my own life and I realize that each human life is a similar tragedy. The infinite suffering and deprivation of great masses of men and women upon whom existence has been thrust unasked appals me. My greatest desire is to devote every hour of my conscious existence to depicting phases of life as I see and understand them."

"What are you trying to show in what you write? Do you point out a moral?" I inquired.

"I simply want to tell about life as it is. Every human life is intensely interesting. If the human being has ideals, the struggle and the attempt to realize those ideals, the going back on his own trail, the failure, the success, the reason for the individual failure, the individual success—all these things are interesting, interesting even where there are no ideals, where there is only the personal

Otis Notman, New York *Times Saturday Review of Books,* June 15, 1907, p. 393.

163

desire to survive, the fight to win, the stretching out of the fingers to grasp—these are the things I want to write about—life as it is, the facts as they exist, the game as it is played! I said I was pointing out no moral. Well, I am not, unless this is a moral—that all humanity must stand together and war against and overcome the forces of nature. I think a time is coming when personal gain will rarely be sought at the expense of some one else."

"Where among people is there the greatest readiness to stand by one another, among the rich or the poor?" I asked.

"Among the poor. They are by far the most generous. They are never too crowded to take in another person, although there may be already three or four to share the same room. Their food they will always share, even though there is not enough to go around."

"Are you writing something else?" I inquired.

"I have another book partly finished, but I don't know when I shall get it done. I have not the time to work on it, much as I want to."

"Have you been satisfied with the reception of 'Sister Carrie'?"

"Well, the critics have not really understood what I was trying to do. Here is a book that is close to life. It is intended not as a piece of literary craftsmanship, but as a picture of conditions done as simply and effectively as the English language will permit. To sit up and criticise me for saying 'vest,' instead of waistcoat, to talk about my splitting the infinitive and using vulgar commonplaces here and there, when the tragedy of a man's life is being displayed, is silly. More, it is ridiculous. It makes me feel that American criticism is the joke which English literary authorities maintain it to be. But the circulation is beginning to boom. When it gets to the people they will understand, because it is a story of real life, of their lives."

The Man on the Sidewalk

*In July 1909 Dreiser secretly became the principal owner of the
Bohemian, a near-bankrupt magazine published in New York. [His
position with the* Delineator *precluded his open involvement in
another magazine.] Although he installed Fritz Krog as nominal
editor, he in fact played a major role in the preparation of the
issues of October, November, and December 1909. In particular,
he contributed a number of brief unsigned articles to "At the Sign
of the Lead Pencil," a column which was a feature of these issues.
Dreiser's authorship of the three items from this column which I
have included is based on two kinds of evidence. The articles were
not written by Krog and H. L. Mencken, the other two principal
contributors to "At the Sign of the Lead Pencil" [Krog to Dreiser,
September 21, 1909, at the University of Pennsylvania Library;
Mencken to Robert H. Elias, February 22, 1945, at the Cornell
University Library]. And the contents and prose style of the articles are distinctively Dreiserian.*

    An unidentified man, about fifty years old, dropped
dead of heart failure yesterday in front of No. 309 Bowery. He was
tall, thin, and emaciated. He wore no overcoat, and his clothing
was thin and shabby. There were seventy-two cents in his
pocket.—*Daily paper.*
    One of the most commonplace items of this, our city life, is
one like the above, which records the falling from exhaustion, or
the death by starvation, of some one who has reached the limit of
his physical ability to cope with life. It is no longer a notable thing.
It is so old, and frequently, as you may see, it is a trivial thing. The
papers give it no more than a passing mention.
    I like, at times, this brief way of recording the failure of an
individual. It is so characteristic of the city, and of life as a whole.
Nature is so grim. The city, which represents it so effectively, is
also so grim. It does not care at all. It is not conscious. The passing

"At the Sign of the Lead Pencil," *Bohemian* 17 (October 1909): 422–23.
Unsigned.

of so small an organism as that of a man or a woman is nothing to it. Beside a star or a great force of any kind the beginning or end of a little body is so ridiculous and trivial, that it is almost like that of an insect or a worm.

And yet to the individual who is thus ground between the upper and the nether millstone of circumstance, the indifference of the city, and of the world and of life, comes as a terrible revelation. He learns that one may really die of starvation in a great city full of wealth, full of power, in a way full of sympathy (misdirected, perhaps). The houses with which the streets are lined may be full of the comfort which attaches to happiness; the stores and offices crowded with those who are industrially bettering their fortune. On every hand are piled up the evidences of wealth—great structures, well-stocked stores, energetic factories, and the masses of material for sale, which can only be had for a price, and yet you may die.

I remember entering a great city once when I had neither place to go nor where to stay. My clothes were poor and my purse empty. In addition, I was ill and despondent, and although I might have and did attribute my misfortunes somewhat to my own indiscretions, that fact did not avail to ameliorate my immediate needs. I wandered helplessly about, and in that period of pressing distress, lasting over a month, I sank to the bottom of human misery.*

It was in this hour that my soul tasted the very dregs of life's little ironies. When in health and comfort my eyes had seen many things which my senses longed for. Now in illness and distress they were multiplied a thousandfold. The stores were no longer great economic institutions which were sensibly arranged to deal with accuracy and fair-mindedness in all that society requires, but holding-places merely of that which if secured would serve to relieve immediately my wants. It was impossible then for me to look in any window or to see any mass of food and not covet it earnestly—a fraction, just so much as would keep body and soul together, a mere handful. I could not help speculating on how little it would take to keep me alive, and how little it would cost the giver to give it. However, here, in my way, I found an inexorable law of trade—nothing for nothing. If I chose to beg there were endless explanations and bitter comments, without (always) satisfactory results. If

---

*In February 1903 Dreiser moved from Philadelphia to New York after a long period of ill health in part caused by his depression over his literary career. He wandered as a derelict in New York until rescued by his brother Paul, who began his recovery by sending him to a health farm.

I chose to steal, the hand of every man was against me. There was no immediate way.

And yet to recover my lost position, or my health, or my self-respect, or my friends, required not only food, but health and labor. Once I had fallen so low, a long wearisome struggle lay before me and I who had reached this place did not always think it worth while. Pride stood in my way when begging was conceived, sensitiveness and lack of strength in the way of a forceful struggle. So it came that often I looked the grim procession of circumstances in the face and wondered whether it was worth while.

However, about me was noising and flaunting what to me, in my troubled state, appeared as a perfect pandemonium of joy. Everybody seemed happy, everybody seemed well pleased. There were inspiring processions of those who were going to business, to the theaters, to the cafés, to the homes—to all the beautiful and interesting things which the world contains, and I, only I, was going nowhere. Not to a good home, or a good business, or a good restaurant, or a good friend—to nothing at all except loneliness and friendlessness. Of such was my portion of poverty.

And so it was borne in upon me how it comes that those who reach the lowest level of distress sometimes die of starvation. The world does not care. It does not understand. It is busy adding to, not taking away from its store, and that which you seek to do in the extremes of poverty is to take away. You have nothing to give. It is only when you are well and strong that you have that.

Therefore it is that in those short, crisp items I see displayed the world of misery which lies behind them, the heart aches, the brain aches, the sad lookings with hungry eyes, the trampings, the waitings—all that poverty means in heat and cold. If nature were not obviously something which invariably works through other things, you would expect it, in its boundless ability, to flash succor out of the sky; but, alas! only the medium of other people (nature's tools) are there to appeal to. Men are its mediums—men and things. And it came to me as a flash of wisdom that these are useless except as they are charitable; and that it behooves us to keep a kindly heart within our bosom and an open eye, for who knows but that at our door, even now, may knock with wavering impulse that boundless wretchedness which but for our generosity and tenderness must travail and die, unthought of, unheeded, even as those whose failures and death are here so immaterially recorded.

The Defects of Organized Charity

This country is pretty well organized now from the point of view of the charity workers. They have systems in most of the big cities—New York, Chicago, Boston, Philadelphia, and a great many of the smaller towns. The work has taken various forms, settlement houses, children's playgrounds, children's hospitals, day nurseries, flower guilds, kindergartens, factories, clubs and what not, to say nothing of legal aid societies, educational alliances, educational theaters, Y.W.C.As. and Y.M.C.As. Intelligent and in many instances generous-minded people are making a great effort to reach the downtrodden.

It is interesting to note this for, in spite of it, the world's misery does not seem to be so very much lessened, although substantial progress has been made. We find the same element of weakness at the bottom. The vast mass of people are born unfit, physically and mentally. If you go through life communing with sensible people and making a study of conditions at first hand, you begin to see partially what is the trouble. Society does not get enough to eat and there is no apparent way of making it get enough to eat. The Socialists have the idea that if you put the mass in charge—make the men who are now supposed to rule us mere servants—things will be all right, but they do not point out how the mass is to make the master do this. Universal education—well, education, is a matter of capacity. Some people will hold a whole hogshead of it and keep it all well in motion, while others will hold a thimbleful or less, and can't do anything with that after they have it; so the big fellows with the hogsheadful are bound to get the best of the little fellows with the thimbleful unless the big fellows choose to be merciful, and there is no evidence in nature as yet that they do. Nature seems to be instinctively, inherently brutal. The man who worked out the details of the law of the survival of the fittest worked out the details of an absolute fact. There is no hope for the man with the small brain or the weak body, and there is no way that we have devised as yet which will give him a better one.

"At the Sign of the Lead Pencil," *Bohemian* 17 (October 1909): 429–31. Unsigned. See headnote to "The Man on the Sidewalk," p. 165.

The Defects of Organized Charity

Some scientists to-day favor a legal enforcement of the law of physical selection. They want to breed people. The idea is, in the first place, to lock up the degenerates or to destroy their power of reproduction, which is just as good. The second thing on the programme is to take the fit specimens—the fittest as it were—among the males and females and mate them as you do cattle. The third thing is to head off from the resulting children all the dangers which flesh is heir to, disease, poverty, hunger, and cold; and the fourth thing so to direct these children's efforts that they themselves will profit most by the opportunities which are put before them.

Fine, you say; a noble programme. Fine indeed. But who is to do it? The state. And who is to make the state do it? The people. And when will the people make the state do it? When they are educated. And when will they be educated? When the scientists and philanthropists and the humanitarians who are now working in their behalf get them so trained, so roused up, so eager and enthusiastic that they will rise up and do this thing.

Fine. We welcome this theory. We hope it comes to pass. The one thing we are afraid of, however, is the inherent brutality and inconsideration of nature itself. It doesn't do these things so gently where it is left to its own devices, where *brain* doesn't come in, where it is left to its own significant instincts, and that in the face of the fact that it creates brain. Nature is brutal, terribly so, striking down the unfit with the most joyous zeal, and we cannot see how this same eager, brutal, avid nature is to be kept out of the resulting children of all these fine notions. Can all these children be kept humane? Can they be kept gentle? Can they be kept equal? If they can't, look out. They are just as apt to fall upon one another as we do to-day, pulling and hauling, the weak beings over-mastered by the strong, the bright dominating the dull.

Ah, but! you say, education. We've just settled that. The state! These very people are the state. Will they be willing to rest equal? They will not. Or if they do so for a while they may not do so forever. The problem then becomes this: What will happen if they do not remain equal, and what will happen if they do?

We can get an answer for the latter if we take a look at the bee and wasp families, and we can get an answer to the former if we look at ourselves. The organization of bees and the social wasps is peculiar. The families or bodies politic of these insects have a state or hive system. They have a government—a rule. This government or rule fixes absolutely the status of the individual—what he may and may not do. But they do not progress. It is, then,

169

interesting to inquire why not? The answer is because no individual in this system is allowed to do anything new, and if he does he is thrown out or killed. If he is thrown out he can go and start a hive on his own idea, but it won't have anything to do with the old hive. And if he doesn't he will die. That is equally true of the social wasps. Now what, you may ask, has this got to do with the discussion of organized charity? Just this. If the hive or the state brought to a perfect balance does not progress, there is no known reason for its existence except a routine—repetition of certain given functions, dull or sweet, which have little or nothing to do with our so-called mind. This is a condition which few think ought to be sought for. Yet there is no other way out. If progress is necessary it can be had only by competition, and competition cannot be had without strife. And strife cannot be had without misery. And misery cannot be had without all that we see to-day, or things like it, or things worse.

Well, what about organized charity? you ask. Oh, nothing, except organized charity leads definitely to one or the other of these propositions. It leads to aimless repetition on a highly selected plan or to natural selection and contention as we see it now. There are no other ways. And this is why we think our present condition is not to be vastly affected by its labors.

Pittsburgh

The City of Pittsburgh is surely exceptional. In spite of the wealth which it has created for certain individuals it is almost always in trouble. If it is not a steel strike it is a car famine, and if it is not a car famine it is a society scandal, which is almost as bad. Recently the Charity Organization Society of New York investigated conditions there and decided that they could not be much worse anywhere. Poverty, filth, wretched laboring conditions on one hand, and, set over against this, great wealth and great display. Thaw came from Pittsburgh, and Carnegie. Could anything point more clearly to exceptional conditions?

As a matter of fact Pittsburgh at the present time illustrates more clearly the inequalities and injustice of our present social system than any other city of our nation. Geographically it is attractively located. It is in the heart of the Alleghanies, so to speak. Those two beautiful rivers which unite to make the Ohio, the Allegheny and the Monongahela meet there. At a point of land central to all the surrounding population they have located the commercial heart, and from it cars—a splendid trolley system—set forth in all directions. You may go where you will, east, west, north, or south, you come upon beautiful landscapes, quaint angles of scenery, great gullies known as "hollows" and "runs," and lovely resident sections, where the population seems to be well fed and well housed. It is only in the manufacturing districts, such as South Pittsburgh, McKees Rocks, Carnegie and places of that sort, that the true bitterness of the industrial situation is set forth.*

It is not the purpose of this editorial to picture the conditions as they exist to-day and have existed for twenty-five years. The world is pretty well aware now of what they are. The thing that is really worth while indicating here is that these conditions, depressing and brutal and inhuman, have existed side by side, or rather

"At the Sign of the Lead Pencil," *Bohemian* 17 (December 1909): 712–14. Unsigned. See headnote to "The Man on the Sidewalk," p. 165.

*Dreiser had been a reporter in Pittsburgh from April to November 1894. He spent much of his time in Allegheny County, the location of these manufacturing suburbs of Pittsburgh.

171

Part 2: 1898–1910

have been the accompaniment of the greatest wealth-producing
agencies of two generations. The steel skyscraper and the steel
battleship have practically come out of Pittsburgh. It has had the
coal and the iron handy. And shrewd brains and cool brains got on
the job early and built up a monopoly in these products, so that
before long they were able to fix the price of not only manufactured
steel and iron but the raw constituents as well throughout the
world. That condition has not changed. To-day they dominate the
steel world just as they did twenty-five years ago; only we have
gotten used to the idea now.

The most interesting thing is the tremendous fortunes that
have been built up out of these conditions and the men who still
dominate them. Beginning with the redoubtable Andrew Carnegie,
vain, stingy, calculating individual that he is, there is truly an imposing array of steel wealth; Henry Phipps, Henry C. Frick, H. B.
Oliver, Charles Schwab, W. E. Corey, H. K. Thaw, and now that
still other powerful individual, Mr. F. M. Hoffstot, who appears to
be having his preliminary struggles with the masses before being
able to grind them utterly under his heel.

All of the fortunes represented by these names were made in
Pittsburgh; all were made out of steel. And if you go there you will
find the works representing their names, tall, dark, many-
chimneyed, belching smoke and flame by day and by night, and
you may see in what fiery furnaces these fortunes were wrought.

It is a wonderful sight, these steel works of Pittsburgh. If you
go there a stranger and can be led by some fortuitous circumstance
to the elevated esplanade on the west bank of the Monongahela,
known as Grand View Avenue, and if by great good chance it has
rained that day or the day before, you will see a sight which you
will not soon forget. It should be night and clear. The lights of
Pittsburgh and its surrounding towns will twinkle below you. The
stars sparkle overhead. Here and there, to the east, the south, the
north, and directly below you will see bursting forth tongues of
flames from a hundred fiery chimneys. They flame for a moment—
these great tongues—lighting the landscape for miles about with a
red glare, and then die down again. No sooner has one or ten or a
score disappeared than a dozen or a hundred others are in
magnificent evidence. The "red heads" a local newspaper writer
once named them; "hell with the lid off," was another euphonious
description. They are to be seen nightly—these fascinating evidences of these great manufacturies—and when they are most numerously in evidence Pittsburgh is most prosperous.

172

The pity of it is that this prosperity does not really represent prosperity for those who are most earnestly and arduously engaged in this gigantic labor. Aside from the officers and the shareholders there are practically no decent returns made to anybody. The men who work here get little or nothing. They are imported especially from downtrodden, ignorant sections of Europe in order that they may be housed and fed cheaply. When they are first introduced any sort of wages will keep them, and when they are made aware by the life around them of normal American conditions, they are discharged. One-twenty-five, one-fifty, two dollars a day are good pay. And when there is any trouble made over intolerable conditions, the electric barbed wire fence, the strike breaker, the State constabulary, and the writ of eviction are freely used. Company houses, company stores, company rules, these govern everything, and the process of sweating gold out of muscle is joyously entered upon.

You would think that in a business out of which so much profit is to be had there would be more regard for the common humanities of life. No one need hope to maintain to-day in the face of the literally tremendous fortunes that have been made out of this business that there is not a handsome profit; unquestionably an enormous profit. The libraries of Mr. Carnegie scattered all over the known world, the model tenements of Mr. Phipps, built in a dozen cities, the chateaux of Mr. Corey, the palaces of Mr. Schwab, the extravagances of Mr. Thaw, Jr., are some evidence that this business has yielded money easily and freely.* Why, then, underpaid men? Why strikes and lockouts? Why foreign labor and company houses and company stores? There is but one answer, GREED. These men are greedy and they will not give decent conditions because they will not get rich fast enough, or, being rich, they will not be able to maintain the showy standard they have set for themselves. There is no other answer.

You would think in the face of all the evidence of wealth that has come out of Pittsburgh—all the extravagance and ostentation— that these men who have made it would take it upon themselves to see that decent working conditions and decent living conditions were enforced locally so that this scandal might cease. You would suppose that they would scarcely wish to face the constant agita-

*A notorious playboy, Harry Thaw, Jr., had killed Stanford White in June 1906 because he believed White was the lover of his wife, Evelyn Nesbit Thaw. The ensuing case was one of the most sensational of the decade.

tion which the unchanged conditions produce. Pride ought to get to work and shame. But no, the conditions remain exactly as they were. Mr. Carnegie continues to build libraries, Mr. Frick to collect pictures, Mr. Schwab and Mr. Corey to live luxuriously and hold their own. But no change for Pittsburgh.

Of course, any change that could be made now would not affect all the horde of workers who have come and gone in the period during which these fortunes were building. There have been thousands and thousands who have lived in poverty and hunger. There have been other thousands who have died of sickness, disease or strike riots. Some have risen to better conditions, some sunk possibly to worse, but at least the conditions now could be changed. Mr. Carnegie in his large educational outlook should think a little on this, and Mr. Frick in his race for greater wealth. As for Mr. Corey—but we won't talk about Mr. Corey, or Mr. Hoffstot, or Mr. Thaw.

The Factory

1910 *was a New York little magazine which appeared for several issues during that year. Both of Dreiser's contributions to the magazine—"The Factory" and "Six O'Clock"—attempt to render in prose the kind of cityscape which Dreiser was to attribute to Eugene Witla's work in oils in* The "Genius."

There is a factory whose outlines fall within the purview of my eye, whose tall walls and towering smoke-stacks give it a peculiar configuration of grimness and beauty. It is a manufacturing plant, devoted to the labor of turning out cotton sheeting, and within whose walls labor some hundreds of human beings whose sole recommendation in the eyes of society is that they can tend a machine. If you were to watch this factory at early morning, you would observe a great plume of smoke curling majestically upward about the hours of 6.30, when the engineer first comes to make his boilers ready for the day. At seven, when a long line of more or less discouraged or indifferent people are filing in, you would hear the clarion call of its whistle, rising like a great cry, which means labor. Thereafter until noon, and again during the afternoon, you would hear the thrash and rumble of its machinery, roaring like a torrent over great rocks, a sound not unlike that which you may hear at Niagara, or could before that current was displaced.

The interior of this factory presents a scene for which the world has long waited in art, and for which the talent of the genius is reserved. It is a long, darksome chamber, set with high, small-paned, prison-like windows, whose mass of light falls like a radiance of evening over the interior. The floors are set with long, evenly arranged rows of clanking machines, whose thrashing shuttles and whirling bobbins make up a roar that is deafening to the ear. Solemn, impressive shadows of men and women go about among them—principally women and some children, whose appearance stamps them as a lesser order of being, the kind, shall we say, who are made to work.

1910, no. 5 (n.d., n.p.).

They are wonderfully constructed—these chattering, intelligent almost human machines. They do deftly and swiftly what hundreds of keen-eyed men could not. They know when one of their three hundred threads are broken, and stop. They know when the tiny cord is fastened again, and go on. They revolve a number of hundreds of times to the minute, carry three hundred spindles, thin out cards of cotton to gossamer threads and toss a shuttle to and fro millions of times a day. The one great engine, somewhere down in the shadow of the basement, drives them all.

These chambers, wherein they revolve, are gray even in halcyon weather. Outside, the earth may be flooded with sunshine, the flowers blooming, the trees stirred by cooling breezes. Inside is dust, shadow, the odor of oil and this deafening roar that never ends. Men move about silently, the women of the machine shuffle listlessly to and fro, occasionally fixing something. Dust and oil are in the air. Dust is upon the floor, which is black and shiny with oil; dust is upon the walls, which are streaked and spatted with it and oil in combination; dust is upon the ceiling, which is stuccoed with oil-impregnated motes of cotton. You could not move anywhere and not come in contact with it, except in the case of the soft, white baskets of cotton, which are bundled about here and there—cotton as white as snow.

It is not so much the factory as the people in it with whom we are concerned. I do not know how you feel about life, but these people strike me as having a woefully sad end of it. They are such poor, slovenly looking creatures. Their minds are apparently so hopelessly inadequate to the task of living well. You see them bundling about here, some stout, but wholly colorless in the face; some lean, but so angularly bony and frail withal as to be pitiable. Dark, colorful, liquid eyes meet yours, filled with a low, inadequate fire. They run these machines—these people—driven by some sense of duty, or some force of want, or because parents make them—strange reasons when you know how dutiless and indifferent some portions of the remaining world really are.

And this labor. It is so impressively commonplace when you examine it. There is so little of real thought involved—so much less of real, joyful exercise. They may not truly stretch their muscles and make them good and tense all day long. They may not use their minds for one swift fancy in the same period. All is watching, a silent, catlike watching, which is neither thought nor strength, but a constant creeping to and fro, reaching in here, bending over there, testing a thread, putting in a new spindle. A weak woman can take

176

care of three, another five, another seven machines. An ordinary man could handle as many as nine or ten. It all depends upon one's ability to see and move fairly quickly—not swiftly at all. It matters not if the fingers are white and lean; no difference if the body is frail. The lungs may be weak, the body wretched—if the eyes are good and the fingers nimble, all else will follow as a matter of course. It seems at times as if it were a silent waiting and watching—for nothing.

And yet, these people are human beings. You see them hurrying away at night with an eagerness that suggests great possibilities in the way of desire. The streets which they occupy, the cities which they infest, run with a wild current of excitement at night, as if the weariness and meanness of the day were being compensated for at night by a riotous abandon—the search of the soul for something wherewith to satisfy its existence, to compensate itself for being alive.

I sometimes look at this factory in the glow of the evening sun, or through the pleasing drizzle of a rainy day, and ponder over the philosophy of it. Its stature is so graceful; its tall chimney so artistic. If you view it as a picture solely, it is one of those satisfying anomalies which the heart of man greatly rejoices in. The color of its walls is so adequate, the height and form of its chimney so wholly pleasing and ornate. Seen through the glow of the setting sun, or when the rain or fog are softening it to a mere shadowy outline, it appears a sweet concoction of Nature, like a flower or a tree. The beauty of it makes it agreeable to that idea.

And yet we know how homely it really is—how wretched to some minds. There are hearts there, no doubt, that despise its very walls, like the prisoner does his prison. To them it is toil, weariness, wretchedness, privation. They see nothing but the grime and the hurt. We who are not of it may witness the sweetness and beauty, which they may never know.

How will we adjust this anomaly, say you? How give each his due? By realizing sometimes, I think, that a portion of work should fall to us all, and by seeing that that portion is never stinted. We should not take from our neighbor that which he should justly have, nor withhold that which he may enjoy. Never to reap where we do not sow; nor idle where we have not labored. I know that this is an old ideal. I know that despite its wonderment or pity, the world smiles complaisantly. Life will take care of itself. The world cannot be bettered by theory. Perhaps not. The problem of the factory, however, is here before us. May we adjust it according to the highest dictates of our soul.

3

1911–1925

A Confession of Faith

The typescript of this statement contains in Dreiser's hand the note "Theodore Dreiser/3609 Broadway/N.Y.C." Dreiser lived at this address from July 1911 to March 1914.

I.

I believe in an insoluble, indestructible universe, good undoubtedly, but past all understanding. I do not believe in a father, son, or a holy ghost as those terms are conjoined. They may be. I have no inward conviction of them. I believe in the theory of evolution as it relates to this mortal state. What relation that state bears to the omnipotent, omniscient, omnipresent intelligence in which I do believe, I do not know. I am inclined to believe that it is all a dream and that "there is no life, truth, intelligence nor substance in matter."*

II.

I believe that the first and cardinal principle of life is change and that all human forms and all human institutions, and all human beliefs are subject to it. It is a current idea of all times, holden of the masses, that if you leave things alone you leave them as they are and that they do not change. The contrary is true. If you leave a new house alone it will soon be old; if you leave a great institution alone it will soon lose its significance; if you leave a human law alone it will become obsolete. There are laws and principles which relate to the universe and which, apparently, do not change. We do not know. I have faith to believe that the principles of beauty are eternal. Else were this feverish existence unendurable to me.

Unpublished manuscript, July 1911–March 1914. Copyright the Trustees of the University of Pennsylvania.

*Mary Baker Eddy, *Science and Health* (1875; reprint ed., Boston, 1971), p. 468.

III.

I believe in the inspiration and genius of men—intoxication of beauty—and of this inspiration I call all revered names in testimony,—Buddha, Zoroaster, the prophets, Christ, St. Paul, Socrates and all who have dreamed or sung or worked deeds of mercy and beauty in the history of the world. I believe that there is no truth more thoroughly established than that there exists some strange link between beauty and happiness; between kindness and a sense of peace; and between a magnanimous and thoughtful policy and public welfare and prosperity. That this has any close relationship to individual thoughts and deeds from hour to hour and from day to day I do not know.

IV.

I believe in the supremacy of art and that from first to last and from everlasting to everlasting the universe is artistic. I believe that in art there is neither low nor high; wretched nor distinguished; pure nor vile; but that all in their proper relationship are beautiful and good to look upon. We see but little and having ears hear not. I believe that this art is above the willing of man and that fortunate is he who is called to be its humblest servitor.

V.

I believe in the essential evil (so called) and the essential goodness of man at one and the same time. I believe that all men are liars, robbers, bearers of false witness, murderers, lechers, ingrates, and the like in part and I believe at the same time they are kind, gentle, peaceful, longsuffering, truthful, noble and self sacrificing. I believe that evil and good are variously compounded in us all and that but for the accident of chance we might be anything but that which we aspire to—either good or evil. I believe that time and chance happen to all men.

VI.

I believe in the compelling power of love. I do not understand it. I believe it to be the most fragrant blossom of all this thorny existence.

182

VII.

I believe in the necessity and dignity of labor for everyone. It is the only solvent of life's woes.

VIII.

I believe that we should believe in change, that we should look at life searchingly, work energetically, love joyously and hope eternally. That we can at all times do this, I do not believe.

IX.

I hope that I shall never cease to hope; that life in all its glory shall pass as a cloud at last; that I shall not live clear minded to see that which I have loved so much become the witness of an inane and futile age.

Now Comes Author Theodore Dreiser Who Tells of 100,000 Jennie Gerhardts

* * * * * *

"There is no intelligent sequence of cause and effect in life," says Theodore Dreiser, explaining his philosophy of life as brought out in the struggles of Jennie Gerhardt. "Life is not reasonable. All our actions are regulated by some previous happening. If Senator Brander had not died, he would have married Jennie Gerhardt, unless some other accident had happened to prevent it. And if he had married her, society would have been none the wiser, and she would not have been ostracized for her fault.

"But that one thing, for which no one was responsible, left her at the mercy of her friends and called down upon her their so-called righteous indignation. It shows how little influence reason has over us as compared with chance."

"Isn't that rather pessimistic?" I asked.

"It may sound so at first," returned Mr. Dreiser, "but it doesn't affect me that way. I don't feel any the less happy about life on account of it. Life interests me intensely for that very reason. It is dramatic. It is more thrilling than the most gorgeous spectacle that man ever planned. And these accidents merely serve to make it more entrancing. I consider the beggar sitting by the roadside one of the most dramatic things that could be imagined. He has a precarious existence and it depends entirely on chance. It is really thrilling to see the way in which he ekes out a living.

"Besides being dramatic, I consider life beautiful, and I believe that beauty is eternal. If I didn't, this feverish existence would be unendurable to me. As it is, I think the beggar I just mentioned is beautiful. His dirt and his rags, his bandaged feet and his sores are all beautiful to me. They are artistic. They complete the picture and make the whole perfect. It may not be pleasant, if you like, but it is artistic. Everything in life appears to me just that way. That would be the reason for life, if there were any reason. But I believe that life is merely an accident from the beginning."

Cleveland *Leader*, November 12, 1911, Cosmopolitan section, p. 5. Unsigned.

"If there is no other force than chance, how do you account for the progress of humanity?" I asked.

"I do not believe that there is such a thing as progress, in the sense that we use the word. It is merely a change. Who can say that it is better to worship the home as we do today than it was in the old days to worship a bull? Our ideas have changed; that is all. We believe that it is better for us to worship the home, but that does not mean that it would have been better for the people of other times to worship the home instead of the bull or the spider. It may be wise in the present day to try to educate our sons in the teachings of Jesus Christ and keep our daughters virtuous, but we cannot say that it will always be our principle. I cannot believe that the teachings of Christ are eternal; that they have really held for two thousand years. It certainly isn't true in this day that one should turn the other cheek."

* * * * * *

"Jennie Gerhardt" is [a] worthy successor to "Sister Carrie," and develops further the philosophy of chance as it was advanced in the earlier book. Mr. Dreiser has not had these views always. He admits that in his youth he was just as bound up in traditions and conventions as any one else. But his ideas changed as he grew older, and a wider experience gave him a broader view on life. He was born in Terre Haute, Ind., but went to Chicago early and started to work there.

"I cannot say just what I thought of things then. Life was a drift, a swirl. I read a great deal then. I was eagerly devouring Emerson, Hawthorne and Stevenson at that time. But better than these books were the tall smoke-stacks, the crowded streets, the boxes and bales and the river and lake of Chicago. I loved these and the knowledge that I was young and alive. The glory of life cannot be put into books. It cannot be even faintly suggested.

"Then I got into newspaper work and that gave me an insight into the brutalities of life—the police courts, the jails, the houses of ill-repute, trade failures and trickery. Curiously, it all seemed wonderful to me—not sad. It was like a grand magnificent spectacle. All at once I began reading Spencer, Darwin, Huxley and Tyndall, and life began to take on a new aspect. As they say in the slang of the day, I got a line on it. I shall never forget Spencer's chapter on the Unknowable in 'First Principles.' I was torn up root and branch by it. Life disappeared in a strange fog.

185

"Just about then, in Pittsburg, where I was working as a newspaper man, I came across Balzac and then I saw what life was—a rich, gorgeous, showy spectacle. It was beautiful, dramatic, sad, delightful, and epic—all those things combined. I saw for the first time how a book should be written. I saw how, if I ever wrote one, I should write it. I did not expect to write like Balzac, but to use his method of giving a complete picture of life from beginning to end.

"Balzac lasted me a year or two, then came Hardy, and after him, Tolstoi. From them I learned what, in my judgment, really great books are. In later years Daudet, Flaubert, Turgenieff and now only recently De Maupassant and George Moore have added to this knowledge. I have never read a line of Zola, unfortunately."

"Which do you consider the world's greatest books?" I asked.

Mr. Dreiser leaned forward and named them off on his fingers.

"I rank 'Anna Karenina,' 'Madame Bovary,' 'Evelyn Innes,' 'Fathers and Children,' 'Père Goriot,' 'The Woodlanders' and our own American 'Quicksand,' by Hervey White, as among the great books of the world."*

---

*Besides the novels of Tolstoy, Flaubert, Turgenev, and White, Dreiser includes George Moore's *Evelyn Inness* and Thomas Hardy's *The Woodlanders*. Dreiser frequently claimed that White's *Quicksand* (1900) was a major work of American realism.

Novels to Reflect Real Life

When the English novelist Arnold Bennett came to this country the other day and said he considered Theodore Dreiser a leading representative American novelist, as truly reflecting current literary tendencies, he called attention by the remark to subtle changes in literature, illustrated by the case of Mr. Dreiser.* For the latter's "Sister Carrie" when it appeared less than a decade ago, was quickly suppressed by its publishers, neither an old nor a markedly conservative [house], because it represented too realistic, too grim a type of fiction, and only about 500 copies of the book lived among a little group of followers. Now his "Jennie Gerhardt," of the same realistic type, has just appeared from the house of Harpers.

Whatever may be the real significance of the work of the American realist in American fiction, his explanations cannot but be interesting. However, he is not anxious to explain; like Robert Herrick, he would much rather let his work alone speak for itself. But when cornered he tentatively ventures an explanation, the while nervously folding and refolding his already much folded handkerchief; sitting quietly in a stationary armchair in a fashion which somehow or other constantly calls to mind the nervous, rocking chair habit of Sister Carrie; twisting the ring which he wears on his forefinger—and it is probably as illuminating a point as one could mention in regard to the author that he can wear a ring on his forefinger with an air of sincerity, so to speak, with no suggestion of affectation.

"I fell down," he admits. "That is, my novel was suppressed. And I didn't offer another to the public for years.

"Perhaps I could have written an unobjectionable, a desirable book if I'd tried. But I didn't try. And I never will. Why in the name of truth and art should I stoop to such travesty? Why

New York *Sun*, November 21, 1911, p. 5. Unsigned.

*Bennett's frequently noted comment occurred on his arrival in New York in October 1911; see the New York *Times*, October 22, 1911, and "Bennett's Opinion," *Outlook* 99 (November 25, 1911): 701–2.

shouldn't I do my best, both by myself and by the thing I profess to work for?

"For what have we all against this literature of ours that we won't let it express itself truly, naturally? Great American novels can't be written while we refuse to countenance the true expression of the American temperament; while we refuse to hear of what goes on in the cities to-day—except by reading in the newspapers and the magazines. And let me say that for real worth in what literature is supposed to stand for[,] to-day's newspapers and magazines are so far ahead of all the novels that have been published that there is no comparison. For they are vital, dramatic, true presentations of the life that is being lived to-day.

"Why can't that thing be put into our novels—supposed to reflect life? Lord knows—I don't. I know that we hold up our hands in awed admiration of what Russia has achieved in the way of a national literature—a vital expression of the national temperament. I know that we exclaim at the French masters for what they have done to immortalize and perpetuate their own peculiar national temperament. England too has had her honored craftsmen— all of whom we honor and respect for what they have done.

"But as for ourselves—Lord help us! Have we no temperament to be expressed? Look around you, go through the country; the question answers itself. And yet we don't want to read about it in books, the only worth while thing of the age to read about now or in time to come. We don't want such books on our shelves—the while we eagerly find places for the French masters, the Russian masters and what not, lamenting that we have not such in our own dear land.

"Certain of the earlier reflections of temperament have not been without their representation. There is Hawthorne and his 'Twice Told Tales,' which I should name even before his 'The Scarlet Letter,' Harriet Beecher Stowe and her 'Uncle Tom's Cabin,' Mark Twain and his 'Tom Sawyer,' and Bret Harte in a part of his work.

"Poe of course is a reflection of nothing but himself—that strange genius which might properly have been met with in any age or any country. And works like those of W. D. Howells, no matter of how much distinction in themselves, have absolutely no place in a reckoning of this sort. For Mr. Howells won't see American life as it is lived; he doesn't want to see it.

"His is like the attitude of a family in which I once visited. I mentioned a certain episode. 'We don't talk of that,' I was told. The fact existed, was known to exist; but it was not recognized.

Novels to Reflect Real Life

"So that great stretch of country which is universally called to mind by the term 'American,' in which a real and a throbbing life exists, has been allowed no literary expression. If one wanted to put finger on the name of the man who first recognized this, strove to work true to his ideals and pioneered the way to a real American expression of American life, I should say put it on the name of Henry B. Fuller.

"I remember reading his 'With the Procession' back in '88, I believe.* Then I read Frank Norris's 'McTeague,' and Hervey White's 'Quicksand,' and Brand Whitlock's 'The Thirteenth District.' These are all names of pioneers who were blazing the trail in the ten years or so immediately following my reading of —."

Mr. Dreiser then realizes he has said more than in his first guarded moments he had intended to say, but having said it, he sticks by it.

"What's the use, anyway, of trying to do anything unless you try to do it the way that strikes you as being right? I don't care if the public doesn't want to read my books, if the publishers don't want to publish them.

"I'll write them the way I know they ought to be written. And I'll not starve. I'll go back to editing first." And he accompanies the threat with a forceful gesture which prominently involves finger ring and handkerchief.

For a man who protests he cannot talk seriously about his work, cannot even seriously think about it, unless actually at it, pen in hand, the author of "Jennie Gerhardt" manages to achieve an air of enthusiasm, and savagery even, if occasion demand.

He maintains that his conception of life when he is seriously at work is entirely different from his attitude toward life when going about ordinary workaday matters; that he does not realize the hows and the whys and the facts of present day existence until he starts into the actual writing of them.

"But how can that be?"

"I don't know, but it is."

"How can you be sure then that your viewpoint when writing is the accurate one?"

"I don't know, but it is."

"How do you know it is?"

"Because it is. It is."

*Dreiser consistently misdated the publication date of Fuller's novel as the late 1880s. It appeared in 1895.

189

And there you are.

Anyway, the author says he does not like to explain. What is the purpose of fiction? he repeats. Well, what is the purpose of the Hudson River out there? What is the purpose of anything? Everything just naturally manifests itself—or should do so naturally. Books are only forced expressions of individuality moulded by their times and environments. Of course they reflect tendencies, for they are temporal in their conditions of making and fashions of making change.

And must they be true? he asked. Naturally; for to be worth while they must be both artistic and humanitarian, and nothing could be thus and not be true. And ultimately the truth wins. So fundamentally every worldly success is artistic and humanitarian. Which discloses an admiration on the part of the author for a certain Mr. Woolworth, a commercial genius who conceived the notion of operating five and ten cent stores.

"I don't know the man," he says. "I don't know whether the idea that he has first of all done a beautiful, artistic and humanitarian thing has ever entered his head. But he has—and he has achieved a great success. Think!

"Scores of manufacturers annually overproduce along certain lines. They are glad to sacrifice on these, for even a small per cent is a profit above dead loss. At the other end are the millions of the poor, anxious for the necessities and the pretty trifles which they have not enough money to buy in the usual departments. Along comes the middleman with his great idea. He buys the stock of overproduction and brings salve to the manufacturer, and he buys at a price which brings these articles within the range of the poor, for a price ridiculous and never before heard of—five or ten cents.

"Now of course I don't know the man nor the real facts of his case. But they must be something like this and he has done a truly beautiful, artistic, humanitarian thing. The matter may be beside the question, but it shows at any rate that all successful things have these basic elements."

Mr. Dreiser, who in addition to saving up his seriousness to use when he works, saves up a lot of strength and works hard and long, already has ready a successor to "Jennie Gerhardt," and others under way. They are all realistic exploitations of the same idea. For he'll write no other kind, even if he has to go back to editing.

Deeper than Man-Made Laws

A contribution to a symposium on divorce.

Marriage runs deeper than man-made laws[,] and difference and Divorce spring from sources which laws cannot remedy. You can say this man and this woman must, ostensibly, live together; that one must do reasonable financial justice to the other, but when that is done, what of it?

You cannot, by law, bind up the broken sympathies, the broken affections. They will not always heal. They come without man-made law and they go without it. To me a man ordained judge or jury sitting in solemn cogitation on the inscrutable woes of the mismated is a spectacle for gods and men. He or it is like a doctor with a pill box standing by the dead.

Convention may hold some men and some women to a conventional sense of duty—whatever that may be. It differs in different places. Fear (which is not justice) may bind others. Sympathy and sorrow others when love is dead. These have little to do with written law. They are like strange winds blowing from nowhere. They are of life, psychology, chemistry, what you will. Law cannot make nor break these and so it cannot remedy the ills of Divorce. To reflect—Fear will govern some, the weak, which is not justice and is not what the law should be seeking. Sentiment and sympathy will hold others. The rest will go their way as they have done through all the ages, law or no law, and in my judgment this will be as long as life is. And by life I mean this spectacle of so-called evolution which is a grand clatter of illusion, sound and fury, signifying nothing.

Hearst's Magazine 21 (June 1912): 2395.

Theodore Dreiser

To Theodore Dreiser, "Jennie Gerhardt" is an accomplishment of the past. He declares that he will never write another book like it; that such a type of woman no longer appeals artistically to him. But at present, it is very probable that he feels this simply because he is so deeply immersed in a volume he is writing for the Century Company on his recent travels abroad. He certainly trailed through the Continent with the enthusiasm of a boy, exhibiting a freshness of vision which bids fair to produce a book of impressions by no means stereotyped. And there is small doubt that some of his varied experiences will figure in the first of a three-volumed novel, "The Financier," which in August will be published by the Harpers.

In one paragraph, I am trying to detail all the news it took me several hours to extract, for Mr. Dreiser approached his work only after he had taken a flying trip through Europe. And this personally conducted tour led me to believe that in "The Financier," the scenes of which will be laid in Philadelphia, Chicago, and London, with the persistent accompaniment of New York, there will be some minor touches of Paris and Monte Carlo.

* * * * * *

Our conversation led us to the subject of art, for from what Mr. Dreiser let fall I inferred that in "The Financier" the collecting instinct of a Morgan or of a Frick will have some play.

"Art! there's to be a great deal about art in my book—that beauty which has been shut out so long like the pottery in Nero's Palace. The rich display is absolutely endless. When I reached Rome, I was not there long before I began to realize that there the remains one sees are native, and fit in with the climate, while the painting in Rome is not as impressive as it is in Florence.

"America is being judged very closely by the English, who in a way like us, though they say no. They seem to resent our false,

Montrose J. Moses, New York *Times Review of Books,* June 23, 1912, pp. 377–78. © 1912 the New York Times Company. Reprinted by permission.

blatant, strident vulgarity. They are civil and well mannered, even on their trams. But here in America there is the divine right for any one to insult you. You know, I rather like it, for it gives us the divine right to slap insolence in the face and go our way.

"I'm half German," Mr. Dreiser confessed, "so I'm not going to say a word right now about what I think of the Kaiser's country. But I must confess that I don't care for the 'I'll eat you up' attitude of the nation. My one great impression was that the soldiers are wonderful in their appearance, and I often speculated as to whether some of them, in their spic-and-spanness, wanted to be quite as nice looking as they are. I distinctly felt the desire for war with England, and let me tell you, there'll be some war if they do fight! Do I believe in the peace movement? I would, if life were peaceful, but is it?"

The handkerchief was now quite bedraggled looking, so Mr. Dreiser discarded it for his glasses, which conducted him through his discussion of his work.

"You may think it strange that I am avoiding New York as the locale of 'The Financier'," he averred. "I haven't struck the city of cities yet, but I have a novel stored away for it. I'm going to write about it some day. But now I'm crazy about Chicago with its great personality. The only reason my book is to be in three volumes is that 500,000 words couldn't conveniently be put into one.* It is all about American conditions, the rich and poor figuring equally, and the working problem in Chicago being discussed. As for the English part, you will hear much of English convention and English civility. But Chicago is my love; I don't believe any one could be crazier over a girl than I am over that city. You know I came from Indiana, but for eight years I was a newspaper man in Chicago, and then turned to New York via Toledo, Cleveland, and Pittsburgh. I've started many magazines, Every Month, Smith's Magazine, the Broadway Magazine,† and I organized—or disorganized, as you will—the staff of The Delineator.

"It was just after 'Sister Carrie' was completed that I began to work on 'Jennie.' I can't dash off manuscript; I hate to push the

---

*It was not until later in the summer that Dreiser acceded to Harper's request that each of the volumes in the Cowperwood trilogy bear a distinctive title.

†Dreiser was a Chicago newspaperman for five or six months (not eight years), and he did not "start" Smith's or the Broadway but rather initiated new editorial policies when he became editor of these magazines—Smith's in April 1905, and the Broadway in April 1906.

pencil. If a thing doesn't grip me, if it is not vital to me at once, it is very difficult for me to go on. That was the fate of 'Jennie.' The only reason the book ever got finished was that, begun during my free-lance days, it weighed heavily on my conscience. I hate to leave a piece of work undone.

"Maybe I sound disloyal, but Jennie's temperament does not appeal to me any longer. I found, however, when I came to finish it, that I had to be true to the first part of the book—in other words, to the character—rather than to my personal likes. That is why I didn't shift the key. Structurally the book is sound, I believe. But in the new novel, the note of the plot will come from the man, and man shall be the centre of the next three or four novels. It would have to be a most remarkable woman for me to write a book about one after Jennie! Possibly that is because I know more about women now.

"You may call 'Jennie' sordid if you will, but there is a certain charm even in sordidness, if it is used with art. A marvelous story might be laid in Fall River or in Jersey City. I have been asked over and over again what I believe realism to be, and I only say that you will find the reply in your own temperament. You can't answer life in a book. No one can solve anything in a single piece of literature. I think I'm a believer in art for art's sake. It's impossible to say that conditions can ever be perfectly moral, so long as there are differing temperaments. And from the same pot— meaning the same era—you get the religionist and the anti-religion- ist. Nature grows all types. They are all using up good land. One is supposed by his goodness to triumph and he doesn't; another is supposed by his wickedness to destroy and he doesn't. There are weeds and flowers in the same spot, and whether we get the weeds out depends on the gardener. I believe in being what I am; in expressing what I feel!

"I have never encouraged all that talk about the American novel. Of course, I'm a citizen of this country, and I suppose there is a certain race temperament that we cannot escape. But isn't Mme. Bovary as true in Louisville as elsewhere? The only thing that race difference does is to make you palatable to the land in which you are born. My one ambition is to represent my world, to conform to the large, truthful lines of life. And if I do that, no matter whether my characters live in Columbus, Ohio, or not, I will be true everywhere.

"I have written about nine short stories, but it's hard work. I need a large canvas. As I said, before I can go on I have to get a huge enthusiasm, and a short story is too small for the necessary run before the jump. I know that I am ultra-serious, that some people who meet me think I am too heavy. If I could, I'd get away from that; I'd rather be something else than I am, but I can't. And so you will find 'The Financier' serious.

"The book is going to create a great amount of comment. The first volume is the segment of a much larger thing. I've read through nearly every book that has been written on financial conditions—Hyde's book, Lawson's book—and the rest.* And it all seemed to me that they had only nibbled at the barrel of cheese. If the searchlight on this new book of mine is blistering, in the endeavor to see whether my statements are valid, I can only say that I have taken no end of care to verify my data. In my day I have written on trade conditions, and I have interviewed financiers. As to the truthfulness of my data there can be no question. But I am not a critic; I'm not quarreling with life, even though life is sad. I take my own misfortunes with less agony than I do other people's. Everything that is may not be all right, but it is beautiful. Life's all right if you are all right yourself physically."

The economy of space alone prevents me from continuing. Mr. Dreiser had something to say of Frank Norris's "McTeague" and Henry B. Fuller's "With the Procession," two of his favorite books. He had equally as much to say about publishing conditions, and about the fate of three-volumed novels. And when we parted at the door he eulogized postcards and the service they were to him while he was abroad. He may be serious, and, as he says, sometimes ponderous, but by the rocking of his chair at emphatic moments, by the squeezing of the bedraggled handkerchief whenever an experience pleased him, by the hearty laugh, I should say that Theodore Dreiser is not as lacking in humor as his walk [talk?] would suggest. In observation he goes a brisk trot.

---

*Dreiser appears to be referring to Henry M. Hyde's novel, *The Buccaneers: A Story of the Black Flag in Business* (1904) and to Thomas W. Lawson's *Frenzied Finance* (1903), an exposé of the Amalgamated Copper Company.

Theodore Dreiser Now Turns to High Finance

The race for wealth at the pace set in America has interested Theodore Dreiser, novelist and philosopher. The author of "Jennie Gerhardt" and "Sister Carrie" has been devoting a long period of thought and study to a dramatic picture of exploitation and high finance, particularly in the reckless years following the civil war.

In his forthcoming novel, "The Financier," which is to be issued on October 24 by his publishers, Harper & Brothers, Mr. Dreiser traces the evolution of a "Napoleon of Finance" from small beginnings before the war to vast dealings which include banks and street railways and close alliance with politics.

His book covers a wide field, and those who know Mr. Dreiser's work know the characteristic breadth and force of his treatment. The new field which he has entered has piqued the curiosity of readers who have learned to regard him as the leading exponent of the newer school of realistic art, and an interview was sought with the author of "Jennie Gerhardt" in order to obtain some information as to his new book, "The Financier." The title clearly indicated a distinct difference in theme from his former books, and this prompted the first question.

"Have you not changed your field of work, Mr. Dreiser?"

"Yes, to a certain extent. But 'Sister Carrie' came very near being a man's book, and I think if I had it to do over that I would now make it one. Nevertheless as it is I think it gives satisfactory evidence that my tendency was to make an elaborate study of a man.

"In 'The Financier' I have not taken a man so much as I have a condition, although any one who follows the detailed study of Cowperwood's life would fancy perhaps that it was more a man than a condition that I was after. It has always struck me that America since the civil war in its financial and constructive tendencies has represented more the natural action of the human mind

New York *Sun*, October 19, 1912, pt. 2, p. 3. Unsigned.

*Theodore Dreiser Now Turns to High Finance*

when it is stripped of convention, theory, prejudice and belief of any kind than almost any period in the world's history.

"In Rome around the date of the accession of the emperors we have an illustration of the strange, forceful ruthlessness of the human mind when it has freed itself from old faiths and illusions, and has not accepted any new ones. There you get mental action spurred by desire, ambition, vanity, without any of the moderating influences which we are prone to admire—sympathy, tenderness and fair play.

"Many of the emperors were murdered, as the ordinary schoolboy knows, and thereafter the world passed into the shadowy realm of religious belief which endured until the Renaissance. Thereafter the amazing figure of mediaeval Italy appeared, including such astounding personalities as Machiavelli, Alexander VI, Caesar Borgia and others. There again you have direct action of the human mind untrammelled by our so-called sense of justice and unmodified in the matter of ambition by any faith or any fear.

"There have been other periods, but few so glitteringly significant until we arrive at the year 1865 A.D. and thereafter. Then here in America we began to breed a race of giants acting directly, wholly financial in their operations, because finance was the one direct avenue to power and magnificence.

"Such men as Rockefeller, H. H. Rogers, Jay Gould, William H. Vanderbilt, E. H. Harriman and perhaps Russell Sage, are conspicuous examples. They knew no law and they would smile with contempt on any one who did. I do not think that the mind of H. H. Rogers or John D. Rockefeller or E. H. Harriman was far removed from that of either Alexander VI, Caesar Borgia, Machiavelli, or to go back to the Roman Empire, any one of twenty Roman emperors, including Galba and Nero.

"Our giants have been strong, eager, enthusiastic and without compunction. They have taken where they could, and silenced their victims with a bludgeon or ignored their cries. It is nothing new in the world; it will never be old or new. It will be simply different. New times make new methods and new conditions. Our Americans have looked straight at what they wished to do and have proceeded without let or hindrance to secure it.

"It is this atmosphere that I have begun to indicate in 'The Financier.' That book is not a complete picture. The full matter, if it could be condensed into one volume, would give possibly an interesting and I hope dramatic interpretation of what has been and still is happening. If I had the time and strength I would select other characters illustrating the same tendency under other conditions. If this is a change from my older method then I have changed."

"What is the theme of 'The Financier' " asked the interviewer.

"I have fairly indicated it in just what I have said. The locale is Philadelphia, the period from about 1847 to 1873, the character a national type, the conditions not different except in detail from those that have occurred in San Francisco, St. Louis, Boston, Chicago, Philadelphia and New York. I only hope they are accurate. Aside from the few specific facts with which most of us are familiar[,] the color and the characters of the story are created out of whole cloth.

"I spent some time in Philadelphia studying the location of the scenes and familiarizing myself with the machinery of local government, but beyond that I guessed, as I had a right to do. The political atmosphere is simply typical, not accurate. The historical dates[,] in the main, are correct. I spent most of my time reading of financial characters of one kind and another in order to familiarize myself with the workings of finance sufficiently to make it intelligent without giving so much accurate detail that nobody would read it."

"Is this typical, do you think, of American finance in connection with public service?"

"Fairly so, yes, I believe there have been many worse conditions than I have described. The machinations of Cowperwood are child's play so far as the Philadelphia end of this story is concerned as compared with the subtle manipulation of financiers in other cities, and even in Philadelphia at a slightly later period."

"Does your book attempt to picture the civil war?"

"Not at all. Most of the financiers of whom Cowperwood is a fair representative were not interested in the civil war nor the question of slavery or any matter of human right. They were concerned as to what avenues of personal profit the war might open to them. P. D. Armour, for instance, got his start by realizing that because of the war pork would be in great demand. It went I think to $9 a barrel. Consequently he stored pork until he had a corner and found himself rich. That is but a single instance. I drew on the civil war just enough to show that this was the attitude that was taken. And the introduction of the figure of Lincoln is merely to prove what I have just said."

"Did not your preparation for 'The Financier' require a great deal of time?"

"In all about a year. My greatest difficulty was in acquiring a working knowledge of finance and getting accurately the mental point of view of the proper character. I found a history called a 'Day by Day History of Philadelphia' to be of considerable value* and the biographies and autobiographies of such men as Daniel Drew, Jay Cooke and others.

"I owe really a great debt of gratitude to a private collection of newspaper clippings that was open to me and which covered many phases of the data I was seeking. It was no trouble to indicate the atmosphere of Philadelphia, although I have never lived there. Most of the histories of that city give a very good picture. My greatest difficulty was in making the machinery of my story work so that it gives a sense of movement and not of a vast complicated structure without life."

"What will be the character of your next book?"

"I shall probably follow the evolution indicated in 'The Financier.' Naturally a story which deals with finance and which has its beginning since '73 and carries its life to the present hour, or nearly so, would be more involved, more ruthless and more orgiastically magnificent than one located between 1847 and 1873. But I do not know that it would be more human or have more of an intellectual or passional appeal."

*I have been unable to identify a book with this title. Dreiser may have been referring to the very detailed work by J. T. Scharf and Thompson Westcott, *History of Philadelphia 1609–1884*. 3 vols. (Philadelphia, 1884).

"The Saddest Story"

Ford Madox Hueffer changed his name to Ford Madox Ford in 1919. Dreiser's comments on the portrayal of English life and character in the novel stem in part from his Anglophobia during the early years of World War I.

The Good Soldier, by Ford Madox Hueffer. New York: John Lane Co. $1.25 net.

Captain Edward Ashburnham, heir of a wealthy British family, is wedded for reasons of family courtesy to Leonora Powys, the daughter of a financially embarrassed Irish landlord. The Captain is a sentimentalist, his wife a practical-minded moralist. Uninterested and unhappy in his wedded state he approaches or takes up with (1) La Delciquita, a Spanish coquette, (2) Mrs. Basil, wife of a British Major in India, (3) Maisie Maidan, wife of another British officer, (4) Florence Dowell, wife of an American globe-trotter who is the friend of the Ashburnhams, who tells the story, and (5) Nancy Rufford, a ward. Both her religious training and her social code compel Mrs. Ashburnham to keep up all those appearances which she deems that these and her dignity and social rights demand. She devotes her life to the task of standing by, saving, and reforming her husband. This results in her supervision of both his finances and his love affairs, to the end that her own soul is tortured while she tortures his. The minor characters suffer also, and in the end the Captain kills himself, his last love goes mad, and Leonora accomplishes her ideal, a happy marriage. Previous to this, one flame has died, another committed suicide, and the wise Spaniard has milked the Captain to the tune of twenty thousand pounds.

"I have, I am aware, told this story in a very rambling way, so that it may be difficult for any one to find their path through what may be a sort of maze. I cannot help it. I have stuck to my idea of being in a country cottage with a silent listener, hearing between the gust of the wind and amidst the noises of the distant sea, the story as it comes. And, when one discusses an affair—a long, sad affair—one goes back, one goes forward. One remembers points that one has forgotten, and one explains them all the more minutely since one recognizes that one has forgotten to mention them in their proper places, and that one may have given, by omitting them, a false impression. I console myself with thinking that this is a real story, and that, after all, real stories are best told in the way that a person telling a story would tell them. They will then seem most real."

Thus Mr. Hueffer in explanation of his style; a good explanation of a bad method.

In this story, as has been said, the author makes Dowell, Florence's husband, the narrator, and it is he who dubs it the "saddest one." This is rather a large order when one thinks of all the sad stories that have been told of this mad old world. Nevertheless it is a sad story, and a splendid one from a psychological point of view; but Mr. Hueffer, in spite of the care he has bestowed upon it, has not made it splendid in the telling. In the main he has only suggested its splendor, quite as the paragraph above suggests, and for the reasons it suggests. One half suspects that since Mr. Hueffer shared with Mr. Conrad in the writing of "Romance," the intricate weavings to and fro of that literary colorist have, to a certain extent, influenced him in the spoiling of this story. For it is spoiled to the extent that you are compelled to say, "Well, this is too bad. This is quite a wonderful thing, but it is not well done." Personally I would have suggested to Mr. Heuffer, if I might have, that he begin at the beginning, which is where Colonel Powys wishes to marry off his daughters—not at the beginning as some tertiary or quadrutiary character in the book sees it, since it really concerns Ashburnham and his wife. This is neither here nor there, however, a mere suggestion. A story may begin in many ways.

Of far more importance is it that, once begun, it should go forward in a more or less direct line, or at least that it should retain one's uninterrupted interest. This is not the case in this book. The interlacings, the cross references, the re-re-references to all sorts of things which subsequently are told somewhere in full, irritate one to the point of one's laying down the book. As a matter of fact, except for the perception that will come to any man, that here is a real statement of fact picked up from somewhere and related by the author as best he could, I doubt whether even the lover of naturalism—entirely free of conventional prejudice—would go on.

Part 3: 1911–1925

As for those dreary minds who find life morally ordered and the universe murmurous of divine law—they would run from it as from the plague. For, with all its faults of telling, it is an honest story, and there is no blinking of the commonplaces of our existence which so many find immoral and make such a valiant effort to conceal. One of the most irritating difficulties of the tale is that Dowell, the American husband who tells the story, is described as, first, that amazingly tame thing, an Englishman's conception of an American husband; second, as a profound psychologist able to follow out to the last detail the morbid minutiae of this tragedy, and to philosophize on them as only a deeply thinking and observing man could; and lastly as one who is as blind as a bat, as dull as a mallet, and as weak as any sentimentalist ever. The combination proves a little trying before one is done with it.

This story has been called immoral. One can predict such a charge to-day in the case of any book, play, or picture which refuses to concern itself with the high-school ideal of what life should be. It is immoral apparently to do anything except dress well and talk platitudes. But it is interesting to find this English author (German by extraction, I believe) and presumably, from all accounts, in revolt against these sickening strictures, dotting his book with apologies for this, that, and another condition not in line with this high-school standard (albeit it is the wretched American who speaks) and actually smacking his lips over the stated order that damns his book. And worse yet, Dowell is no American. He is that literary packhorse or scapegoat on whom the native Englishman loads all his contempt for Americans. And Captain and Mrs. Ashburnham, whom he so soulfully lauds for their love of English pretence and order, are two who would have promptly pitched his book out of doors, I can tell him. Yet he babbles of the fineness of their point of view. As a matter of fact their point of view is that same accursed thing which has been handed on to America as "good form," and which we are now asked to sustain by force of arms as representing civilization.

After all, I have no real quarrel with the English as such. It is against smug conventionalism wherever found, too dull to perceive the import of anything except money and social precedence, that I uncap my fountain pen. It is this condition which makes difficult— one might almost fear impossible at times—the production of any great work of art, be it picture, play, philosophy, or novel. It is the Leonoras, the Dowells, and the Nancys that make life safe, stale, and impossible. They represent that thickness of wit which prospers impossible religions, and moral codes, and causes the mob to look askance at those finer flowers of fancy which are all the world has to show for its power to think in the drift of circumstance. All the rest is formalism and parade, and "go thou and do likewise." We all, to such a horrible extent, go and do likewise.

But you may well suspect that there is a good story here and that it is well worth your reading. Both suppositions are true. In the hands of a better writer this jointure of events might well have articulated into one of the finest pictures in any language. Its facts are true, in the main. Its theme beautiful. It is tragic in the best sense that the Greeks knew tragedy, that tragedy for which there is no solution. But to achieve a high result in any book its component characters must of necessity stand forth unmistakable in their moods and characteristics. In this one they do not. Every scene of any importance has been blinked or passed over with a few words or cross references. I am not now referring to any moral fact. Every conversation which should have appeared, every storm which should have contained revealing flashes, making clear the minds, the hearts, and the agonies of those concerned, has been avoided. There are no paragraphs or pages of which you can say "This is a truly moving description," or "This is a brilliant vital interpretation." You are never really stirred. You are never hurt. You are merely told and referred. It is all cold narrative, never truly poignant.

This is a pity. This book had the making of a fine story. I half suspect that its failure is due to the author's formal British leanings, whatever his birth—that leaning which Mr. Dowell seems to think so important, which will not let him loosen up and sing. The whole book is indeed fairly representative of that encrusting formalism which, barnacle-wise, is apparently overtaking and destroying all that is best in English life. The arts will surely die unless formalism is destroyed. And when you find a great theme marred by a sniffy reverence for conventionalism and the glories of a fixed condition it is a thing for tears. I would almost commend Mr. Hueffer to the futurists, or to anyone that has the strength to scorn the moldy past, in the hope that he might develop a method entirely different from that which is here employed, if I did not know that at bottom the great artist is never to be commended. Rather from his brain, as Athena from that of Zeus, spring flawless and shining all those art forms which the world adores and preserves.

[Symposium on the Medical Profession]

I cannot say that I think there is anything wrong with the medical profession as a profession, any more than I would quarrel with lawyers, or engineers, or architects, or authors as such. The trouble with most professions, including priests and soothsayers, is not the tenets which govern them, but the weak, confused, aspiring, selfish animals who are called to be made into professional men. And back of them is nature, compounding and breeding the above described animal. Some of the best men I have ever known have been doctors, and some of the worst. An evil-minded or shallow or careless doctor is to me as bad as a burglar or a murderer. Indeed, I have more respect for the latter for they are often so passionate and confused that they know not what they do. Similarly, a thieving lawyer—of whose kind there appear to be thousands—is lower than the ordinary criminal.

The ideal of each day and age since the world began appears to have been and still is strutting pomp,—richly caparisoned power. For this men murder as they go, in an endless variety of ways. The low-minded ignorant doctor—in order to live and be happy—steals in the sense that he takes what does not rightfully belong to him. He doctors where he should not, pretends to a knowledge he does not have, fumbles with life, and when his victims die turns his back on memory. The higher skilled, but equally unscrupulous professional, seeking local station and wealth, over-charges, brow-beats, carries profitable cases along, and bleeds his victims to the last dollar. I know four such eminent practitioners in New York alone. They make a shame of a great art.

But at the bottom of all our wiles is conniving nature—necessitous, flagitious, hungry. Men are so hungry. The mass is so dull. We live as sharks on blue fish—we strong. We round up sheep and eat them. We chase the deer and the roe with hounds of subtlety and arrows of the swifter mind. The strong eat the weak. The weak nibble at each other as much as they can. Occasionally giant locks horns with giant over vast possessions. If I were to indict anything it would be nature—brilliant, pyrotechnic, lustful, shameless. But I cannot indict nature because I love it and am glad to be alive. So I accept it, run as best I can when in danger, fight as hard as I can when cornered, study as hard as I may to avoid its endless pitfalls, and dance with joy when no danger is nigh. If I were to commend any policy to the rest of my fellows it would be my own. And above all—avoid doctors and lawyers as long as there is any other course.

Suggesting the Possible
Substructure of Ethics

The typescripts of "Suggesting the Possible Substructure of Ethics," "Some Additional Comments on the Life Force, or God," and "It" bear on their cover sheets the notes "Theodore Dreiser/ 165 West Tenth Street/New York City." Dreiser lived at this address from July 1914 to October 1919, but the essays no doubt date from late in this period. Dreiser's allusions in the essays to the work of Jacques Loeb, George W. Crile, and A. A. Brill resemble similar references in essays which he wrote during 1918–19 and collected in Hey Rub-a-Dub-Dub. *Note particularly his reference in "It" to a work by Brill initially published in early 1918.*

Ethics may be, after all, not so much a result of the (by some assumed) accidental processes of evolution as conditioned in and by the forces and elements out of which it has been possible for that evolution to take rise. In other words, may they not be an expression of mathematical laws which inherently and inescapably govern all Nature, the elements as well as the primary impulse which moves them? At the same time it should be clearly pointed out that the human mind with its very limited equipment of senses, suited only to minute measurements in connection with itself, is not and cannot be a fit implement for the detection and measurement of forces and matters which create and limit it and which lie outside the range of its various organs of perception. For consciousness and its accumulated data are as much exclusive as inclusive. The "unknowable," or at least unknown, is all outside. Life is so much larger than the little included realm which man's few senses are capable of perceiving and measuring that it behooves him to be modest, not so much in his theories as in his assertions and dogmas, as to what is or is not beneficial for the human race, what is moral and what is not. We do not and perhaps cannot know what is beneficial for the human race. Herbert

Spencer in his "Synthetic Philosophy" endeavors to show that everything done by or through the race or its allied species, either by itself or by outside directing forces, makes for the ultimate improvement of the race. This may be so, but since he distinctly predicates or pre-admits the immense unknowable from which anything may rise or into which everything may sink[,] how is one to be sure?

Insofar as society or the relationship of one individual to another is concerned, we find codified laws and suggested rules and methods of procedure, all intended, or presumably so, for the benefit and improvement of man, and all nearly equally difficult in the matter of application. Aristotle laid it down as a fact that whatever it was that was troubling human beings it was due to one of two things: either too much of something or too little, and in that he suggested what should in its way be quite obvious, a law of balance or equation as holding for all, as being inescapable even. Yet as against this it must be said that if it were only too much or too little that ailed us, the medium "just enough" should solve all our difficulties for us. But will it? There may well be sharp dispute as to that. There is no doubt that life seeks and maintains a rough equation, but does it seek or ever attain an absolute one? Philosophy and science answer no. Coeval with a rough balance there is always the tendency to change in everything, thus preventing an exact equation. It would look as though man were not intended to live on or even near a median line, not all of him at least, but for interest's sake, for others as well as himself, to oscillate between (limited) extremes to one or the other side of it. This oscillation, due to the inherent compulsion to change, is what gives rise to the variety, disputation, contention, color and what not else which we know as life; and that in the face of a constant attempt at balance or equation.

Indeed one might safely assume, from the scientific data available thus far, that life is no more enamored of equation than it is of change; that, oddly enough, it seeks both the normal and the abnormal. Its medium is little more than a rough compromise between extremes constantly straining, the one against the other. To pause stock-still at the centre would mean for us no life, an end of all those doubts and pains, and, by contrast, ecstasies, which make this seeming existence very real indeed to most of us. Our life does and must include apparently robbery, murder, lust, as well as charity and self-sacrifice and asceticism.

Yet it is this very fact, coming into contact with our very

limited conception of what may be extreme or median, which proves so disastrous to our reasoning processes, confuses us so that we may by no means agree with each other or with the powers or forces above or below us as to what may be extreme for us or for them, each individual presenting in the main a separate problem. Each strikes, or seeks to, or must, a balance between himself, his internal forces and aspirations, and all external things. Within the limits of our sensations and conceptions all of us are at times seeking either a medium or an extreme, according to our internal compulsions or capacities or weaknesses, in matters of wealth or love or power or peace or entertainment. All would say no doubt that they wished neither too much nor too little, but it would not always be true, especially as viewed by others. Yet in individual cases, as opposed to mass interests and mass life, too much or too little compulsorily sought or attained by any one may, and often does, prove disastrous.

Take a few idle examples: A tyrant by disposition seeks power, yet power for one necessarily proving inimical to the love of power in many others, it must be opposed by many. The more power the more opposition, with the inescapable result that the power invested in one must be eventually undone by the fusion of the many minor powers of others due to its own growth. (Note Vogt's theory of pkynotic energy, any encyclopedia[.])* A man of thrift is well liked, but one whose thrift tends to hoarding or miserliness is eventually disliked, a tendency to extreme non-equation in anything having both economic and art aspects which are unsatisfactory. Youth, let us say, admires long thick hair on a woman, but if a maid with hair as plentiful as that of a bison were introduced to one he would flee, the normal or accepted equation between too much and too little, as per the size of the body, being broken or upset. We say we admire a student, yet how few admire the intellectual recluse lost in profundities? It is too great a fracture of the norm. A disciplinarian is liked, but not one so strict as to be tyrannical or a martinet; similarly a brave man is admired, yet not one so courageous as to prove foolhardy. Yet all are interesting in their way, the medium and the extreme, and serve to provide the necessary contrasts and varieties out of which the seeming of life is

---

*J. G. Vogt held, as Dreiser notes, that large masses of substance or large charges of energy generated counter masses or charges. Ernst Haeckel discussed Vogt's theory in The Riddle of the Universe (New York, 1900), pp. 217–20. Dreiser appears to have derived his knowledge of Vogt from this source, since Vogt's works were not translated into English and his ideas were not generally known.

made. They stimulate argument, friction, color and change; all spelling, if anything, life and human interest.

The thing which we cannot, very fortunately, attain is a dead level or flat balance. Man is so constituted that he cannot endure it. He is a chemical compound, bottled and sealed in realms outside his ken and placed here willy-nilly but subject to the laws of his own substances and such others as govern them. These require both change and equation. Yet it is imagined by some—the religionist for one—that intellectually he is free not to subscribe, not to change, to avoid equation if he chooses. But sensorially and physically, as all chemists and physicists now know, he is stimulated to and chemically moved by or driven to certain actions and forms; in short, compelled by the forces which have produced him to respond as he does and be as he is. Not he, but they, are responsible. We bluster and deny and threaten, but we are all harnessed and driven, as much so as any ox, not only within minor and inconsequential limits but within all limits. Only seemingly are we free to make those choices which our emotions compel us to make—not all of them without pleasure, to be sure. Pleasure is the great bait or result, and when achieved allays most ethical uncertainties.

In accordance with this we find that in so far as ethics are concerned (the things which govern our relations one to another and to life in every form of civilization, or the lack of it) man, under whatsoever condition he has found himself in the past, has sensorially and chemically responded to or refrained from things or acts which in some cases have been extreme, in others approximative, of the median. Among instinct-guided animals, where murder and unreasoned herd opposition are common, there is a certain amount of parental and filial affection as well as herd relationship and solidarity which bear an ethical look, and these in so far as they contribute to a sustaining and race-forwarding equation between herds and the individuals of herds are no doubt as ethical as any other mechanistic or chemic impulses. One is all but compelled to assume that life as we see it is an aimless, accidental, mindless functioning of force in motion, or that the various elements, now listed by chemistry, think and plan and that all the movements of force and matter are mental—and, more confusing still, merciless and even horrible, since they pass entirely beyond our power to grasp or control them—and they do not seem to heed or know us. Yet running through it all there is nevertheless a huge rough equation which seems to avail us minute atoms very little, but which does serve to keep the tremendous and apparently at times conflicting forces on an even keel. Stars do swing in their courses. The elements contend, but balance each other, even in the human body and the minutest organism. In so far as social polities, low or high, are concerned, most individuals of the same school or herd—as in fishes, birds, cattle—excluding hunger and sex rivalry, will not assail each other. A wolf will not desert or devour its young. The male will care for the female during the rearing season. Yet this, if one may trust the mechanistic chemists (Loeb; Crile), is not a matter of conscious cerebration, ethical or the reverse. It is an unreasoned chemism. They cannot do otherwise. The ethics of it is in the elements, if anywhere. So with all of our physiological functionings.

The mystery of mysteries of all this is, how in the face of so great a chemical or mechanical accuracy, if any such thing can be said to exist (if it is not all mindless turning and twisting), such astonishing varieties of self-conception or misconception of an ethic or religious character concerning itself could have risen. If it is all so mechanic and unending, the constructive and physical processes of life being old, old, the various elements should know beforehand what it is they are going to do on any planet whereon they begin to function. According to the neo-chemists (the chemists of the mechanistic view or mood) germs of sufficiently small dimension can be and are driven by radiation pressure through space to one planet and another, and these germs, if they fall upon new cosmic bodies possessing water, salts and oxygen and the proper temperature, give rise to a new evolution of organisms. These germs then may, indeed must, be of ancient and interstellar derivation and know beforehand the old, old processes of evolution, since they have been endlessly subject to it—trained, as it were, in its ways. And yet the philosophic, ethic, religious conceptions of life (the thoughts of the constructive process about itself, as it were) differ so greatly, give rise to such inane and insane wars, religious and other, between different knowing and supposedly thinking parts of itself! What a mystery!

Yet, this one fact apart, and once this purely mechanistic theory or proof is accepted, all the ethic and unethic functionings of life become plain and understandable enough. The lowest groups and organizations of creatures as well as the highest, from cell to man, with their chemic "loyalties," unities and self-preservative and constructive functions become as understandable as the highest. They are blind, yet inescapable, processes. Their crimes, if anything they do can be considered criminal, are not individual but chemic; their impulses the same. What they are[,] God or Nature is. The mechanism of which they are the shadow may and probably does, accidentally or no, slowly evolute itself into finer and finer equations and balances. It can even take on the look of a highly reasoned and deliberate process, when all the while it cannot escape itself, is itself a mechanic process, enduring from everlasting to everlasting, slowly and helplessly and blindly (?) following the laws of its own universal being. It may even assume the look of free will when there is but one will, or lack of it, a huge, inescapable compulsion.

Some Additional Comments on
the Life Force, or God

I am the light and create the darkness; I make peace and create evil; I the Lord do all these things.   Isaiah 45:7

Darwin gave to the world a new law, that of the survival of the strongest, also the fact than animals and plants have arisen by mechanical laws without any preconceived design on the part of anything; yet (according to its occidental mood at least) the world immediately transmuted the strongest to mean that Nature is moral, in the local, passing or period sense, and that God intends for the moral, in that sense, only to survive. Of course the theory of Darwin carried no such interpretation. Plainly, whether for good or ill to the individual or the mass, the chemic impulses of all individualists who collectively constitute the mass are for things very different from those which the religionist or moralist considers either religious or moral—i.e., for self-satiation in many purely material and earthly ways: better shelter, more food, finer raiment, more and more diversified pleasures, fame, wealth, title, power, the right of precedence; things which, according to the religionist and moralist, have no moral significance in themselves whatsoever. Yet if you were to examine closely you would quite plainly be compelled to admit that the thing which is creating and supplying these instincts and impulses to man is none other than Nature Herself, or God, or the chemical and physical forces which underlie life, or whatever it is that makes life. And if man is seemingly to blame for exercising these instincts, Nature, or God, or the force or forces which create man, is or are plainly to blame for supplying them. From this there is no logical escape.

But, waiving the mechanistic or evolutionary interpretation of life and its compulsions or no, the question still remains: who receives the benefit of man's actions here, evil or good, as they may be? Man? In the first instance perhaps. We see him, as a reflection or representative of various processes in Nature, enjoy-

Unpublished manuscript, 1918–19. Copyright the Trustees of the University of Pennsylvania. See headnote, p. 206.

ing himself in material and even savage ways. But who in the second? Is it not Nature or God or the chemic substances which underlie him, or the intelligence (if it be) which underlies them, agencies who or which, accidentally or intentionally, has or have built or invented man, supplied him with these quite plainly chemic impulses and must receive satisfaction in some form at seeing or *feeling* via man himself? For, argue as one will, he is their or its accidental or devised implement, functioning or operating or sensating and enjoying himself as their combinations and arrangements dictate. For before man was the cell, and before the cell the protoplasm of the cell, from which strangely enough it was generated (mechanically?). And before the protoplasm were the elements of which it is composed: water, carbonic acid and ammonia; and these operated upon by sunlight between given limits of temperature, above freezing and less than boiling. And man is to these huge elements from which protoplasm rose or synthetized itself about as one of the ions or electrons of his internal cosmos is to him, an infinitesimal thing, yet organized into various mass forms externally about as the inner ions and electrons of his body are organized to make a heart, a liver, a brain. But to give who or what pleasure? Man, or the elements behind him? The ion may get some joy out of its life and work, or out of man's of whom it is a part, but compared to the collective reaction which accrues to man as the representative of all these how small. And similarly man, while a larger unit or electron in the forces which plainly create and govern him, may obtain some minute individual pleasure, it cannot be that it is for his pleasure alone that he is created. Something else must be receiving, enjoying—or if you will, suffering—the total collective sensory reward which he in his mass or race aspect suffers or enjoys.

For man does not make himself, except via provided impulse; did not make the present scene of his activities, and often, often does not willingly stay here; yet being so conditioned as not to know what other ills await him he does remain. Is there any logical escape from this? Then God Himself, or the creator of man, or Nature, cannot escape the responsibility for any indictment leveled at man for his so-called material or evil tendencies any more than it (God or Nature) can escape credit for the virtues, self-sacrifices, dreams, weaknesses or self-abnegations of man, which are the antithesis of the other qualities announced. Both or all are the product no doubt of an inherent necessity for balance and equation in all things, a balance and equation which is as necessarily main-

213

tained among the chemical and physical substances of which man is composed as among those of which Nature or the Creator is composed. They create, or at least make up, God and man. And what chemistry and physics now seem to imply is this: that God, or Nature, no more than man, can escape itself, its destiny. One cannot examine chemistry, physics, the creative processes revealed by biology, without reaching some such conclusion.

But, assuming that this is not true and surveying life at the surface where man is to be seen in his manufactured or completed state, what a contradiction of the idealists, dreamers, saints, humanists and religious and moral theorists in general who preach an all-wise, all-good God, the so-called triumphant outcome of his impulses reveal—the passions, savageries, hungers, lusts, unsatisfied longings, despairs, deaths—which cannot then be attributed to Nature's as yet inscrutable chemistries. What type of individual is it that under the direction of the all-wise and all-good really succeeds here?—the saint, humanist, moralist, religionist who preach and live morality and spirituality here and now and believe in them as an integral part of the hereafter? If you were to accept the moralistic and religionistic interpretation of life at its own value you would be compelled to assume so. But is this true? Will life bear any such interpretation? Is it not far more true that in actual practice the world all but hates the true moralist or religious teacher, enjoying his teachings and assumed practices as theories and ideals only and abominating self-restraint, self-abnegation and the like? Is it not true that, insofar as the fixed restful mass is concerned, even those with advanced or distinguished ideas in any form, which tend always to produce change and so make the mass uncomfortable, are an irritation to it and hence despised by it? Do we not all too well know how the world treats its guides and leaders? And does it not above all things love change and even unrest, whatever the cost in the way of individuals or ease, ethics or theories, religious or other? And is it not true that just in proportion to their actual value, intellectually and therefore ethically, individuals are neglected or punished? A Galileo tortured, a Columbus chained, a Bruno sent to the stake and flames; to Spinoza, Cervantes, Poe poverty, contempt, even disgrace.

On the other hand, who receives the rewards, such rewards as only a material world can give and crave?—the thinkers and leaders or those who quite frankly are the most material, the most ruthless, the most selfish, the most sordid, the most changeable and invariably the most unscrupulous? Look under the surface of life, not at it. Who possesses wealth and power?—the so-called intellectually self-sacrificing and world-serving, or a very different type often masquerading as the above, adding subtlety and treachery to brute force? Who craves food in plenty and obtains it; show and obtains it; wealth and obtains it; fleshly gratification and obtains it? Is it not those who most avidly seek these in the first instance and who in their desire to obtain them prey upon their weaker fellows, the very strong materially, those who crave money and material possession above all else, a sense of purely material grandeur? It may be said of life that it involves beauty, does not seem to be able to escape it; but as for the units who compel or present beauty, are they not helpless or savage, envious, uncharitable, ungrateful, presenting only so much charm of balance or equation as is compulsory in Nature itself? And are not the strongest among them, however arbitrarily you may choose to describe the strong, the only ones who survive and propagate their kind? Does not the world smile at generosity in others as, to put it at its best, an amiable weakness? Does it not scoff at an ideal, nearly any ideal, as being impracticable, not material enough? Does life trust its idealists—or any one really? The phrase "Greeks bearing gifts"—what does that mean?

Yet because weak man hopes for much and is not able to achieve it, he anoints his sufferings with one of two things: that only the morally wicked, the wastrels and socially unfit, come to grief, those worse than himself in the ethical and moral sense; or that a devil, a rebel against God and Good, prevails at times and perverts His intentions, and that for every ill so come by here there is a haven of glory and ease for him elsewhere.

But of course this last is not true; the thought is what it is, an illusion, a bandage prepared by minor ignorant atoms for immedicable wounds, a narcotic that gives the peace of dreams to those who endure all but unbearable ills. May not the wastrels and self-gratifiers count their lives a great success, as representing earthly and material or natural impulses gratified according to Nature's strongest impulses? They may say that they have not sighed in vain or looked to a mythical heaven for their reward; indeed they have had those prizes for which they were fit (strongest) and for which the materially fit, Nature's most vigorous types, are plainly striving. For if the so-called civilization of all ages presents anything at all it is the spectacle of the strong taking where they could, by conniving, by stealth, by flattery, by illusion foisted upon others, by sheer brute power; as against the weak taking what pittance the former choose to return to them by reason of lack of strength. Indeed is it not a fact that in secret the strong, the avaricious, the hungry, smile at the moral or religious humility of others, even while they encourage it? For this is the chaff upon which the dull are fed, the chains with which they are deadened, while the true grain of satisfaction is being garnered and carried away by these others, the material and physical greedy and powerful, the savage hungry souls so ably generated by Nature to express, chemically, its deepest impulses.

In that brilliant synthesis, "The Riddle of the Universe," Ernst Haeckel is at great pains to show us not only the unity of the universe, the inextricable connection between spirit and matter and the merging of energy and matter into substance, but he is at still greater pains to make plain that substance as well as matter can never have had any beginning and cannot have an end, and that a mechanistic and therefore unthought and hopelessly conditional state or process is at the bottom of everything, never beginning and never ending. Also he proclaims the underlying unity in inorganic and organic Nature, the latter, according to him, springing from the former. He emphasizes the common origin of all organisms: all plant and animal forms are twigs of one and the same genealogical tree, the race of man a shoot of the vertebrate animal branch. There is no absolute difference between plant and animal, animal and man; and just as little is there a schism between body and soul: the psychic development is dependent on the physical and the human consciousness differs from the animal only in degree. That which we call a soul is a sum of plasma movements, and consciousness is a brain-function, depending on the mechanical work of the ganglia cells; and these, in their turn, can be traced to chemical and physical processes. The individual soul disappears with the individual body; man's demand for immortality is reduced *in absurdum,* as well as his faith in a personal God who interferes in human affairs. Yet, having swept away all possibility of faith in a thinking, guiding, loving Creator, he is also at pains to recommend as a logical course if not duty the worship of "The good, the true and the beautiful."

Well, one might agree with this if one could always identify for oneself in life "the good, the true and the beautiful," but, failing that, the suggestion becomes rather inane and foolish. Logically, he might have gone one step farther and announced what is true, that Nature, being itself so conditioned, is, and we as a part of it, compelled to accept, admire, desire itself as beautiful, accu-

216

rate, true. And since there exists in Nature an inherent necessity for proportion or balance from which our minor ideas of the good, the true and beautiful take their rise and is everywhere holden, we must crave and admire aspects of this balance and proportion which are the only good, beautiful, true that we know or can know. Yet this is not a matter of free will but of condition, and we cannot escape it. The flaw in Haeckel's process is that having previously denied free will, as well he may, he yet calls upon the individual to exercise it; a flaw, one might point out, common to most dogmas and theories. That which science and philosophy have to offer, if anything, is not a definite perfection of adjustment here and now but the hope of it, conditioned on the obvious necessity for balance and equation which everywhere we see holding in a huge, rough, at times seemingly inconsiderate (in so far as we are concerned) way in Nature. Nothing else gives us hope or the illusion of good which sustains so many. If he had said so much his philosophy would have matched his science, great as that is.

The astounding fact is of course that man, in spite of all his skepticism as to things earthly, will never believe this. It is too grossly contemptuous of himself, either as a failure or a hopeful, strutting power. In spite of all his frailty, his meannesses, the manner in which he is constantly preyed upon by others, the manner in which he in turn preys upon them, his so obvious degradations, and the fact that Nature cares no more for him than any fly or rat, still it is his petty life which is to come to nothing (and why, under the shining sun, since he is made by quintillions almost within a century and all alike as two buttons, should he not?), he is willing to pay almost any price, practice any self-deceit, in order to escape the plain implication on every hand that dust he is, or rather a poor, endlessly duplicated chemic compound or machine, easily broken and easily replaced, with a very limited set of "senses" or reactions, set here to fulfill the impulses, desires, hungers of something—his Creator, no less—which or who cares no more for him than any manufacturer of cans or plates or cups or spools cares for any particular specimen of his endlessly reiterated product.

Actually he is without import save as a medium by which something else is gratified, only he will not believe it; it may be that it is intended that he should not. But one thing is plain: he cannot be important. He is too easily made, too easily duplicated, too easily replaced; the very best of him, great generals, poets, dreamers, is as easily made by this mechanic master-something as tin cans or spools. If you had learned to manufacture men by

217

billions and quintillions you certainly would not be concerned about one. It is entirely possible that the formula might be worth something, but not necessarily not even that. You might be able to devise a better formula than this; in fact, if one reads evolution aright, Nature or God has as often been doing that very thing continuously and indifferently in so far as man's hopes and dreams are concerned, making one type of eating, seeking animal and then, finding it not quite as satisfactory as might be, casting it aside and wiping it out completely. The history of the two-horned rhinoceros, behemoth, the sabre-toothed tiger, the flying fishes and reptiles, birds, apes—a hundred million forms—are all instances.

Yet man, in spite of this endless evidence of his unimportance, is unwilling to believe it. It does not flatter his self-love, flies in the face of the centripetal energy which keeps him whole. His hope, he says, contradicts it. From somewhere he has faith—sprung from fear and fear only—although he is not willing to believe that either. He at least is to endure, is of some importance. There is a God, who loves *him*. This same God wants his (man's) death, in order to exalt him. He allows him to suffer here in order to make him happy somewhere else!

The truth is that if we judge this Creator or Ruler whom we have set up by man alone we will be compelled to admit that of all things man's creator is a lover of mediocrity of the rankest, shabbiest, most ridiculous character, for He loves billions of so average a trivial and shabby character as to make life all but a jest. And markedly He shuns highly specialized or generalized individuals as being above or beyond His needs here. Take the commonest truth, the most universal: that the accidentally strong physically, the shrewd, the cunning, the highly specialized in purely material and narrowly self-aggrandizing ways, are always the most successful and best preserved here, whereas the more generalized, the truly wise—artist, philosopher, seer—the individual with exceptional intellectual vision and aspiration, is as out of place as a giant in a land of pygmy dwellings and furniture. By the same token, the so-called unfortunate (meaning in the main the unselfishly generous, the ignorant, the sympathetic, the tender and the poorly equipped physically or mentally, the wretchedly born) are, mediocre-wise, left to go under. Again, are not those whom the mass hails and admires as the spiritually or intellectually good only those who here, and in some purely fortuitous way, have been able (or to pretend) to serve them in some feeble way, to remedy things a little *here,* to assuage the obvious brutalities of existence for the mass

218

and so bring gratitude (a lively sense of favors to come) in return? One need not ask whether a true solution has ever been offered; since there is none they have only needed to sympathize, or pretend to (the Catholic Church, for instance), in [a] world where so much sympathy is needed. Indeed if the chemical and physical laws of life be carefully examined they will show, as I have elsewhere pointed out, that the appearance of such individuals as Christs, Buddhas and all so-called lovers of mankind are but chemical and physical reactions against or equations of a too-gross materiality in other directions, accidents really or equivalents or equations of the other or greedy, self-aggrandizing types, and are conditional and inherent in the scheme of things as well as are these others and cannot be escaped by the so-called Creator Himself. No black without a white, no strong without a weak, no material without a spiritual wherewith to contrast it, no hot without a cold, no short without a long, no round without a square, no high without a low, no great without a small, no savage without a tender, no greedy without a generous, a something wherewith to contrast it, however minute in quality; the one being inconceivable even without the other. Does not this sound as though life were fixed, conditioned, mechanistic, from everlasting to everlasting? Try to think of the one without the other, or in other words life without its contrast, no life.

The only value in the whole life movement or generation apparently is that it makes for multiplicity, duplication and mediocrity for something other than man, something that is a synthesis of him and that offers no least advantage to the individual in so far as his special state here is concerned. Vast, vast quantities of everything in minute forms and under general laws, they being the all-desired, the be-all and the end-all, so that no one thing may rise to any great or individual height. God dancing as a vaudeville performer, serving as a bartender, tending a machine as a mill-hand! Nature apparently hates, and seeks and proceeds to check, soaring ambition in any one thing or individual. Balance and equation between all things is apparently all that is desired, so that only dull functioning, without reason if not without rhyme, ending in death or nothingness, as a thousand physicists and philosophers have clearly pointed out, is all that prevails. Yet again, Nature, in the ultimate and for the preservation of her own superiority or integrity perhaps, plainly seeks to avoid this also for Herself and so has evolved or invented the dependent equation, or a system of alternating balances or equations in all things, whereby Nirvana or

219

exact equation or nothingness in all things may be avoided for Her, leaving room for endless anachronisms and changes—jokes, really, hence humor perhaps—in other words, life as we see it.

In short, these anachronistic indictments may be carried by any one to any length. A close examination of the results of life can only lead to a low estimate of ethical and intellectual import of the guiding mechanistic processes. Far better had man concern himself with direct scientific investigation, the earnest study of all mechanical or physical and chemical laws of his own and the universal being. In due time, with good luck, a body of fact may be gathered upon which may be erected a new synthesis—whether of theory or fact, who knows? But of God, or our Creator, as we speculate concerning Him today, the less we theorize or moralize, aside from maintaining a reasonable social equation or harmony, noninjurious and possibly beneficial to ourselves, the better.

It

We say so often that we control our minds, but do we? Is it not a fact that our temperaments, come by heaven only knows how, control our so-called minds or moods for us? The Freudians would have us believe (Brill: "The Psychopathology of the Selection of Vocations")* that even the so-called temperamental leanings which influence us to take up our various professions or labors are accidental, due to psychic wounds in infancy or youth, repression or woes, which burst out later in retaliatory decision and works. Perhaps this is true. Whatever It is, life-spark or ego, that sits at the centre and does the deciding (self-interestedly and selfishly always), there is no least evidence that we control It, Its wishes and instincts, but that It controls us. *It* is, or rather we are, for It is in us and we in It, "polymorphous perverse" (to use Freud's apt phrase) in infancy and later.† Its chief and only power is that of wishing and preferring, but by this same strange force nevertheless compelling the body to act, and act vigorously, often violently. How powerful this is[,] the passions and longings of the world, expressed in effort and deed, illustrate clearly enough. See all the neuroses that later spring from It when thwarted, the insanities, the evils, the horrible lusts and impulses. It has no other energy than "connotive tensions"; its active control is all desire. But this same desire, if too long ignored, appears later with vast and crushing power, rising and breaking through and making us do the things which formerly we ignored, only now with disrupting and crushing energy.

These internal wishes and dreams are built-up plans and schemes which seem so futile in themselves and so helpless in the face of life, do at last burst forth and compel us to act—these things which are apparently Its only method or means of getting

Unpublished manuscript, 1918–19. Copyright the Trustees of the University of Pennsylvania. See headnote, p. 206.

*In *Medical Record,* February 1918.

†In his "Three Contributions to the Theory of Sex," Freud used the term *polymorphous perverse* to describe the indiscriminate sexuality of infants.

what It wants. We say so often that we have made up our minds to do a certain thing or things. But have we? Is it not It merely, this internal spirit or chemic compound, which has made up Its mind, or rather generated those moods, built up Its force, reasoned out Its course, and swelled and so compelled by Its very need or longing the thing which otherwise we would not do? What is that? Logic, reason, the workings of a free-willing and -thinking spirit, or only some internal and accidental chemical synthesis built up by some other power which we call, and which looks to us like, a soul? And later we say that we guide It, Its desires. But do we? It compels the body to move, to do, and life (external circumstances) modify, even fix, how It may do. It has free will in nothing save wishing and to a certain extent compelling our machinery, the machinery of our body, to motion. Life fixes it so that It has not so much free will as free choice. It can only choose between various things which are possible for It to choose or do. It cannot ordain or will anything possible or impossible and then achieve it. There is a great difference there.

One of the things which tends to convince me that the biologic force shown in us and everything is one and the same and that its seeming separateness or division into egos or personality, so-called, is more of an illusion than anything else, is the manner in which the human brain in separate individuals functions in the first place, biologically the same in every instance. They respond, for instance, to the same stimuli (sex, hunger, ambition) and then in turn to all compulsions and inhibitions built up by this same biologos in the past via other forms of itself and in the same way. Our so-called independent souls have no control over It whatsoever, but It has control over us in every instance. In each of us, via Its pivotal position as soul or centre (our soul) It carries on thought processes suited more or less to the conditions (other phases of Itself) by which It finds Itself surrounded. Subconsciously, as the psychologists and Freudians have well shown, It matures Its moods unknown to the superconsciousness that shows itself in the brain and its so-called thought and orders; and whether that organism will or no, when the time is ripe, it is compelled to launch the moods and compulsions of this deeper thing which outside forces alone can hinder. The brain cannot. Apparently the body must act when this internal force or energy has brewed enough force or units to compel the brain to execute or issue its orders.

Yes, down in the depths of the so-called unconscious, or the elements of which we are composed, rests or works the real representative of biologos. It is ever at work apparently, wishing, dreaming, ceaselessly planning. And of a sudden, growing weary of wishing or Its method of procedure finally thought out, It presents you, the general organization (the body), with Its idea. You are to do thus and so. And thus you do and so you must, or suffer the tortures of inhibited desires. If the body complains that it cannot, that it lacks strength, It, in the subconscious where It dwells, grieves or curses, sets up a darkling mood of sorrow, a giant despair that may wreck the very machinery of the organism itself and so free It from Its bondage. The ego which lifts the poison to Its own lips (the machinery by which It eats), that whips from Its pocket the knife or the revolver, that defies laws, scoffs at governments, taboos, philosophies—what does It know or sense that we do not? What is it that insures It the courage for all this? And when It destroys the machine in which It finds Itself here, does It know perchance where It is going after It leaves here?

Dark, central force that rules in our midst, that sings whether we will or no, plays whether we will or no, decides, whether the circumstances seem propitious or no, reads, dreams, mourns. . . . It!

The wonder of It!

The Right to Kill

A few years ago, in the city of Chicago, a baby was born so very defective that those nearest—its own father and mother among others[—]decided that it should be allowed to die. Among other things, it was partially blind and deaf, there being no external auditory canal on the right side, and, in addition, a very defective development of the skin over the right shoulder, causing an apparent shortening of the neck. Again, a part of the coccyx was missing, and there was a destructive discharge through the nose. The nurse in charge of the child at birth did not believe it desirable that it should live. The doctor in the case agreed, but left the matter to the parents, who thought it would be better to allow it to die. To save it, an expensive operation would have to be performed, and there would be no assurance that it would prove effective, or that the child would not grow up hopelessly deformed, and very likely idiotic. In this case the physician, after having consulted 15 other doctors, refused to operate, and the child died.

Pursuant to this stand of the physicians, there was a widespread discussion of the case, in the hope, apparently, of settling once and for all the question as to whether the healthy and normal in charge, for the time being, of the social forces of life have or should have the right to decide whether the unhealthy and defective, particularly in infancy, be allowed to live or not. Indeed, the discussion grew so furious, as it always does under such conditions—in the United States especially—that it threatened to result in the prosecution of some one—the doctor, the parents, or all together.

The customary morbid female with convictions as to the applicability of the Commandments to the lives of other people was on hand, weeping and denouncing. The smug, pro-moralistic newspaper, always with one eye on the cash-box, hemmed and hawed and babbled pro-moralistic tosh, in the hope of catching a few more Christian readers. The whiskey advertisements and the patent medicine advertisements were balanced by editorials making it

New York *Call*, March 16, 1918, Call Magazine, pp. 1, 12–13.

quite clear that God is on His throne, and that He commands the enforcement of the Commandments and all the Beatitudes as written.

At the time it occurred to me, and now I repeat it, it is time that this bugaboo of the pro-moralists—the existence of exact and spiritual laws of right and wrong—the whole Ten Commandments and the beatitudes, no less, as final interpretations of life and conduct, be kicked out of doors and the world permitted to face the fact that there are no invariable rules. Even the Golden one is merely a suggestion, to be followed at their convenience by the wise, and solely on the ground of expediency. Might is right, because, strangely enough, might is always involved with a form of outward racial, chemical or geological compulsion which may be right or wrong, but is the only "right" which will be permitted to endure. The strong do rule, superior brain controls inferior brain so long as brains are manufactured, and the depths of life and death are not to be plumbed by any theories, religious or otherwise, however consoling they may be.

One might write volumes on these several and sundry propositions, had it not already time and again been done. The Schopenhauerian and the Nietzschean know much of what is meant. It is a fruitful theme. But in regard to this silly outcry in America a few interesting things might be said. We are such fools in America, and, when not fools, such amazing hypocrites.

In Greece, under Spartan rule, defective children were exposed, but there was a tribunal which passed on those who were to live and those who were to be allowed to die. We do much the same with horses and cattle to-day, saving those best suited for maintaining the standard of the breed, while sending the rest to death, and from a material point of view this is unquestionably sound. This was almost equally true of Rome, where many mothers exposed their children without, apparently, other than family consultation and decision, though it is to be supposed that public opinion regulated the danger of too careless a decision. At any rate, there was no great outcry against it. Here in America, where the precepts advanced by Christ are always quoted as laws, and where the phrase, "Christian Nation," is perpetually flung in our ears, it is always decided beforehand, and without regard for the difficulties involved, that life, however painful to the holder of it, is abnormally sacred and must be persisted in, though the holder of it himself object. It is Christian and merciful to save a child to self-torture and pain, and though the child might curse its life after, if it could. It is un-Christian and brutal to end life, however horrible to the possessor. Christ said: "Suffer the little ones to come unto me, and forbid them not," and because this was supposedly said in some place, at some time, all defective children must be allowed to live regardless. They must be made to live, if possible.

I do not know what to think of a world that reasons so indirectly, that fails to consider the obvious facts of life, and insists on harking back to rumor and religious theory. Christ was an opponent of pagan reality, but that does not alter the fact. On the contrary, the world was all but undone by His theories, as witness the dark ages, when pagan or real knowledge all but died, and vain theory flourished. It was the revival of learning, pagan learning, no less—reality, from the 13th century on—which began once more to rehabilitate the world intellectually and otherwise. In short, all truth is inherently un-Christian, for Christianity—its theory—is a delusion. It is absolutely opposed to free scientific research, and as such should be kicked out of doors and forgotten.

* * * * * *

There is an awful lot of dust thrown into the air whenever the question of the poor defective who ought not to be allowed to live, a helpless drain on others, is raised. "Christ said," is the greatest present argument, and whenever any one arises and opens his mouth and says "Christ said," that is supposed to be the end of the argument. Further than that human wisdom cannot go. No one ever steps up and offers to pay the cost of maintaining the poor defective for the rest of his days. The state, guided by religious theory, has to compel this. No one seems to meditate for one moment on the horrors and tortures put upon a parent who must care for and contemplate a wholly wretched and unhappy being. "Christ said," "Christ said"—and that is the whole and perfect answer—"Christ said," "the moral law requires," etc., etc.

As a matter of fact, the so-called iron clad moral law does not exist at all. It never has, and it never will. At best it is a convention by which society saves itself from too much visible chaffering, a rubber band easily stretched for the strong, but too strong for the weak to get through, a net which is ripped by the sharks, but retains the little fish in place at times and under certain conditions. There is really only the golden suggestion (not a golden rule) which softens life greatly and makes it more endurable, but it is not a law. Love may be a law, hope a law, fear a law, chance a law—I don't know—but the golden rule is certainly not, nor any precept handed on from Christ, Buddha, Mohammed or any other prophet or religionist. They did not deal in laws. They dealt in theories, dreams, which have led the world into various miry places. The first impulse (which makes it really the first law in so far as humanity is concerned) is self-preservation, and only the greater self-preservative strength of the other fellow overcomes this. Precepts have been devised, but the hard fact of life remains, that life is a struggle and that only the fit, or those favored by accident or chance, regardless of moral or inherent worth, can or do survive, not necessarily the strong or the clever always, but those whom some accident aids, as well, and who are able by some temporarily, perhaps, "fit" condition to take advantage of it. To this rule, where the processes of nature are not temporarily disarranged or clogged, there is no exception and there is no high moral theory connected with it, I am sorry to report. At least my observations lead me to that conclusion.

If this is true, it is perfectly plain that there should not be so many institutions crowded with the hopelessly sick, halt, insane, degenerate and criminally and congenitally deformed. I am not advocating that the sick and halt now grown to maturity be taken out and summarily murdered, but I do think that in infancy a greater selective judgment as to the character of babies worth rearing might well be exercised. I know the cry that is certain to be raised in connection with this—that by so doing some of the greatest geniuses and mental guides the world is ever to see will be slain before they have a chance to indicate what they are. That is probably true. Sometimes, also, I think that there are guiding "accidents" which keep the essential from harm, mystical and illogical as that may seem.

No matter, let that be as it will, let us wait, then, until certain marked and unmistakable deficiencies or tendencies appear, and then translate via anaesthesia or destroy the reproductive power. Why not? We hang murderers and incarcerate defectives in a far more inhuman way now, as it is. Why not let a jury or a grand jury say whether they are to be put to sleep or no, or at least be prevented from rearing progeny in any form? The burden will have to be lightened at some time or other, or nature will introduce a much more stark remedy. For, after all, merely calling for unimpeded procreation, a larger birth rate, is begging the question. It is throwing the children to the wolves of chance. Life is a grinding game, and the weak and defective *are* ground out after much suffering. Why, then, not beforehand? I am not saying that I would

227

leave this to the judgment of any individual or even the parents of the children, but to a court where mental and physical examination by intelligent and sympathetic experts could be secured. Otherwise, the defective is eventually thrown into the strong Moloch arms of society, and there no real mercy is to be found. The defective is tortured to death, anyway, only where the latter process is adopted it is a matter of years and years, rather than of a few minutes or hours. Have you ever listened to the pleas of those who preferred to die?

* * * * * *

Horrible? Not at all. We have reached the place where, because we have removed ourselves once, twice or thrice from the sight of the slaughter by which we are maintained, we have come to think—we in our warm apartments and with open plumbing near at hand—that there is some basic law of tenderness or mercy which rules all life, defective or otherwise, and ordains that the weak and insane and criminal must be preserved, whether the people on whom the burden is unloaded are able to carry the burden or not. It is the theoretic duty of *the other person* to live and let live, although we may never practice the Golden Rule ourselves. But this is not a true law; it is only a notion—a fat and very comfortable idea—but nothing more. Nature does not work so.

The golden suggestion cannot—and should not, for that matter—save your life in extremity, any more than it can or should save mine, or that of the chicken or the egg or the grain of wheat on which you and I live. Life is not lived by divine electric waves coming from nowhere in particular and sustaining us without effort. Life is an eating game. One cell eats another. One organ (even in the human body) preys on another or enslaves another. One animal eats another. We, as animals eat other animals—the weaker the weakest, of course. If you don't believe this, note how one man eats up another man's business, his very livelihood, and so often brings about his death in this fashion. Have you never heard of a business man killing himself because he had been ruined, or dying because he had failed under the great pressure brought to bear on him? We have reached a tacit understanding among ourselves as brothers and sisters in a so-called social organism that we will not—save in parlous times—eat each other, but that is a mere agreement, subject to abrogation. We have found ways other than those of direct attack, one on another, of finding food and clothing

228

and shelter, but, should those ways become insufficient, you would soon see whether the Golden Rule applied or no, or any other so-called divine precept, for that matter.

* * * * * *

But to return to the pivot of this argument, which is that society has, then, not the right, particularly, as we understand that word, but the power and often the necessity of taking the lives of others, either in self-defense or as a measure of offense, and against this there can be no sane word. It has, in the last analysis, the instinct so to do, a thing the roots of which are in something deeper than we know or can understand at present, but which invariably supersedes all man-made law or theory. Man dreams of what he would like to do, and builds up paper defenses, ways and means. But nature knows, apparently what she *must,* or wishes— and, alas, sweeps his feeble defenses all away. Have you ever read the history of any war, the ambitions, fears, lusts, of any nations? If a state can protect itself (the individual) against criminals, so called, or predatory or diseased forces of any sort, how about the defective child or grown person? Would you personally want society (yourself) to reach the place where you would be overrun by such? Heaven forbid!—yes? Well, then, in my judgment, at least, it is time that we cleared away the cobwebs of altruism and all fine-spun religious notions, sweet as they may be, and faced the facts, disturbing as they may be, but healthy; that life is a chaffering bickering game; that if there is mercy at times and other kindly emotions or impulses there is also the lack of it and them—and by sheer necessity; that the man animal lives by killing and eating other animals; that self-preservation is his strongest instinct, etc., a la Darwin, Haeckel, and all other naturalists. We need always the tonic draft of ice cold and brutal bitter fact—murder, no less— brutal and fearful as that is to us, no doubt, but perhaps the merest skin shrug to a planet or a psychic entity of some kind, to keep life on its strange, aggressive and, let us hope, progressive way.

Americans Are Still Interested in Ten Commandments.—For the Other Fellow, Says Dreiser

I can truthfully say that I can not detect, in the postwar activities or interests, social, intellectual or otherwise, of the younger or other generations of Americans, poor, rich, or middle class, any least indication of the breaking of hampering shackles of any kind—intellectual, social, monetary, or what you will. The American as I encounter him, young or old, is the same old American, thin lipped, narrow-minded, money centred, interested in the Ten Commandments as they apply to the other fellow, and absolutely blind to everything that would tend to enlarge, let alone vastly extend his world outlook. Here and there there may be an individual, one or two maybe to a town or city, who by some accident of nature is interested in something outside his business, his store, or his church. But, as I say, he is an accident. The vast majority are interested in but one thing—to get into business where they will be able to "sting" the other fellow good and plenty. And after that their dream is to build a stuffy house wherein they can lie down and take the count. He hopes to be a Rotarian, a Shriner, an Elk, or an Odd Fellow, and wander off with trainloads of others like himself to conventions, picnics, reunions, where his outstanding hope is to parade in an outstanding uniform. World outlook? Now, really? Are you kidding me?

He still forms, daily, outside some fourth-rate moving picture house immense queus in which he waits for hours in order to be permitted to see Blossom Springtime or Cerise Fudge illustrate the humor, virtue, heroism, self-sacrifice, charity, etc., of American manhood and American womanhood. And he is only happy when for the billionth time at the end he has seen that no one has done anything wrong and that all the really good people have come off pure and uninjured, if a little naked, as it were.

And in his cities his politicians still continue to give away his franchises, where there are any left to give, the while they lecture

New York *Call*, March 13, 1921, Call Magazine, p. 7.

him in his nearest church on the duty of patriotism, thrift, morality, virtue, guarding the home, filling his civic duties, etc. His gas company sells him carbon monoxide for gas and charges him for eight hundred and fifteen thermal units as against seven hundred and fifty delivered. His street railways raise his fare from 5 to 7 to 10 cents—on account of rising prices—and then when prices fall, his wages included, keep it there. His railroads raise his freight and passenger rates on him, ruin his business or his district, making it impossible for him to travel or to ship and then when their own business slumps rush to his government with a plan to reduce wages and to have their own annual income guaranteed. His telephone company lets his business and his home wait months without a telephone, the while it retains his large deposit without interest, and should he complain meets with the sobriquet: Socialist or Bolshevist.

The lumber trust taxes him 80 per cent profit whenever he seeks to build one of his dear American homes. His landlord adds 75 to 100 per cent to his rent. The milk trust jumps the price of his milk from 5 to 20 cents the quart. The clothing trust stings him three prices for his clothes. (And to defeat them he threatens to wear overalls—just like that.) His shoe trust charges him four prices for his shoes and makes them of imitation leather. And if he gets too outspoken in his complaints his local district attorney arrests him for being a Socialist or a Bolshevist—particularly if he suggests that his government do something for him as opposed to his 971 might-is-right trusts.

His lawyer refuses to take his case unless he can put up a retainer of $1,000. His banker, if he has one, advises him to let well enough alone. His preacher assures him that Christ reigns, the while his doctor and his undertaker raise prices and so make his exit heavenward difficult. His newspaper and his magazines assure him that he is all right; that he is living in the best of all countries, the land of the free and the home of the brave, and that all he needs to get on is grit, nerve, honor, decency, thrift, spunk, wit, tact, brains, patience, etc. His librarian locks up every decent book relating to politics, economics, and life, and then urges him to inform himself. Lastly, in face of it all, he himself insists upon subscribing to a conservative paper wherefrom he comes to favor a blue Sunday and the censoring of the already brainless movies and the stage, to say nothing of his one refuge, a decent book.

No, frankly, I see no least sign of those post-war activities on the part of the younger or the old generations which threaten the

231

hampering and unnecessary shackles, social, economic and religious, which now hold the good American safe and sound. I see no change in the point of view that looks upon all phases of art as essentially immoral and upon political change as dangerous and even evil. In the eyes of the American, young and old, the salvation of the world lies in religion—more spiritual activity—not in any widening of his social and economic faculties. He seems to feel that all he needs to do is to trust in God and the innate goodness of his fellow men—especially his allies. God is on His throne. The less one knows of life and the more of Heaven, the better. In God we trust.

Oh, well——

America and the Artist

Dreiser's contribution to a symposium conducted by the Nation *in which a number of American writers responded to the question, "Can an artist function freely in the United States?"*

With all its defects, whatever they may be, social, religious, moral, I still cannot see that America so much more than any other country is lacking in those things which should stimulate or at least make bearable the life of an artist. I know that from the point of mental freedom it is supposed to and does present many difficulties and draw-backs—two or three million K.K.K.'s, for instance, watchful of morals, liquor, the Jew, the Catholic, the Negro; twenty or twenty-five million Catholics and Knights of Columbus, all set upon clean books, the parochial school, lower or purely sectarian and mechanical education—or none; innumerable Rotarians, Kiwanisians, Baptists, Methodists, each with a theory as to how the life of the other fellow should be regulated and what the national or State government should do to make the Ten Commandments work. And it is true that where these flourish, as they do largely outside New York and San Francisco, there is little doing intellectually or artistically.

You can live well enough materially and socially anywhere in America if all you want to do is to talk to your next-door neighbor about his cabbages, his motor car, his radio, or how he is getting along in business. And if you are intellectually cautious, and watch your step as to what you think, you can avoid ostracism. But tread upon any of his pet theories or delusions, or upon those of the community, and then see. Yet, of course, this is old stuff critically and argumentatively among those who know. And no different, I fear, from what you would find in Russia if you failed to agree with the Communists at present; or in the back regions of France or Italy, or anywhere in India or Egypt, if you ran counter to the religious and moral notions of the middle classes. Indeed, I cannot see that at any time or in any clime or land it has been an easy

Nation 120 (April 15, 1925): 423–25.

matter for the artist to live and do his work. Only consider the thinker or artist under the Caliphate, under the Catholic church throughout the Middle Ages, in India under the caste system, in Russia under the czars up to Catherine, in France under the kings, in Spain, Portugal, Turkey today.

If I recall aright, Socrates with his original notions about life was scarcely *au gratin,* as we say over here, with the Athenians; and assuredly Rabelais, Molière, Shakespeare, Kit Marlowe, or— to come a little closer to our own day—Voltaire, Dean Swift, Flaubert, Anatole France, Baudelaire could scarcely be said to be *en rapport* with their time and people, or very welcome either. And one needs only recall Copernicus, Galileo, Bruno, to know that in these darling States today we are not nearly so badly off as we could be—Mr. Bryan and cactus and jimsonweed legislatures to the contrary notwithstanding.

At first at least, and speaking solely as a humble devotee of the pen, I found America very difficult and unfriendly. The editors as well as the critics of 1900—to say nothing of the rank and file of the wide open spaces—seemed to be determined that that which smacked of continental realism or naturalism should not take root here; and for all of fifteen years I felt rather badly treated—being kicked and cuffed unmercifully. However, I did not die; and since then I have seen a change. Only think of the army of young realists now marching on New York, the scores of playwrights and critics even who vie with one another to keep the stage and the book untrammeled. Decidedly I have no complaint to make *now* and hope to have none—if only the K.K.K.'s, the hundred-percenters, and the Catholics and Methodists be quiet until I pass on.

But apart from past experiences, inimical as they were to mental freedom and artistic energy in such forms as I could master, I still found—and find yet—America as satisfactory to me, as stimulating, I am sure, as Russia ever was to Tolstoi or Dostoevski, or Germany to Goethe or Schiller, or France to Flaubert or De Maupassant. It has, or at least to my way of thinking it has, all of the social as well as the geographical and topographical variations which any artist could honestly desire. Where can you find a more cosmopolitan city than New York? And as for social, religious, moral, and political variations, pyrotechnics, idiosyncrasies, it is as colorful to me as any other land could possibly be.

But aside from that I would call attention to the fact that life is life wherever you find it—in whatever land or clime. Winds blow, storms come and go; the fortunes of men rise and fall; your worst enemy is fortuitously slain at some opportune moment or he harries you to your grave. But all in all it is *life* that the artist is facing in any land or clime—life with all its variations and difficulties, social, climatic, idiosyncratic; and these various aspects are not likely to prove colorless or without stimulus for the artist, assuming that he chances to appear. Of course I am well aware that social, or if not that then racial and climatic, difficulties or repressions are entirely capable of preventing the appearance of the artist in any form, just as climates are capable of preventing races in any form. Only consider the Middle Ages and the Caliphate. But even so. In America such conditions as are here have already been sufficient to nourish a Poe, a Whitman, a Norris, an Emerson, a Thoreau, a Saint Gaudens, an Inness; and I doubt not that within a reasonable period of time it will produce as glistening a galaxy of geniuses as any other country can boast. At least I hope so. In my particular field I see material literally for millions of novels—millions of plays. For to me every life is a book or many books or many plays. That the psychic compost of a given nationality is not such as to produce interpretations of the same in great volume is neither here nor there. Apart from Greece, England, and France, what countries have ever done so?

Not Rome. For all of its amplitude and wealth, what a painfully petty showing of names or thoughts! Virgil, Horace, Cicero, Sallust, Livy, Juvenal, Plautus, Tacitus (only contrast them with the Greeks); and Rome lived a thousand years! Not Spain. For apart from Cervantes, Herrera, Goya, Velasquez, and a small company of moderns—just who? The Netherlands, during a period of a hundred years, produced Dutch art—since then nothing. Russia, with nine hundred years of life, has a Golden Age of about a hundred years during which it produced some seven writers of real distinction as well as some painters and some musicians. Germany, or rather the Teutonic strain, all of two thousand years old, has produced within the last hundred and fifty years—no longer—perhaps ten authors of the first literary rank, and no more. These nationalities, and others like them, are no better and no worse than America. Each has its ignorant mass, its constructive, commercial, materialistic middle class, its thinkers and its artists. Each has but a few artistic shrines at which it worships, and already we have several. I have named them.

Personally, if I had the time and the skill I should like to write a novel of the South as it is today, of New England as it is today, of Lower California and the movies, of Utah and the Mormons, of

235

Part 3: 1911-1925

Arizona and the desert, of the great grain and cattle countries that make life southwest of the Mississippi so interesting, of American society as it existed between 1885 and 1900, of the Klondike and the gold rush, of Washington and its altering political phases, of New Orleans fighting a temperamental river to maintain a semi-tropic paradise, of Florida as it is today, of Kansas or Nebraska as they will be tomorrow. Certainly of material there is no lack, even if the object be nothing more than satire. And supposing there were a Voltaire who could write an American "Candide." Does anyone maintain that the material is wanting? It is not that the grain is not ripe for the reaper or that there are not endless fields as far as the eye can see. The reapers by some strange national lack are for the moment at least wanting.

But that appears to revive the question as to whether for one reason or another these federated States are difficult or impossible for the artist—whether it is harder for him to survive here than elsewhere. I will say that for one not incorruptibly fevered with artistic convictions, standards, desires, and ideals, the material and sensual gauds of America this day—the enormous prices offered for shoddy as opposed to silk and fine wool and linen—certainly tend to wean him from more serious efforts. One must desire, and desire much, to do that which is beautiful and honest—today, here—as opposed to that which is tintinnabulary and meretricious; for the fumes of those twin, and to so many irresistible, flesh-pots—notoriety and cash—will assuredly call him from his lean and soul-searching labor. But when *ever* has the true artist failed to adhere desperately and without shadow of turning to that which is true and beautiful? For these shall he not put aside kin and coun-try, and with these only as his guides—his pillar of cloud by day, his beacon of fire by night—go forth?

A charge that has been (and possibly to within very recent days at least, justly) brought against America is that it lacks his-toric background and patina—the older lands of the world shaming it in the matter of architecture, history, art, the fanes and relics of great men and great things. Well, maybe. Yet for me at least Amer-ica has always had the novelty and charm of youth, virility, igno-rance, innocence, and that zest for life which is as characteristic of youth, together with all the interesting and astonishing problems inherent in its newness: exploration, government, transportation, organization. So many lacks to be supplied, so many opportunities to be seized—those of art and letters among them. And to say truthfully, apart from my own personal difficulties, I have been

236

most heartily entertained rather than tortured by its ignorance, its gauche enthusiasm for impossible ideals of liberty, equality, fraternity, its wild dreams of its mission on this planet if not in the universe, its profound conviction (all below the thinking line, of course) that all things of real consequence in the modern world originated here. Do not the exponents of these illusions and convictions daily provide a percentage of us at least with a hearty laugh?

It may be and no doubt is a hard place at times for an intelligent man to work. There are so many strident voices—or have been in my all too brief day—bawling about the proper fields and materials with which an artist here may dare concern himself. The one hundred per cent American home, the one hundred per cent American mother and father, the one hundred per cent wife, daughter, son, the honest and God-fearing husband, brother, official, etc. And at the same time this handsome betwixt-oceans stage the scene of perhaps as ruthless and greedy and merciless a war for pelf as the earth has thus far been privileged to witness. The money barons, the trusts, the landlords, the stock jugglers, together with their handmaidens, the Comstockers, boards of moving-picture censors, busy ministers, vice-crusaders, sly agents (tools and fools) of religious and financial organizations—all so eager to compel or cajole or trick a rank and file likely at any time to become restless or contemptuous into a program of mental shoddy and soufflé such as no healthy animal nation bent upon even a semi-respectable career of constructive thought and constructive action could possibly accept and mentally live. It cannot be done, or at least I hope it cannot; yet of course that is why so many American intellectuals, to say nothing of some—a few—really important writers and artists, have heretofore gone abroad to live—James, Sargent, Whistler, Lafcadio Hearn, Bret Harte.

Essentially I know (assuming for argument's sake that tragedy is the greatest form of art) that a thoroughly prosperous country such as America is and is presumed to be might not prove creatively as stimulating as one in which misery reigns. The contrasts between poverty and wealth here have never been as sharp or as desolating as they have been in the Orient, Russia, and elsewhere; the opportunities for advancement not so vigorously throttled, and hence unrest and morbidity not so widespread and hence not so interesting. And are not "the sorrows of life the joys of art"? On the other hand, considering the individual as he must always be considered, a creature separate from his racial as well as economic environment, tragedy or the materials of art in any form

237

are always at hand. For while a nation, of which the individual is a part, may be and often is a huge success, it does not follow that he is so. Amid the plenty of a nation the individual may well starve. Amid seemingly unbounded resources for the entertainment for the many he still may be wretchedly unhappy, alone, and devoid of that which entertains him. His temperament may be, and all too frequently is, at variance with the dreams and ideals of a thoroughly regimented mass about him. It only requires the temperament of the genius to select and portray this condition.

And obviously the artist, if he is one to arrest attention, is one with a message—some new mood, theory, or form to present, something that is new, not old, and hence of necessity at variance either with what has been said or believed or with what is currently believed and practiced. Hence all too often (invariably when the message is of any real import) he is a pariah, as much so as is the unbeliever to the Mohammedan, the atheist to the true Catholic, the theatrical producer to the Baptist; and he must shift for himself as best he may. But he is not here or anywhere long before he realizes that this is true, and in consequence seeks to make the best of an untoward scene while he does what he can.

Yet personally I must say I have found the working atmosphere far from unbearable and still so find it. (I talk of the South Seas, the Spice Islands, Egypt, China. Yet here I am and here I am likely to remain. Ah, me!) I am like the man who thinks—at times—that he hates all his relatives. He can do without them. He never wants to see them again. But every once in a while he runs into one—or one gets sick or dies and he goes calling or attends a funeral; and he finds that they aren't so completely offensive to him as he had imagined. He may not see eye to eye with them or have exactly the same tastes or wear as good or as poor clothes; but after all they are blood of his blood, flesh of his flesh, and he has all the things common to his country in common with them. They are better than aliens at that—or so he will think—tolerable, and even amusing. He may even strike up a friendship with one here and one there, or at least think kindly of them. And thus do I.

4

1926–1945

1935-1990

Woods Hole and the
Marine Biological Laboratory

The Collecting Net *was published by the staff of the Marine Biological Laboratory at Woods Hole, Massachusetts.*

      I am here really on the advice and at the instigation of my friend, Boris Sokoloff, of the Rockefeller Institute, also to sense the trend of current biological thought and effort in America.* Since my arrival I have been most courteously and wisely chaperoned and introduced by both Dr. Sokoloff, Dr. Heilbrunn of Michigan University and others. Long before this present large laboratory building was here, as early as 1900, I came once with a fellow writer to investigate the Bureau of Fisheries Station work which had been called to my attention in Washington.† At that time Woods Hole was a lone and spare hamlet indeed, frequented principally by fishermen—although, because of houses on the point and islands to the South, there was what was known as "The Dude Train" which then ran once daily to and from Boston. The arrival of the automobile did for it, I fear.

      Mentally as well as scientifically for me at this time the Marine Biological Laboratory is quite the most impressive as well as interesting institution of its kind that I have personally encountered. Its interests and results are so various and so genuinely stimulating; the number of concerned students and thinking investigators gathered here so impressive! More than this, the purely scientific or mentally unbiased nature of their approach to the mysteries of life is one of the most hopeful things in connection with the human mind as it functions today. The patience, earnestness,

Collecting Net 3 (July 21, 1928): 1–2.

*Sokoloff was both a distinguished scientist and a popularizer of medical research. Dreiser wrote the introduction to his *The Crime of Dr. Garine* (New York, 1928).

†Any article which resulted from this journey was either not published or has not been identified.

and, I assume, honesty of these men and women impress me more than anything else I have seen in America.

And the enormous psychological value of their devoted and, as I gather, poorly rewarded efforts, to man as thinking animal—to the entire race of which they are so minute a part! Positively to come here out of the blare of inane and purely utilitarian politics, or the limited and wholly selfish phases of commerce, or the vague, and in so far as my mind is concerned futile potherings of most of our literature, arts, and of dogmatic religion, and here to contemplate the direct, undogmatized gaze of these workers toward the unknown—what a relief! For me just to walk these halls used by the various seekers, to look into their rooms with their microscopes, their chemical and physical equipment, the various flora and fauna assembled for purposes of experiment and thought; to observe the occupants—each with his problem, his hope of an answer to some mystery that has never yet in all the life of man been answered, is to me to breathe a freer mental or spiritual air than is breathed elsewhere in America at this time. Truly, I marvel at the patience that hour after hour, day after day, year after year, permits these seekers to hold to the chase—each with his chemical solutions, his notebook, his implements; each thinking, varying his mediums, recording his results—in order that possibly at some time or other in the life of the race some larger co-ordinating intelligence may arrive, and so man may win at least a part of the secret of his descent and his being—

Marvellous! Beautiful! The most honorable and respectable employment of man; his greatest, most admirable distinction—that he can thus employ himself; that he has the urge and the equipment so to do. Positively, when I consider the average man with his usually defective mental response to what is: his worse than petty interests, his indifference to the vast and mysterious universe 'in which he finds himself—and then out of all the millions, the billions even—contemplate this self-selected, knowledge-absorbed group which would like to *know* and is willing in this fashion to work and to sacrifice in order to *know,* I am visited by an elation of spirit such as does not ordinarily befall me. In truth, I am reminded of men who go forth to fight a battle, or who, courageous and yet poorly equipped, venture into a strange and difficult land in search of gold; or, I vision a group of cast-aways upon an unexplored island who have chanced upon a mighty house of many chambers, every one silent and locked—yet, since their need of aid is great, with the urge and the necessity to explore but with no implements or keys save of their own devising. Yet, the room so various, so vast, so mysterious. And their self-devised keys so inadequate: yet to be tried and altered and re-altered or abandoned and others made and tried, while many die, until at last one with more skill, patience or endurance than another may unlock at least one door, only to observe beyond it many, many doors which in due time must be unlocked if further progress is to be made. The strangeness! The wonder of it all! Indeed, you, each of you is like the figure in the Grecian fable who kneels before his Gordian Knot, but without a knife, or the permission to use one. Or again (and there the poorest of my similes) like a hunter who stalks game, a trapper who sets traps or gins, a cat that sits without a rat or mouse hole and listens and waits in the hope that from it will emerge and be seized that which to it at least is a need.

A profound and impressive spectacle to say the least; a great and most admirable and honorable labor—something that, as set over against the ordinary interests and business of my fellow-men, makes of them colorless and tawdry beings, they and their interests scarcely worthy of the thought, let alone the rewards, gauds and adulations with which as yet an unthinking world is all too ready to bestow upon them.

My compliments to the workers of the Marine Biological Laboratory at Woods Hole! A profound and reverent obeisance!

Statement of Belief

One of a series of statements by "America's leading authors" which appeared in the Bookman.

I can make no comment on my work or my life that holds either interest or import for me. Nor can I imagine any explanation or interpretation of any life, my own included, that would be either true—or important, if true. Life is to me too much a welter and play of inscrutable forces to permit, in my case at least, any significant comment. One may paint for one's own entertainment, and that of others—perhaps. As I see him the utterly infinitesimal individual weaves among the mysteries a floss-like and wholly meaningless course—if course it be. In short I catch no meaning from all I have seen, and pass quite as I came, confused and dismayed.

Bookman 68 (September 1928): 25.

What I Believe

One of a series of "Living Philosophies" by various public figures. I omit four poems which Dreiser published originally in his 1926 edition of Moods, Cadenced and Declaimed: "All in All," "Suns and Flowers, and Rats, and Kings," "For Answer," and "Related."

I

The original inquiry which is responsible for the ensuing fanfare requested information concerning my beliefs as to the nature of the world and of man—a spiritual (if only I or anybody knew what that word meant!) as opposed to a material (whatever that is!) last will and testament.

And because all my life I have speculated concerning the mystery of my being here and the (to me) lamentable finish to all the serious moods, sentiments, struggles, beliefs, and what not else to which from time to time I have lent myself, I do not now hesitate to undertake this serious, if ultimately unilluminating, labor. For, Messieurs and Mesdames, to be quite frank, I have thought of but little else. The mystery of life—its inexplicability, beauty, cruelty, tenderness, folly, etc., etc.—has occupied the greater part of my waking thoughts; and in reverence or rage or irony, as the moment or situation might dictate, I have pondered and even demanded of cosmic energy to know *Why*. But now I am told by the physicist as well as the biologist that there can be no *Why* but only a *How*, since to know *How* disposes finally of any possible *Why*.

Yet, just the same and notwithstanding, here I sit at this particular moment, pen in hand and scribbling briskly concerning something about which finally I know nothing at all, and worse yet, about which no one can tell me anything, and yet wishing to know *Why*. To be sure, I can turn to almost any religion and hear that God lives and reigns, that He is all-wise and all-good, and that, assuming ourselves to be sufficiently humble and worshipful, He

Forum 82 (November 1929): 279–81, 317–20. *Living Philosophies* (New York, 1931).

may "save" us to a more agreeable hereafter—though why He should have chosen to invent such irritable and even ridiculous creatures as ourselves or the several chemical and physical processes of which we are compounded in order to ultimately "save" us is beyond me. He need never have troubled to create, and so might well have saved Himself the trouble of "saving" us.

But not only that. For I am not only puzzled, but even startled and all but struck dumb by the number and variety of the *creations* of the Creator of the religionists, or if there chances to be no such Creative Being, then by the will-less mechanism of the physicist and the chemist which just is and does, but without any traceable intention of doing so—a blind and yet deathless energy possessed of most amazing powers and attributes, but not that of intelligible intention. Sitting in a modern home or automobile, walking through a modern street or building, seeing for oneself what appears to be intention, direction, order, intelligence, and what not else in the way of forms and implements wherewith to protect and preserve as well as entertain and even educate—I will not say *all* of the inventions of this alleged Creator or this blind mechanism, but rather one only—Man; seeing this, one might almost be inclined to exclaim and even insist that here was order and intelligence at work. One might say that here was the obvious handiwork of an amazingly wise, although not necessarily a kindly, intelligence; for some of the adventurings and compulsions of Man in connection with himself and his fellows—those of his own species as well as others—would soon make clear that kindness, although a fractional part, possibly, of the nature or at least the relationship of one individual of this species to another, was by no means the whole of it.

For here among men you soon find vitally and—strangest of all, perhaps—constructively operative: cruelty, greed, vanity, lust, gluttony, false witness, envy, and hatred; with their evoked and hence attendant wars, murders, injuries, and deaths; together with the possibly more admirable qualities of friendship, affection, admiration, charity, generosity, etc.—if, indeed, these qualities often be not mere figments or illusions of the human mind, or *élan vital,* or blood stream, or whatever it is that keeps us functioning in the very peculiar and not necessarily (except to ourselves) admirable forms or shapes in which we find ourselves. For, friends,—and much to my own astonishment it is that I am compelled to conclude this—I find life to be not only a complete illusion or mirage which changes and so escapes or eludes one at every point, but the most amazing fanfare of purely temporary and always changing and ever vanishing and, in the main, clownish and ever ridiculous interests that it has ever been my lot to witness—interests which concern at best the maintenance here of innumerable selfish, self-centered, and cruel organisms whose single and especial business it is to exist each at the expense of the other—no more and no less. If only it were by cutting each other's hair—and no more.

For what other incentive has Man than to feed, clothe, and entertain himself at the expense of others—whether little or much? And when you pass into the realms of animals and the vegetables—of whom Man, by reason of a built-up process of offense and defense, is supposed to be the overlord—what other incentive or incentives do you find there? Love? For the propagation of the species, the progeny of the individual—yes. But for anything other than the progeny of the individual of the species as against the welfare of the individuals and the progeny of all other species? No. And as for understanding of how or why—to what end? Does anyone know what other creatures apart from Man apprehend or understand?

What we plainly see is birth and death—the result of chemic and electrophysical processes of which at bottom we know exactly nothing. And beyond that—murder, the chase, life living on life, the individual sustaining himself at the expense of every other, and wishing not to die. And then beauty, beauty, beauty, which seems to derive as much and more from this internecine and wholly heartless struggle as from any other thing. And yet, beauty, beauty, beauty—the entire process, to the human eye at least, aesthetic in its results if by no means entirely so in its processes.

On the other hand, if I turn from this to the physicists and biologists—or to science *in toto*—I am at once and almost equally confused and confounded. For here, while I find a world whose assertions, if not thoughts, are based (in so far as possible) on previously verified experience in the physical or chemical worlds, or in that third world jointly erected out of the two of them—the biological realm—I am still, at bottom, sunk in mystery. For, as I have said, here is no *Why,* only a *How*—and the ultimate basis of the *How* not known! Instead, only a chemico-physical process which requires endless observation and correlation but with no least belief that it can lead to more than a very limited knowledge of *How*—which, should sufficient ever be known, is to abolish *Why*.

247

II

But let me say here that I have no intention of becoming too technical—or rather, attempting to become so. My intention is solely to present my reactions to a world that is as yet completely immersed in mystery—physicist or no physicist, biologist or no biologist. And as for astronomy, history, geology, sociology—well, we gaze or observe and attempt to set down certain laws, but little more. For we have but five weak little senses and with these during the past few thousand years we have begun to perk and pry—the mystery and the aesthetic beauty of it all luring us on. But the wonder to me is that Man is not even more astounded and dumbfounded than he appears to be each hour of his presence here; that he is not more withdrawn from his so-called necessities than he really is, in order to sit beneath a tree, Buddha fashion, and gaze in wonder and astonishment upon the wholly inexplicable world about him.

For here I am, as I now choose to inform you, at the corner of Broadway and Fifty-seventh Street, in New York.* And the world, or at least a typical portion of our very human American world as it is to-day, is marching or rolling by—busses, street cars, autos, men and women, boys and girls. All, however, human beings, of the seemingly favored *homo sapiens,* who in the wasteful and yet possibly shrewd processes of nature have either succeeded or failed, or half succeeded or half failed. At any rate, here they are.

And now what I wish most particularly to point out in connection with this is that this scene taken as a whole is scintillant, brisk, interesting, forceful, And yet, as I here and now once more ask myself: "For what reason, unless it be that each of these individuals thus hurrying here and there—to work, to pleasure, to acts of duty, virtue, crime, or what you will—achieves a somewhat of something which he or she thinks of as pleasure, here and not elsewhere; and, so thinking, actually at times achieves? Apart from that *here,* what is all this about? What else can it possibly concern? A possible future state entirely different from this?"

Impossible. These creatures that I see here and now have little capacity for imagining, let alone sensing, any such entirely different state, assuming such a one to exist. Their reactions relate

*Dreiser was living in an apartment at the Rodin Studios, 600 West 57th St.

to what they see, hear, feel, taste, and smell *here*—not elsewhere. And except for various vague and curious and, in addition to that, all too terrified, thoughts as to how such a different state might— and worse—is certain to dispose of them, they have no interest in any other state. It does not exist here. Possibly there is no such other state? Yet in the face of much pother and blather on the part of self-seeking religionists or theorists with this and that quack nostrum as to the why and how elsewhere, after death—these creatures know all too little as to the significance of good and evil here (and try to find the ultimate difference!) and are all too willing to contribute something toward the support of these same nostrum venders, lest, in the strange and unbelievable welter and mystery of things, there may be something to what they say—a God or Devil or supervisory (and therefore more or less inimical) Ruler sitting or moving above Man.

The greatest factor in all this is, as you see, the fear of annihilation. For here, now, is one walking with you. He is tense, alert, strong, charming, alive. Then for a very little while, maybe, he is gone from your presence. And then of a sudden that ever appalling word—dead. He is dead. He or she was alive and now is no more. The look, the feel, the voice, the temperament, the dreams, the plans—all gone. No word, no sound. No trace. The effective and valuable and always amazing body that you knew—dissolved. You stand—astounded—but without answer. No word of truth in regard to it all from either science or religion—but with science arguing eternal dissolution and religion barefacedly lying as to the what and how of the future. But no absolute truth. And struggle and contest and fear stirred in with a little pleasure for those who remain.

A dour credo?

It is all I have to offer. All I have ever intelligently accepted.

III

Let us now approach the chemical and physical combinations and processes which make the individuals and parts of this scintillant scene. And what a mystery! For here we have— what? Bricks, stone, glass, wood, plaster, paints, and what you will of the surrounding buildings. But representing what? In the last analysis, electrons, protons, quantums of energy in some amazing and constantly shifting arrangement of atoms and molecules which makes it possible for man, responding as he must to his instincts, pleasures, or necessities, to arrange them in this fashion.

And yet, when you go further and ask: "What is Man?"— behold, you are informed that he also is a diversified arrangement of molecules or atoms or electrons, protons, quantums (I am using the current scientific lingo for these amazing mysteries)—but in him masquerading as blood, gray matter, liver, kidneys, muscles, viscera, bones, hair, cartilage, and all their attendant powers, emotions, duties, etc., yet each constructed of the primordial cell, in numbers; which cells in turn are composed, in the last analysis, of molecules, atoms, electrons, protons, and finally (the last word of to-day) quantums. But all finally and inexorably, as the physicists see it, electrical—so that someone has already said that God is electricity. In other words, and to go back to the sentient Greeks, He is Jove with his bolts!

But, then, what is electricity? Atoms.

And what are atoms? Electricity.

Wonderful!

But then, as I say, here I am, still looking at the passing crowds at the corner of Broadway and Fifty-seventh Street, and now asking why should electricity, or primordial energy, or what you will, wish to form itself, via electrons, protons, quantums, into atoms, molecules, and eventually cells—in other words, into such a troublesome and mysterious, if varied and aesthetic, scene as this? And why again, composed though we may be of this, that, and the other proton, electron, etc., etc., why should we not in some way be able to sense why we are as we are—assembled as we are of the same ultimate atoms and doing as we do? Why? Good God—surely in the face of all this sense of aliveness and motion and this and that, there should be some intimation of *Why*. But no—none.

And, furthermore, there is no intimation as to why these several electrons, protons, atoms, etc. should wish, assuming they could do so, to combine and recombine—via the long and voluntary or involuntary process of evolution—into wood and stone, heat and cold, snow, water, air, blood, bones, hair, teeth, viscera, etc., in order and at last, say, to make an individual who has to hurry to an office in a shabby suit to earn a meager wage; or a multimillionaire who thinks that the combining of one hundred and twenty-one minor banks into one large one is a great and even wonderful achievement. At best, whatever man does is something that can only prolong the struggles and worries and for the most part futile dreams of those with whom he finds himself companioned here in this atomic or cellular welter, and which in the last analysis may be just nothing at all—a phantasmagoric or cinematic shadow play. Signifying what? A momentary belief in being? Or happiness? Oh Jehovah! Osiris! Jesus! Jove!

This—nothing less and nothing more—is the significance of the scene at Broadway and Fifty-seventh Street. And as for myself on this bright, sunny morning, I find it pleasant and good, myself a living, if not exactly worthy, part of it.

IV

But now let us shift the scene to the Congo, where, likewise, is a panorama composed of electrons, protons, quantums, or let us say, atoms and cells. And all busy with the work or pleasure, as you will, and whether willing or not, of constructing an amazing succession of species or growths—such as the deadly snake, the killing fly and spider, the savage tiger and lion; in short, such a world of predatory beasts and flowers and trees and vines, poisonous or the reverse, as should be sufficient to lay forever the notion of a kindly directive force or intelligence in the universe. And yet each bent upon the apparently difficult and nearly always miserable labor of sustaining it or himself at the expense of every other. And for how brief a period! At best, from half a minute to a few years. And with seemingly no more knowledge of *Why* than we ourselves—unless sex, the chase, hunger, and the satiation of hunger be *Why*. In short, a kind of electronic or molecular hell, yet atomically no different from that which prevails—or at least produces the scene—at Fifty-seventh Street and Broadway, say, or the body of the Pope, or that of the Archbishop of Canterbury, or Mahatma Gandhi, who is assumed to irradiate only the kindliest and most helpful of thoughts toward all.

And yet—so springs the thought in me at the moment—perhaps, in order to obtain so colorful a scene as this, it is quite necessary to have this angry show of contest and death. Perhaps there can be no true color or zest this side of it. Very well; but why, then, religion or a fixed moral code? Why not rather the Darwinian survival of the fittest, or a man-made series of rules governing the game here and not elsewhere?

As for myself, I see life—for most, at least—as a very grim and dangerous contest, relieved at best and but for a very little while by a sense or by an illusion of pleasure, which is the bait and the lure for all to all in this internecine contest.

Still, as I so often ask myself, can this be what the universe is for? Not really! For here are immense suns, hot or cold or dead, shouldering each other in space; minute planets spinning like moths humbly and meaninglessly—if this is all the meaning there is. And upon this particular and most minute of planets—ours no less, and the same quite invisible in space, I am told—robbery, oppression, false witness, cruelty, vanity, gluttony, sodomy, and what not else, and all seemingly fortified and entrenched—the weak or deficient, as in the jungle, preyed upon by the strong; the strong fortified by the weakness of the weak and their own strength, and motivated by what lunatic and ever-elusive dreams of happiness. In short, each seeking to establish his dreams for himself—and by whatever methods he may—and then rejoicing in the still more lunatic fanfare which his success in downright villainies at times seems to evoke in those who would be like him, the weaklings and dubs beneath him in position and power! Only meditate on the phrase: "God save the King!"—and then consider the departed kings of the world! Lust of flesh, food, show, applause—these seem to be the chief items with which the world I see is concerned. If I am wrong, let me be properly and appropriately flayed therefor!

V

I am not unaware that there are opposing points of merit that are not to be gainsaid. These merits I have many times and in many ways stated or sung. Rain-dark violets under rain-soaked leaves. Crimson fungus growths under drooping birch twigs. A brown path over a green hill down which streams a westering sun. A girl, arms akimbo, gazing at the sky at dawn. A sea a-shimmer in the sun. A beautiful gray rain amid the drooping leaves of the year. A seamed and weary face bent low in sorrow. A light-keeled boat upon an enchanted sea.

I am flooded with happiness—divine, demoniac dreams. I am seized with the very sting and tang of energy and desire, however fateful. So motivated, I can indeed front a universe that knows nothing of kindness, pity, wisdom. With the aesthetic principle here indicated at work among the threads and skeins and shuttles which make this amazing pattern we call Life, I can rest content, though I beg or suffer seemingly meaninglessly at the hands of it.

Moreover, there is the interest that attaches to struggle and defeat as well as to success and dominance among the creations of these atoms and cells—an interest that ranges from wonder at the

252

struttings and show of ignorant power and force to the pathetic complaints and defeats of the incompetent; an interest that swings from applause and acclaim—or the enjoyment of it—to the hatred and vengeance that follow defeat. Indeed, the dominant human mind thus far developed, as I see it at least, is at best a petty piece of machinery, in the main registering states of customs of the silliest possible nature. What does my neighbor do? What is he called? How is he paid, acclaimed? Where is he? How does he feel I should act? Is he more or less successful than I am? Am I better-looking than he, or less? Has he more acclaim, or have I? And the more average the intelligence of the organized atoms, the more prevalent these conventional inquiries and thoughts and dreams. But these are deathless, indestructible atoms, please note, that produce these things or effects—eternal energy in eternal action or change. And this is the result here!

But why, as I now repeat, should eternal energy as presented by atoms and cells concern itself with the hum-drum and nonsense that we see here on this planet? Is this all it has to do? Is it by any chance the best it can do? God!! Actually, as I see it, society or the constructive efforts of these atoms and molecules and cells comes to little more, on this planet at least, than a scheme or method of procedure whereby each form or species or tribe or race of things can, by contributing something—if no less or more than the bodies or lives of a portion of the totality of each—obtain permission to satisfy each itself in turn by feeding on the bodies or efforts of other organized forms that would like to live and flourish on this earth! And if that is true, what a coarse, grim, and even futile procedure, since so small a percentage of true delight is really achieved! And if not that, just what else, exactly, does the grand process of generation and struggle mean?

VI

And yet, in the face of all this, I would not like to write myself down as a total pessimist. Having observed the process here over a period of years, I find that it has, in the main, the quality of interest—taken all in all, a fairly good show, albeit so filled with anachronisms and illusions and lunacies of one type and another as to make it discreditable either as reason or order. Rather, the best I can say is that I have not the faintest notion of what it is all about, unless it is for self-satisfaction in many and varied ways—all more or less achieved by cruelty or greed, as for instance, life living on life;

253

man growing things in order to consume them; men or creatures preying upon the efforts of others in order to feed and maintain themselves with little effort. Think, for one thing, of the butcher shops at every corner. You do not *see* the abattoirs scattered throughout the world, but hourly they serve you, by murder, even though you dress in silks, sniff bouquets, and perfume your hands!

Of course, the anomalous thing in connection with such a viewpoint as this is that (at least in so brief a paper as this) it begs the question of aesthetics in nature as well as the presence of emotions, which, whether selfish or unselfish, religious, sexual, or purely aesthetic, cast over the innate savagery of life a gossamer veil of beauty which softens or blurs the essential blindness or indifference or one might almost guess (at times, at least) devised cruelty of it all. For here are, to begin with, the aesthetic forms of things, and on every hand. Architecture, flowers, mountains, the seas, rippling streams, silvery lakes, the depths and silences of forests, bird song, love, the beauty of every living and seemingly quiescent or dead form. Snows that are compounded of lacelike and inspiring designs; rains that are like drops of silver or thin, bright chains of steel. The beauty of a butterfly's wings; a snake's or lizard's skin; the flashing hues of birds or insects; the striding and contemptuous dignity of lions or tigers, at once proud and cruel in their power.

It snows, and the receded saps of life in tree and animal, flower and insect, leave only somber and yet moving and even colorful lines that somehow stir the heart with thoughts not only of a change that will not permit permanence, but a somberness which the inmost molecules of our being appear to respond to as a charm. Comes spring—mere mechanical and physical rotation of the earth in sunlight—and ash saplings clash their twigs in rippling, flickering winds; a robin's song is heard; dog-mercury and arbutus bud under the dead leaves of an earlier year. A bit more of mere physical rotation, and yellow, full-grained wheat slumbers under a July sun; gold flies whirl and dance for an hour; songs out of bird throats thrill the fields—wood dove, thrush, lark—and cause the heart to faint or bleed the while we marvel at the seeming insensibility and cruelty out of which these same can and do take their rise.

Opposed to this consoling coat of beauty is the phenomenon of religion, which hourly—aye, from century to century—voices the plaint of man that all is not well here and that only elsewhere can there be satisfaction or compensation, in part at least, for the ills endured here. The fanfare in regard to it all! The temples, towers, prayers, and the profound stupidity that accompanies it! And not only that, but the fear and awe which throughout the ages have induced billions of creatures, compounded of these same universal atoms about which we are talking, to believe almost anything in regard to themselves or the order and rulership of the universe, and to subscribe humbly or stubbornly to anything which any charlatan or misinformed or misinterpreting philosopher or ascetic or dreamer might evolve out of his own fears or ignorance, and then choose to set forth as the truth, telling how this mysterious thing we call Life is arranged or come by. And yet, why should not at least some of these indestructible atoms or electrons in combination, and of which we are composed, know something of the order or meaning of the structures they erect, and so, via emotions communicated to the brain, say, suggest something of the meaning of life to us? Why not? And yet atoms or no atoms—silence, no less; no least intimation of their own significance or what they know—if anything—from them.

As for myself, I continue to be astounded by this fact: that here in all of these creatures who are so ignorantly worshipful, or those who like myself are not, are all of these same atoms or electrons and protons, and with them—if I can believe some biologists—their derivatives, the molecule and protoplasmic cell, and all erecting, either intelligently or unintelligently, this thing called Man, or in a broader sense, all flora and fauna. And these underlying units a part (albeit a compound or construction of device) of this same sentient or mechanistic but universal energy which is everywhere—and which, if sentient, should know better, or be more kind, say, than to erect ignorant, pathetic, and groveling creatures who really know nothing of anything. And then afterward leave them here to develop all sorts of erratic nonsense in regard to what they are and where they came from; and, those failing, as they do and have, then to turn to all sorts of amazing and yet decidedly pathetic laboratories wherein this compound man proceeds to search or peek and perk, in order to learn, if possible, some minute nothing concerning his *howness* and almost next to nothing as to his *whyness*.

VII

What a condemnation, this, of that seeming sentience below or above Man, this creative if blind energy that so condemns Man to this—this complete ignorance which he may not escape!

The almost devilish indifference to the fate or state of creatures so erected, if not by its knowledge and will, at least out of its indestructible energy!

* * * * * *

And if we are not so created, but are the result of chance, then what a condemnation of religion in general as an expression of a terrorized state on the part of energy that does not know what it is yet finds itself erected into creatures that without the slightest knowledge of their past, future, or fate in any form, must still struggle (and how bitterly at times) for the continuance of that which they find ill, perhaps, but hesitate to flee from for fear of encountering something worse—or nothingness! And yet, for this point of view, religion proves itself not wholly an evil nor yet an unmixed good, but only an illusion of the rankest character, yet which for the many at least has served as a nervous or emotional escape from a condition much too severe to be endured. In that sense, of course, the illusion has proved to be a medicament of value, however meaningless without the deadly and sensorially unendurable reality out of which it grew. On the other hand, what is to be said of a reality (these same underlying atoms, electrons, protons, cells, etc., either intelligent or unintelligent, and so mechanistic) that must fall back on illusion in order to endure themselves, or the things into which they have made themselves—men, animals, vegetables? Exactly what? Could universal ignorance do worse? Or evil less?

VIII

But now as to our so-called intelligence here on earth. Man, differentiated, as he assumed, from all other lower or lesser flora and fauna, asserts (the majority of *homo sapiens,* at least) a higher and selective intelligence which in its uppermost reaches is not to be differentiated from free will. He knows good from evil and is free to choose between them! The mechanist, of course, denies this. And to me also this has ever seemed the most unfounded and unintelligent of all assertions. For, as I personally have observed life, man responds quite mechanically, and only so, to all such stimuli as he is prepared, or rather constructed, to receive—and no more and no less. And by the same token, the range of his intelligence is limited by his five meager senses and the appetites or chemical calls they are compelled to register and later serve, or he suffers and eventually ceases as an organism. Not only that, but this constitutes the sum and substance of his free will and intelligence—responding to these various stimuli which are neither more nor less than the call bells of chemical, or perhaps better yet, electrophysical states which require certain other electrophysical or chemical atoms to keep them in the forms in which they chance to be.

And as one descends lower and lower the electrochemical or physical stair that leads to the cell and the atom, this same obvious and apparently unchanged sensitivity to stimuli—but nothing more—continues and gives the same seeming appearance of either intelligence or mechanical law, as you will, but that which in ordinary human response or exchange we think of as intelligence. Call any number of chemical or physical or biological masters together and ask. Their unanimous report will be that the sensory responses and reactions which masquerade as intelligence or free will in man never cease in protoplasmic matter of however low a state. Only, as they say, they may, and in most instances do, become less and less complicated, the necessary reactions to stimuli fewer and fewer. But complexity for complexity, the quality or degree of intelligence, or intricate mechanical response, as you will, which they insist is no more than the mechanics of physics and chemistry, remains the same.

As for myself, I really view myself as an atom in a greater machine, just as is the cell in the greater body of which it finds itself a part. But as for myself being a free and independent mechanism with a separate "spirit" of its own?—Nonsense! Science knows nothing of a soul or spirit. And I personally have never been able to find any trace of one, in me or any other. When I am dead, as I see it, I shall be dissolved into my lesser constitutents; I shall then be, if anything, a part of universal force, but merged and gone forever. More, I cannot even think of a desirable continuance for myself as I am here, and therefore ask for none.

Enough that my meager electrochemical and physical content as it shows here must remain an indestructible trace maybe of the all in all—to be a part (however minute—scarcely a trace, say—but possibly that) of all light, heat, energy, planets, suns, flowers, rats, kings. To what extent I shall function, if at all, it will be with all that is; and with the poet (Thomas Hood, I believe) can truly say: "If my barque sink, 'tis to another sea."*

*The lines are not by Hood but are rather from William Ellery Channing's lyric "A Poet's Hope."

Part 4: 1926–1945

IX

The only additional point I would like to make or perhaps re-emphasize—for I have probably made it before—is that in spite of all this mechanistic response which disposes of the soul or entity, and in spite of obvious cruelty, brutality, envy, hatred, murder, deceit, and what not else, I still rise to testify to the aesthetic perfection of this thing that I see here and which we call Life. For look you! Here is this great, this enormous force, which as we plainly see, can and does evolve suns, planets, immensities of all kinds and descriptions, to say nothing of such animalcula as rats, bedbugs, flies, and lice. Still, at the same time it can and does achieve an aesthetic whole—beauty no less—and via the same elements that are in lice and bedbugs as well as in the most distant suns or sidereal systems—in fire and flowers, in Shelley and Christ. You and I may argue that rats and flies and bedbugs are not aesthetic and join no aesthetic whole, but examine more closely with lens and concentrated interest of the mind and its response to organization and effort, and then judge.

* * * * * *

The New Humanism

Dreiser's contribution to a symposium on The New Humanism. Dreiser had been singled out for attack by a number of writers in the 1930 New Humanist manifesto Humanism and America, *edited by Norman Foerster. Irving Babbitt, professor of French at Harvard, and Paul Elmer More, professor of English at Princeton, were two of the leading proponents of the movement.*

Traditionalism as opposed to newness, strangeness and its expression. Or decorum (the voices of the timid and retiring who fear or resent what is new, strange, unusual) as opposed to the voices or actions or works of those who seek to express newness, strangeness, unusualness. "Ladies and gentlemen" as opposed to "men and women." Dr. Irving Babbitt, say, as opposed to George Bernard Shaw or Henry L. Mencken. Religion as opposed to science. Peace and quiet as opposed to energy and effort. The shades of Oxford and Cambridge—or Harvard and Princeton—as opposed to the steel mills of Gary; the front line trenches in the late war or the ignorant marching millions of all lands and our great modern cities. Such is Humanism versus naturalism—its arch enemy.

But decorum or super mental refinement as an article of faith! Or as the proper base or character of all literature and art! What then is to become of Voltaire, or Rousseau, or Shakespeare, or Marlowe, or Villon, or Rabelais, or "The Decameron," or Defoe, or Swift, or Fielding—or, to come down to our own times, Strindberg, Gorki, Whitman, Stendhal, Dostoevski, de Maupassant, Balzac—even our own Mark Twain at his best? All booted into the limbo of the undesired and ignored. And replaced by exactly whom? Dickens, Thackeray, George Eliot, William Dean Howells, Proust, Prof. Irving Babbitt? It may be. Who is to say what is to come next in life?

But in the meanwhile, the same old unchanged and unchanging life roaring about us—Chicago unable to pay its workers because of graft; a dozen powers in London unable to agree on a

Thinker 2 (July 1930): 8–12.

modified way of killing each other;* Communism blazing into the eyes of Capitalism; corrupt judges and magistrates in New York sentencing less dangerous criminals than themselves to jail; the Catholic Church warring on Science.

A score of lands and a half dozen continents, honeycombed as ever with vice, graft, folderol, vanity and lunacies of all kinds and descriptions and a little band of college study philosophers and essayists who would have us carving and polishing amethyst adjectives wherewith to express decorous and not too coarse thoughts. Oh, strike me pink! A slight tap on the wrist is now in order for a world that has been most wretchedly misbehaving itself since ever it began.

What I suspect is that this is a very mild little tempest in a very small, if decidedly graceful and ornate, teapot. The ladies and gentlemen of letters who are pumping up this little crusade do not know any too much of Life—and for the very good reason, I fear, that they have no strength for it. A tea and toast crowd at best. As Mr. Hazlitt so amusingly suggested in *The Nation*—a group of *Caspar Milquetoasts*.† And troubled, in so far as America is concerned, by some twenty or thirty years of rebellion, which at last has begun to get somewhere.

There was, let us say, Norris with his "McTeague," or "Vandover and the Brute"; David Graham Phillips with "Susan Lennox"; Sherwood Anderson with "Winesburg, Ohio"; Masters with his "Spoon River Anthology"; Dos Passos with "Manhattan Transfer"; Sinclair Lewis with "Main Street" and "Babbitt"; and, in addition, such other honest transcripts as "Undertow," "Spring Flight," "Sweepings," "Diversey," "Miss Lulu Bett," "Poor House Sweeney," "One Man," "Oil," "Black April," "Weeds"— in short, a long company.‡ But all—quite-all—lacking in that *decorum* which is "supreme for the Humanist." (The words are Prof. Irving Babbitt's.) Also lacking in that "will to refrain." The words are again his.

*The London Naval Conference had been convened in the spring of 1930 to seek a naval armament limitation treaty.

†Henry Hazlitt, "All Too Humanism," *Nation* 130 (February 12, 1930): 181–82.

‡*Undertow* (1923), by Henry K. Marks; *Spring Flight* (1925), by Lee J. Smits; *Sweepings* (1928), by Lester Cohen; *Diversey* (1928), by MacKinlay Kantor; *Miss Lulu Bett* (1920), by Zona Gale; *Poorhouse Sweeney* (1927), by Ed Sweeney; *One Man* (1915), by Robert Steele; *Oil* (1927), by Upton Sinclair; *Black April* (1927), by Julia Peterkin; *Weeds* (1923), by E. S. Kelley.

In short, they are none of them so highly polished or selective or refrainful as the Humanists would have them—for the most part, raw and crude—having, in part at least, fairly close resemblance to a large part of life.

That they are not, unfortunately, exact equivalents of Villon, Marlowe, Rabelais, Shakespeare, Swift, Strindberg, Gorki, Stendhal, Whitman, Dostoevski, is to be regretted, as well as admitted. But then, that is a matter of birth and genius. But assuming that they were, they would still be anathema to all Humanists now talking or writing—and worse, doubly and trebly damned—since quite all lack that essential "decorum" so "supreme" for the Humanists.

(Oh, Rabelais, Swift, Marlowe, Villon!)

But at that, though, this craze or palaver anent Humanism is not new. And, at worst, it conforms to that law of change which appears to be imbedded in the heterogeneous nature of matter and energy through space. For if I read my astronomy as well as my chemistry and physics aright, there exists no unimpeded progress for anything in this very restless and stifling universe. Chickens must become eggs; eggs, omelettes; live cattle, beef; trees, lumber and lumber houses.

Nothing can go in an unimpeded direction anywhere. Ennui sets in, or enmity. And so Naturalism gives place, for a time at least, to Humanism (maybe, I wish it no bad luck), just as in the past Classicism gave place to Romanticism, Romanticism to Rationalism, Rationalism to Realism and Realism to Naturalism or rough stuff, as *Caspar Milquetoast* sees it. But here comes refinement again—a call for restraint or refraining from too much reality.

But has *Naturalism,* which is what the Humanist shadow-dancers are at the moment so exercised over, flourished without opposition? Only read its history anywhere. And will it not be modified, for the time being anyhow? I fear me much that it will.

All life is change and there are fashions in literature and art which now uplift and glorify one method and now another. Consider only our own dear New England school of blessed memory, with its transcendentalism. And its contemporaneous English cousin—Mid-Victorianism. It is of these, I am sure, that Professor Babbitt and his fellow Humanists are dreaming.

But by what good or bad fortune did he come to be named Babbitt?

At worst, such arguments or intellectual combats as this make for entertainment—a good show. And do no real harm, since anything—whether a diet, a philosophy, a form of government or a theory or practice of letters—if too energetically or persistently pursued in any given direction is likely to become a bore or a tragedy.

Personally, I myself am a little weary of the already stratified and hallmarked Naturalism now holding in America. To shine therein it has already become too necessary to spit, curse, blaspheme and show your predilections after the fashion of a sixteen-year-old rowdy on a country town street corner.

It is too callow and too, too uniformed. This is a universe we are dealing with and not a Chicago or a London slum. And when Naturalism becomes a school of "cross-section" observers whose first rule is to pointlessly and even nonsensically insist on the crudest or baldest terms for every human state or relationship from sex to diet, however functionally well known and admitted, well . . .

But that is not the Naturalism of Rousseau or Stendhal or Fielding or Dostoevski. But only of would-be Naturalists, who by adjectives and not understanding, would outdo the great masters. The method, if method it may be called, has fallen into less adequate hands or thought processes.

But life goes on. And at its worst as well as best, it certainly is as both Humanist and Naturalist see it. For there is the Humanist of the Babbitt variety—and he sees it one way—or as it ought to be if it isn't—whereas the Naturalist sees it as he truly thinks it is. And now one interests a part of the world and now another. But whether one or the other wrote or did not write, life would still go on—and it would contain as it always has all its ancient elements—weakness as opposed to strength, darkness to light, evil to good, ugliness to loveliness, cruelty to tenderness, littleness over against bigness, intelligence as opposed to the lack of it, capacity as opposed to incapacity.

And among its observers will be those who lack the strength to contemplate, let alone share, its darker, more brutal phases, and also those who can not only contemplate, but even share, some of its boisterous energy.

Among the first you may be sure will be the Humanists, Moralists, Religionists—all the too-sensitive and so-retiring souls who prefer dreams to reality; and among the latter will come the Naturalists and Realists—accursed always to the sensitive and the fearsome—but making for that larger understanding which has given the world its great masterpieces—and, unless I fail in understanding, will so continue to give.

Remarks

Dreiser's remarks were his contribution to a dinner held in New York on May 6, 1931, honoring Freud on his 75th birthday. They were read on that occasion by A. A. Brill.

I understand that Dr. Freud has been hailed as the Copernicus of psychology. Also as the equivalent of Darwin in the world of revolutionary thought. To me he seems more like a Napoleon or a Hannibal of the mind, sweeping all before him with the intense penetrative subtlety and strategy of his reason.

I shall never forget my first encounter with his *Three Contributions to the Theory of Sex,* his *Totem and Tabu,* and his *Interpretation of Dreams.** At that time and even now quite every paragraph came as a revelation to me—a strong, revealing light thrown on some of the darkest problems that haunted and troubled me and my work. And reading him has helped me in my studies of life and men. I said at that time and I repeat now that he reminded me of a conqueror who has taken a city, entered its age-old hoary prisons and there generously proceeding to release from their gloomy and rusted cells the prisoners of formulae, faiths and illusions which have racked and worn man for hundreds and thousands of years. And I still think so.

The light that he has thrown on the human mind! Its vagaries and destructive delusions and their cure! It is to me at once colossal and beautiful.

But there are so many here who can interpret so much more intimately and brilliantly his amazing contributions to human thought and the mysteries of the human mind (my friend Dr. Brill here, for one),† that I prefer to sit and listen. But it is a privilege

Psychoanalytic Review 18 (July 1931): 250.

*In Dreiser's sketch of Edith De Long Smith as "Olive Brand" in *A Gallery of Women* (New York, 1929), 1: 82, he recalled that Mrs. Smith had introduced him to Freud's *Three Contributions* during his early years in Greenwich Village—that is, approximately 1914–15.

†Brill was Freud's foremost American disciple and translator. He and Dreiser met in early 1919 and became friends.

and an honor for me along with so many others to be called upon to express my debt to his invaluable work. Also to wish him health and strength and length of days. Immense wisdom he has.

Introduction to
Harlan Miners Speak

Like many labor disputes of the 1930s, the coal strike at Harlan County, Kentucky, in 1931 was a struggle not only between workers attempting to organize and employers seeking to prevent unionization but also between a Communist-dominated union and a more conservative craft union—in this instance, the left wing National Miners Union and the United Mine Workers of the American Federation of Labor. Dreiser's role in the dispute arose out of his position as chairman of the National Committee for the Defense of Political Prisoners, an organization of writers, artists, and professional men founded in the fall of 1931 to publicize the fate of political and labor figures who were being persecuted for their beliefs and activities. Although ostensibly non-political, the organization was controlled by its largely Communist membership. The Committee decided to send a delegation to Harlan because labor organizers of the National Miners Union had claimed harassment by county officials. In early November 1931 such a group, led by Dreiser [John Dos Passos was another prominent member], visited Harlan and conducted an informal investigation. The bulk of Harlan Miners Speak *consists of testimony taken by members of the Committee during the investigation. I omit from Dreiser's "Introduction" several long passages in which he recounts his difficulties in organizing and conducting the investigation.*

The reason that I personally went to the Harlan coal district in Kentucky was because from about June to November, 1931, the newspapers of America carried more or less continuous reports of outrages upon the rights of not only the striking miners in that region, but apparently those of all sorts of other people inside and outside the State who sought to interfere in their behalf. I recall reading that representatives of different newspapers and press agencies, the United Press, the Federated Press, and individ-

Harlan Miners Speak, ed. Theodore Dreiser et al. (New York: Harcourt, Brace, 1932), pp. 3–16.

ual newspapermen such as Bruce Crawford, of Norton, Virginia, were attacked, and in Crawford's particular case, shot in the leg,* the others threatened and ordered from the State, as though a portion of any State, apart from the State itself, as illustrated by this Harlan County coal district, had authority, let alone the right, to set up a military law of its own and order citizens from other States to observe it, all Constitutional guarantees to the contrary notwithstanding.

I really did not pay so much attention to this particular situation at first, because mining wars of this character in America have been a part of my life's entire experience. As a newspaper man in Chicago, St. Louis, Pittsburgh and other places, I was early drawn into this sort of thing and as early, of course, witnessed the immense injustice which property in America has not only always sought to but has succeeded in inflicting upon labor. Besides, in July of this same summer, I personally was asked by the National Miners Union to come to Pittsburgh and witness for myself the cruelties being inflicted upon the strikers of that region—Eastern Ohio, Northwest West Virginia and Pennsylvania. What I saw there of murder, starvation, extortion and the like practiced upon the coal miners by the coal operators was sufficient to cause me to openly indict the American Federation of Labor, which resulted in nothing more than a glossy and self-exculpatory denial from William Green, the present President of the A. F. of L.

In late October, however, I was presented with a thirty-two page document or indictment compiled apparently by the International Labor Defense from various sources,† but all relating to crimes and abuses inflicted on the striking miners in the Harlan district by, obviously, the coal operators' association of the same area. This document contained from three to five indictments to the page and covered, as usual, everything from unpunished murders (eleven all told) to the dynamiting of soup kitchens, the unwarranted search of strikers' homes, the denial of their right to join any union except the United Mine Workers of America of which they were heartily sick and to which they did not want to belong,

---

*Crawford, a member of the National Committee for the Defense of Political Prisoners, was editor of *Crawford's Weekly,* published in Norton, Virginia.

†Another Communist-dominated organization, the International Labor Defense, published *Labor Defender,* a magazine to which Dreiser contributed during the 1930s.

also the denial of free speech, of the right of representatives from outside newspapers or organizations to come there and see for themselves what was going on.

Because the International Labor Defense confessed itself as in no position to evoke public interest in this wholesale brutality, it wanted to know if I, as Chairman of the National Committee for the Defense of Political Prisoners, would not organize a Committee out of the membership of the general committee of that body and proceed to Kentucky not only to question authority there as to their actions, but to see if by so doing we could not center possible attention and so modify if not dispel some of the ills being suffered by the miners there.

* * * * * *

My personal conclusion, after the various individuals had been examined and the mining districts visited, was that this was a very remarkable struggle of the American worker against the usual combination of power and wealth in America which for so long has held him in subjection. As a matter of fact, there, I found the same line-up of petty officials and business interests on the side of the coal operators and as against the miners, as I have discovered in almost every other labor war or controversy that I have had the opportunity to observe. The small town bankers, grocers, editors and lawyers, the police, the sheriff, if not the government, were all apparently subservient to the money and corporate masters of the area. It was their compulsion, if possibly not always their desire, to stand well with these who had the power to cause them material or personal difficulties and, as against those, the underpaid and even starving workers, who could do nothing for themselves.

Possibly this practice springs from the asinine notion in America that every one has an equal opportunity to become a money master, a Morgan or a Rockefeller, although the data concerning America's economic life today show that no more than three hundred and fifty families control 95 per cent of the wealth of the country. Also, that almost every man, short of the officers and owners of our great and all-controlling corporations today, must wear the collar of one or another of these great combinations, and it is only through their favor and power that there is a chance for him or any one to improve his economic state or his

267

social position. He must wear the collar marked with the name of his owner.

* * * * * *

In conclusion,* however, I should like to add that what I cannot understand is why the American people which has been drilled from the beginning in the necessity and the advantage of the individual and his point of view, does not now realize how complete is the collapse of that idea as a working social formula.

For while, on the one hand, we have arrogated to each of ourselves the right to be a giant individual if we can, we have not seen how impossible it is for more than a very few, if so many, to achieve this. Also that, should it be achieved by so much as one, the rest of us would be mere robots functioning at the will and under the direction of that particular individual. It would follow, then, if we had the mental strength to grasp it, that it is really not complete individualism for anybody that we need or want or can endure even, but a limited form of individualism which will guarantee to all, in so far as possible, the right, if there is such a right, to life, liberty, and the pursuit of happiness, and also an equitable share in the economic results of any such organization as the presence and harmony of numerous individuals presupposes and compels.

As it is now, we have gotten no further than the right of the most cunning and strong individuals among us to aggrandize ourselves, leaving the rest of us here in America, as elsewhere, to subsist on what is left after they are through. And if you will examine our American economic arrangement, you will find that they are not through, since by now, three hundred and fifty families control 95 per cent of the wealth of the country, and these families, their trusts and holding companies, are now not only not distributing that wealth in any equitable ratio, but even if they were so minded, they are not capable of so doing. Taken collectively, they do not constitute any central authority. And except through the functions of government which they seek to and do direct for their own private aggrandizement, they have no means, let alone any intention of so doing. More, the government which is supposed to represent all the individualistic ambitions of all of our people, is in

*The portion of Dreiser's introduction which follows had already appeared, in different form, as "Individualism and the Jungle," in both the *New Masses* 7 (January 1932): 1–2, and *Crawford's Weekly,* January 2, 1932, p. 6.

no position to do that. It, too, in its turn, has become one of the instruments of this central group of individuals which now directs all of its functions to its particular and very special advantage. That leaves the American citizen, one hundred and twenty-five million strong, with his faith in individualism and what it will do for him, mainly without his rent, his job, a decent suit of clothes, a pair of shoes, or food. His faith in this free-for-all individualism has now led him to the place where his fellow individualists of greater strength, cunning and greed, are in a position to say for how much, or rather, for how little, he shall work, for how long, and whether he shall be allowed to make any complaint or even seek redress in case he is unhappy or dissatisfied, ill-treated, deprived, or even actually starved. In fact, his faith in this individualism as a solvent for all his ills, has caused him to slumber, while his fellow individualists of greater greed and cunning have been seizing his wealth, his church, his press, his courts, his judges, his legislators, his police, and quite all of his originally agreed upon Constitutional privileges so that, today, he walks practically in fear of his own shadow. He cannot now any longer openly say that he is dissatisfied with his government, or that he thinks it is wrong; nor that he thinks individualism is wrong, if actually, he as yet now thinks it is wrong; nor can he any longer organize in unions which are not suborned and so controlled by the very individuals from whose economic pressure he is seeking to escape. He cannot turn to his church, because his church will not listen to his economic ills here on earth; it calls his attention to a Paradise which is to come hereafter. The present earthly Paradise, in its economic form, at least, the church blandly concedes to the very individualists of whom he now complains. Nor can he turn to his press which, by reason of economic advantages, which only those great individualists whom he has so much admired have in their keeping and can bestow, turns not to him but to these his masters. And for that reason he may not be heard. Personally, as poor as he is now, he cannot bring to the door of the press that cash return which they now demand in order to do justice to those millions whose minute and underpaid labors still constitute the source of the wealth of the treasuries which his giant overlords, once lesser individuals like himself, now control.

In sum, by his worship of his own private rights to individual advancement, as opposed to the rights and welfare of every other, he sees himself, if he is really poor and as he really is, an Ishmael in the land as well as the prosperity of the land which he creates. Actually, as a worker, he is laughed at and, in times of unrest and contest, spit upon as a malcontent, a weakling, a radical, an undesirable citizen, one who had not the understanding and hence not the right to complain of the ills by which he finds himself beset. Herded, in so far as the majority of him is concerned, in work-warrens called towns, watched over as the slaves of the South were watched over in the days before the Civil War, by the spies and agents of the immense coöperative associations of wealth, in the factories and mines and mills for which he now works, warred upon by the veritable armies of mercenaries employed by these giants whom he still so much admires, in order to overawe him and subdue him; he finds himself discharged, starved, and then blacklisted and shot down when he strikes; he finds himself, as I have said before, frustrated, ignored, and denied by his church, his press, his paid officials and his supine and traitor government.

Americans today should make an intensive study of individualism as such. They will find its best exemplar in the jungle, where every individual is for itself, prowls to sustain itself, and deals death to the weakest at every turn.

The cries of the jungle today are no more and no worse than the cries of the miners in Harlan, or of the cotton mill workers of Gastonia, or the textile workers of Lawrence, or the agricultural workers of Imperial Valley, or of the masses in general. They, like the zebra in the jaws of the lion, are the economic victims of these giant corporations, *still posing as individuals,* although armed to the teeth with purchased laws, hired officials, and over-awed or controlled courts. These latter are their teeth and their claws, and with these they strike, and their dead are everywhere, defeated and starved.

Again I say, Americans should mentally follow individualism to its ultimate conclusion, for society is not and cannot be a jungle. It should be and is, if it is a social organism worthy of the name, an escape from this drastic individualism which, for some, means all, and for the many, little or nothing. And consciously or unconsciously, it is by Nature and evolution intended as such, for certainly the thousands-of-years-old growth of organized society augurs desire on the part of Nature to avoid the extreme and bloody individualism of the jungle. In proof of which, I submit that organized society throughout history has indulged in more and more rules and laws, each intended to limit, yet not frustrate, the individual in his relations to his fellows.

In fact, the dream of organized society, conscious or unconscious, has been to make it not only possible but necessary for the

270

individual to live with his fellow in reasonable equity, in order that he may enjoy equity himself.

If that is not so, why then organized society at all? If that is not so, then why the hope and the dream, in every heart, of a State in which the individual may not be too much put upon? And why in the absence of that (this desired State) *Revolution*—the final human expression of its hatred of injustice, cruelty, slavery, usury? Why our present social structure, with its courts, its legislative bodies, executives, its so-called representatives of each and every one?

If these do not indicate or spell a dream of true democracy, of helpful companionship in this all-too-disappointing struggle for existence, what does? And if that is true, then why should not this giant and rapacious individualism here in America, now operating for the whim and the comfort of a few, and the debasement and defilement of the many, be curbed or, as I would have it, set aside entirely?

New York, N.Y.
December 23, 1931

[O. S. Marden and *Success* Magazine]

The physical state of the typescript of this essay does not contribute to a specific dating of its composition. However, Dreiser's mention of Marden's death and his failure to mention Marden's unacknowledged use of many of Dreiser's interviews in various collections edited by Marden establish 1924 as the earliest and 1938 as the latest date of composition. Marden died in 1924, and John Huth revealed to Dreiser in 1938 that Marden had used his material. The article can probably be placed more narrowly in the period between 1932 and 1935, when Dreiser was publishing in the American Spectator *and* Esquire *a series of reminiscent sketches about his early career.*

Dreiser's first contribution to Success *appeared in January 1898, soon after he became a free-lance writer. From that date until the close of 1900, he published 27 articles and poems in the magazine, including interviews with Andrew Carnegie, William Dean Howells, Thomas Edison, Philip Armour, and Marshall Field. Dreiser's account of Marden's career differs in a number of details from that by Frank L. Mott in his* A History of American Magazines *(Cambridge, Mass., 1968), 5: 286–92. In particular, Mott notes that Klopsch did finance* Success *for some time, and that the magazine did not succeed financially until approximately 1902. Dreiser also drastically foreshortened the close of Marden's career.* Success *failed in 1911, but Marden made a "comeback" in 1917, editing a journal with a similar name, and he did not die until 1924.*

Whenever I think of success stories—the writers of books like *It's Yours, You Can, How to Succeed in Life,* etc., I think of the first and most arresting champion of this program that I ever met. His name was Orison Swett Marden, and he was the Dale Carnegie of his day. He came from the environs of Boston, and seemed a dreamy, semi-professional type of person. He had once been a travelling salesman, and had (this was always

Unpublished manuscript, 1932–35. Copyright the Trustees of the University of Pennsylvania.

272

[*O.S. Marden and* Success *Magazine*]

significant to me) placed a certain kind of remedy on the market for a patent medicine company—somebody's swamproot, or elixir. He used to be called *doctor* Marden; I think the *doctor* was a hangover from his patent medicine days, although, for all I know, it might have meant some kind of degree.

Anyway, Marden in the course of his slow and interesting development—by the time I met him he was all of 50—had encountered the works of Samuel Smiles, who, back in the 1850s, had written a book called *Self Help* and one or two others of the same type, and he forthwith became the advance agent of that great idea. In short, he proceeded to write more books like that, *Success, Why Fail* and such allied noble volumes of practical if not wholly disinterested encouragement.

Myself having read *Self Help* at a time when I was trying to find out how one got started in the world, and having been somewhat encouraged by it, I was duly impressed with the value of such volumes to[,] chiefly, the untrained, the necessitous and the enquiring. *Self Help* consisted of a long series of struggles of different individuals to place themselves in life, with detailed analysis of what perseverance and energy and honesty and loyalty etc. had done for them[,] and the same impressed me, whether I had these virtues or not. At the same time it was really of value to me in the sense that it cheered me up, it bolstered my faltering courage, and, to a degree, disposed of a large quantity of doubts that were very bad for the individual starting out in life to consider too seriously.

Mr. Smiles and most of the others who have written on the subject of self help failed in, or perhaps avoided, emphasizing the basic need for ability and ingenuity, as well as real opportunity somewhere. But after all, it is so much more important to a struggling beginner to make him feel that opportunity is ready and waiting for the taking, and that whatever abilities one has are sufficient. Armed with such a delusion, one is so much better fitted to take difficulties; and it is absolutely true enough that if a book like this could evoke enough such courage, you would very likely arrive in the lap of opportunity, and to your wonder, find yourself through the door of success. Whether your ability would permit you to stay there is another question—but since the great thing is to get there—why there you are!

Anyhow, in my starting out days, when, every morning I had to speculate as to which way I would get four or five more dollars and when I had made the amazing discovery that I could write a rather hack type of magazine article, I ran into Orison Swett Marden, in, of all places, the editorial offices of the *Christian Herald,* the most successful all-round Christian paper of its day. Strangely enough, although it was edited by two thrifty Scotch Christians who knew how to turn a Christian penny as well as the next one, it was owned and published by a very resourceful and clever Jew, who had fixed upon it when it was a total loss as a Christian document, and had turned it into a huge success. So much so that he himself was a millionaire and had a very large country place, and was rich and shrewd enough to employ the most popular interdenominational preacher of his day to write sermons for the paper.* These sermons, as I understood it, were written almost years in advance, and were so a perfect mine of material as to be suitable for use by the paper while the author travelled in India, China, Palestine, Egypt, which countries he had in the sermons left behind described and enthused and wept over long before he visited them.

However, be that as it may, here one morning in the office of the *Herald* where, for the sum of ten dollars, I was trying to sell some data I had gathered about Charles A. Dana of the New York *Sun,* my good Christian friends, the editors, finding Dr. Marden in the office, took the trouble to say to him that as long as he, Dr. Marden, was considering starting a magazine, that I was a likely young lad who might do something for him, and not too expensively, either, which last was what caused Marden to shake my hand. He wanted to know all about me, and fortunately for me, I had the two editors, for whom I had been manufacturing what might be called inexpensive chicken-feed, as my sponsors.

And so it came about that Dr. Marden began to tell me about what he really planned to do. He was going to start a magazine which was going to be called *Success.* And, of course, he was to be its editor. What led him to do this was the fact that by then he had already written those three or four or five books previously mentioned which had proved so successful that he had spare capital to undertake this magazine. One of the books he had written had been called *Success* and was his largest seller. But the others—*Opportunity* and *This Way to Fortune*—had done well.† The reason why he

*The *Christian Herald* was edited by B. J. Fernis and G. H. Sandison; its proprietor was Louis Klopsch. The Reverend T. De Witt Talmadge, one of the most popular clergymen of the day, contributed a weekly sermon.

†Although Marden published a book called *Success* in 1897, he did not issue any volumes entitled *Opportunity* and *This Way to Fortune.* Dreiser appears to have derived these titles from such works by Marden as *Rising in the World* (1894), *Pushing to the Front* (1894), and *How to Succeed* (1896).

was in the office of the *Christian Herald* was that he had been
talking the matter over with the publisher who at one time had
been inclined to join with him as a partner, but there and then—this
very morning, he had decided to go it alone, since the publisher
had insisted on a financial control.

He wanted to know, since I was so well recommended,
whether I had any ideas that would fit in with this scheme and what
I would want for them. Actually although I had read *Self Help,* and
was in need of really everything—shoes, hat, food, shirt—I was
without a single self-help idea. As luck would have it[,] however,
Dr. Marden was so full of self-help ideas that he could not help
telling me just the kind of articles he would want. They must be
about people who had made good—people who, like the people in
the work of Mr. Smiles, had gone out and captured what they went
after—had shown pluck, were insistent, and stuck to what they
were doing—literally, had torn success out of the stingy hands of
opportunity, and lived to please the world with their subsequent
gifts to man. He even went so far as to name certain people who
were excellent American examples of his idea—Rockefeller, Carnegie, Edison, Marshall Field, Armour—well make up your own
list. And he said that unlike Mr. Smiles and himself in his writings,
he didn't want rehashed hearsay about these noble go-getters.
What I was to do for his magazine was to go personally to each of
these and wheedle or extort from them the truth about their early
struggles—as he phrased it. What he wanted was the glorious
drama of poverty, the man who in the stable or barn of poverty and
despair could still look about and feel and say, that opportunity
was everywhere, and the great thing was to begin where you were,
like, one might say, Christ in the Stall.

To make a long story short, if I was the man for the opportunity, he would pay me one hundred dollars cash on receipt of a MS.
which was to be anywhere from three to five thousand words long,
as I chose. All I had to do was to go to the people, and get their
"true confessions," the story of how they leaped over the wall
from nothing to something. Actually, in all my literary career no
such glittering opportunity had ever come to me. It raised my
blood temperature enormously. I began to count the people who
were successful in the U. S. on my fingers, and found to my astonishment that without moving a foot I could count twelve which I
could sell him at once. They included some that he had named, and
some that I had—W. D. Howells, Mark Twain, John Burroughs,
and I even suggested Walt Whitman—who, however, he an-

nounced, would hardly do, since poets could hardly be looked upon as representing the kind of success he was after. So Walt was left out.*

Now it is to no purpose insofar as this story is concerned as to how I did these things—well or poorly. I can assure you though that with the $100.00 posted over each subject of success, I managed to do them to his satisfaction. I actually broke in on such remarkable individuals as Marshall Field, Carnegie, Mr. Armour and others and insisted that they inspire young Americans with the wonder of their early struggles. Much to [my] astonishment, I was received not only with kindness, but courtesy and even confidence by each and every one of them. What is more, I made the discovery from Mark Twain to Mr. Field to Mr. Duke of the American Tobacco Co., that great men seemed to like to talk about how and why of their greatness and their achievements, seemed actually to feel that they knew exactly what had brought it about. As a matter of fact, in some instances, they seemed willing to do themselves more than justice.

What is more to the point, is that in doing these articles from month to month covering a period of several years, I came into not only regular contact but the confidence of Dr. Marden. In spite of the fact that he was determined not to raise the price of the articles above $100 he was perfectly willing to tell me that he liked them— at that price. Furthermore, he talked over with me from time to time what he had in mind for the magazine and even asked my advice, which I gave freely enough, because by this time I had all the work I wanted to do anyhow. And it was in the course of these conversations that I managed to take the mental or character measure of the man. A little to my personal astonishment I was deciding that while he was charming and earnest and sincere, that he was partly a dreamer and partly an unconscious charlatan and hence not a little fatuous. Although, as he told me, he had been out and around as a boy, sweeping out stores, tending counters, running errands and finding that people were strong and weak, shrewd and stupid, etc. still he was absolutely convinced that whatever their defects might be mentally, that if they willed so to do, they could overcome with absolute surety, whatever handicap it might be that was staying them—in short, that they could wrest success from failure.

*Whitman, of course, had died in 1892.

[*O.S. Marden and* Success *Magazine*]

It never occurred to me at the time that nearly everybody was nothing more than a minor point in a huge organism, and that the part in it in which one found oneself might offer very serious objections to the achievement of a great financial or mental success. One of the things that brought this matter to the surface was an interview with Thomas Edison, who told me that insofar as electricity and his lamp was concerned, that he had had a gift from birth for the particular work which he followed, that nothing else interested him. Also, P. D. Armour explained to me that luckily enough for him his arrival in Chicago had synchronized with the growth of the cattle market which offered one of the greatest doors to trade and success ever encountered. The outbreak of the Civil War had furnished an enormous demand for pork and beef which he was shrewd enough to see meant a fortune if seized at its full tide, which was when he seized it. Carnegie told me that the growth of the iron and steel business had been impressed upon him while working for $.50 a day in Pittsburgh. Personally he was of the belief that anyone could have done as he did—but of course, there were thousands of boys in Pittsburgh and hundreds of thousands in America and strangely enough they never became world-controlling ironmasters. And in writing the article about him, I had made this observation to myself although I did not dare put it in the script. It would have detracted from the *You Can* idea. But what I am trying to impress is that Marden, in all sincerity, believed that any boy, working like Carnegie, perhaps reading *Success,* or my article, could, from that point, if he would, leap into the arena of life and succeed. May God bless us and save us. His insistence on this point is what made me not a little skeptical of the soundness of the idea, although I had no least doubt about the soundness of the idea that such a magazine as his would succeed, which it did.

Well, as I say, this relationship or what is better, a friendship, continued over a period of years quite long after I had ceased to do anything for *Success* and had become an editor myself. I saw the magazine grow from what was a small room at the American Book Co. building at 4th St. and Washington Sq., to a half-floor, and then to a whole one, and then three floors, filled up with all sorts of offices and rooms, laboring editors, circulation and subscription managers, and in a very palatial chamber giving onto a charming view of the park and with a built-in fireplace and mahogany library, was Dr. Marden himself with his laterally achieved mien of a serious and even a great editor. *Success.* Even a shoeblack came daily to shine his shoes while he read more documents on his beloved subject.

277

Part 4: 1926–1945

When I first knew him I had discovered that he lived in one of the poorer hotels in a poor district. But at the top of his career he was riding in an automobile and living in an expensive hotel. Also at that time he seemed to have proved his theory—that success came to him who was determined to obtain it.

However, after seven or eight years of this, or more, during which we occasionally had lunch together as fellow editors, and talked of the good old days when we first started, he announced that he had conceived an idea which was to result in the crowning work of his life. It was true that the magazine was a success, and he had thought of starting some other kind of a magazine which might contain fiction or general articles, but in view of the importance of the need of this Success thought which he had proved for himself, and which he was satisfied had helped thousands, he had decided to enlarge upon it in a way which had never been done before. He intended to get and publish what would be called the *Encyclopedia of Success!*

During the years that *Success* had been published, there had accumulated, he said, a large number of articles which showed how success could be achieved in every field, and not only that, but how it was related to a very large variety of temperaments—statesmen, explorers, salesmen, preachers, executives and so on. And better, here was this wonderful material, not only in the magazine, and in his own books, and in the works of Samuel Smiles, but in the pages of literally thousands of newspapers, magazines and books and more than that, in the pages of history—since the very dawn of life. How wonderful it would be, he expatiated, as we sat in the Brevoort of that day, if, like the compilers of the *Encyclopedia Britannica,* a group in the success field, with him as director and editor in chief, should now search these sources, the histories and books of all times, and produce this record of man's victory over circumstances—proving no less that whatever or wherever you started—*You Can,* and what is more, *you must.* It was all to be in eight or ten volumes. It was to contain cross references so that anybody who was in doubt about any phase of the truth that You Can could proceed to trace it to its utmost historical lair. In other words, determined youth in all lands and times had succeeded where they had tried to. Perhaps even protoplasm could!

At first, I thought, in my commercial innocence, that this was a fine idea—must be—because, as he said, all libraries would have to have it, all institutions of learning, and, much more than the *Britannica,* it should be in every public school. And then there would be the individuals who, seeking success, would like to have such an historical series of volumes ready to hand—particularly in moments of desperation and doubt. One thing that did come to me, having by then become the chief of some 32 editors and 64 assistants myself, and having a most quarrelsome and watchful business management behind me, engaged in the business of counting the cost of everything I did,* it occurred to me that the *Encyclopedia* was likely to be an expensive undertaking; and so I said. But to that he replied that he had already taken the expense under consideration; he had written to librarians, educators, and distinguished individuals in the realm of success, and had asked them their opinion. Without exception, insofar as he could see, all had agreed that the *Encyclopedia* would be not only a valuable, but a necessary work. So that all that remained now was to get a staff of editors and researchers and begin the collecting and editing of all this data which was to make up the volumes from A to Zacharia.

And as he thought and planned at the time, so it was done, or nearly so, for with my own eyes, I was permitted to see the very large departments in his building which were soon devoted to this work, a great deal of which was done under his direction. Researchers were sent to all possible sources to gather their material and then write it up. After this, it was edited and cut to what was considered the necessary length of a work limited to eight volumes. And in addition, there was the designing, printing and advance advertising, or what might be called the propaganda department which was to spread the word of the coming of this great work. All this required salesmen, bonuses, commissions, rewards for special successes, to say nothing of the other costs, and I saw for myself that a great deal of money was necessary. And although Marden as I found in time had been more or less prepared for that—still it seemed even to him that gathering the material appeared to take an inordinate amount of time. Furthermore, as he latterly informed me, there had arisen the question in the minds of some of his editors as to the sameness of quite a little of his material. Some seemed to think that once in volume form—in eight volumes—it might prove too much of a good thing. At one time, he even asked me whether I thought that might be true. And for my answer, I might be said to share a part of the blame for what followed. For while I said, if there was any basic danger in the thing it was that—

*Dreiser is referring to the period between 1907 and 1910 when he was editor of Butterick's *Delineator*.

279

it might be too much, still, I added that while there might be this sameness in so much of the material, it was also true that *Success* was a very widely distributed publication with a large following and many believers in the idea, and since no such work as the *Encyclopedia* had ever been contemplated, let alone put into form, that, good, bad or indifferent, the novelty of the idea should bring about a sufficient distribution or demand as to carry it to a successful point, where, if one were wise, it could be dropped. Alas to relate, he agreed with me. Anyhow having gone so far, he was in no position to do anything else.

I heard nothing more from him for some time because I resigned from the publication with which I was connected, and retired to write some novels and paid no attention to the magazine world. I didn't stay in New York at all.

But one day, I ran into a man who several years before had been one of *Success*'s editors, but had moved to another publication. And at once he asked me if I had heard what had happened to *Success*. No, I said, I hadn't. Well, he went on, all along he had told Marden that he didn't think this *Encyclopedia* was any good—didn't think it could be since it was too full of the same thing. But Marden in spite of this, as he said, was determined to do it. And accordingly it got so that all the money that came in, not only from the magazine, but all Marden had saved and could borrow, was used to keep the thing going. And so about seven or eight months before it was ready, the printers had gone into court and foreclosed on the *Encyclopedia of Success* as well as *Success* magazine and had thrown Marden into bankruptcy. He went, said the man, around to all sorts of people, but they couldn't see the *Encyclopedia* for anything. They wouldn't touch it. Hence the creditors sold the magazine, *Success*, for a song to somebody, and Marden had retired ruined, and with a nervous breakdown. But this man so soon after didn't know where he was.

I finally ran into a woman, a contributor to a magazine I had edited who had done some work for *Success* too, and we fell to talking about what a tragic thing this was. She said that it was, actually, as bad as it could be, that Marden after a time had begun to see that he had made a great mistake, that all the people whom he thought would subscribe in advance for the *Encyclopedia* had failed to do so, and that that had shut off prospective income. Also that he had gone to live with relatives or something back in Massachusetts where he had come from. She thought he would come back later. But he was very sick, and without money of any kind except what he could borrow.

[*O.S. Marden and* Success *Magazine*]

Finally I found his address, and curiously enough, I got it from a "new thought" healer whom I had consulted in connection with some problem of my own.* She told me that she had known him and preceding his nervous breakdown he had taken a number of treatments from her, but that in the course of these he had disappeared. She gave me his address, in some small house on Varick St. For some time I debated whether it was really wise for me to go there and talk with him because I felt that I had given him the wrong steer, and besides I imagined how he felt after this terrible blow to his enormous faith in this idea of success.

But finally, I did call on him. He had a room in a very bare little house run by a widow, and he was the only roomer. When I saw him he was in a very serious nervous condition. He had aged about 20 years, was thin, pale, shrunken. I told him that I felt sure that if he pulled himself together and held out that he would be able to establish himself again and that he could revive the magazine. His attitude was one of complete futility, loss of faith in himself and his ability to do anything. He complained rather weakly. He didn't see how he had managed to make such a mistake. He was convinced that it was a wonderful idea, but he didn't see why he couldn't have foreseen that it wouldn't work out. Anyhow, now he was old, coming back was hard, and would take too long.

Well, I gave him the usual consolation, and helplessly enough, according to his own formula, and left. The next thing I heard, maybe six months or a year later, was that he had died and that his body had been sent back to Massachusetts. Sad as it was I could not help being moved by the irony of this result, that such an apostle should be thus deceived in his dream. But so it was. He was as I could not help seeing the St. John of *Success* and yet!—. Laughter or tears? But anyhow, there it is. And I cannot say more (alas). Go thou and do likewise!

Success was sold in mid-1911 and ceased publication in December 1911. Dreiser consulted a Christian Science ("New Thought") healer during 1911, after his resignation from the *Delineator*. See *The "Genius"* (New York, 1915), pp. 702–8.

Appearance and Reality

Randolph Bourne was graduated from Columbia University in 1913 and died in 1918. His reviews and estimates of Dreiser's work remain of permanent importance. In 1935 Dreiser collected the poem which appears in this article under the title "The Process" in Moods: Philosophical and Emotional (Cadenced and Declaimed).

That which was crooked
Straightened.
That which was defeated
Joined
With that which was
Victorious.
And that which was beautiful
Blended
With that which was ill-planned.
To be separated
And made crooked
Or straight
Again.

Somewhere back in 1913 or 1914, there appeared a critic whose work interested me greatly. It was humanly sensitive as well as aesthetic. The view was large, and the underlying natural understanding appeared to have been edged and clarified by experience—and that, perhaps, not of a happy character. Nevertheless, along with the deep understanding that springs from that sort of experience, there was a gaiety, an optimism, a high sense of beauty, and even a poetry of phrase. From time to time, I entertained the thought of writing a short note to Randolph Bourne, but for this reason and that, I never did so. Time passed, a great war began, and, somewhere in that period, I began, completed and published "A Hoosier Holiday."*

American Spectator 1 (February 1933): 4. *American Spectator Yearbook,* ed. George Jean Nathan (New York, 1934).

*A *Hoosier Holiday* is based on Dreiser's trip to Indiana in the late summer of 1915. It was published in October 1916.

Appearance and Reality

In the interim, and before ever the book was published, I had a quite casual and yet very impressive experience. It was an evening in late November or December or, possibly, January. I was in the vicinity of the old Night Court that stood at Tenth Street and Sixth Avenue. It was dark, and snow was falling and, as I turned the corner at Sixth Avenue, I encountered as badly deformed and, at the moment, as I accepted it, as frightening a dwarf as I had ever seen. His body was so misshapen, the legs thin, the chest large, the arms long, the head sunk deep between the bony shoulders. More, the head was preternaturally large; eyes, the character of which, because of the general physical ensemble, I did not grasp at the moment. I did note, though, that the skull and even the mouth appeared to be a little askew; large ears flattened against the large skull and, on top of that, a soft hat, of what color I do not recall. Even in the snow and shadow, I could see that the clothing of the man was good.

Somehow, and just in passing, a slight chill passed through me, a chill born of what notions or sentiments within the depths of myself I may not say. But so it was. And just in this passing, as I noted to myself afterward—just as afterward I asked myself why—I recoiled, perhaps moved aside a foot or two, and went on. Also, afterward, although I never expected to see the man again, I reproached myself for having done so. Why should the fumbling hand of nature frighten or irritate me? And why, instead of recoiling, should not sympathy and understanding be the first sentiments to spring into mind, and so control one's emotions? But what had been, had been, and I sought to dismiss the incident from mind, hoping that I had done no real harm. By degrees, it did pass from my thoughts.

It was in 1915 or 1916 that I published "A Hoosier Holiday," and, shortly after that, not more than a few months, there was a knock on my studio door one late afternoon, and when I went and opened it, there stood this same dwarf. I recognized him instantly, and perhaps the more because of encountering him a second time, and this time on my threshold, I again recoiled, affected by some accursed prejudice of which I am heartily ashamed, and was then. None the less, he surveyed me now with what I saw to be large, clear and impressive blue eyes, and announced himself. He was Randolph Bourne, and asked if he might speak to me. When I realized who it was, and that this was the man to whom I had once thought of writing, I experienced a veritable tremor of regret. So this was the body that contained the mind which I so much admired, and this was the way I had twice acknowledged that mind on account of the body!

I did my best to make such social amends as I could, offered him a chair by the fire, prepared a drink, and began volubly to speak of how much his work had impressed me, how much I rejoiced in the beauty and understanding I found in it, how really proud I was that he had come to my door.

In an elfish way which was a condition of his frame and not of his mind, he sat hunched in the chair I had given him, one knee crossed over the other, and continued to look at me with eyes which now were about all that I could see. And, somehow, chemism, mysticism, deeps upon deeps of undecipherable life affecting me, the dwarfed body had by now as completely vanished as though it had never been and, in its place, was a mind, strong, tender, discerning. A mind that had suffered and had learned through suffering. It was truly a beautiful hour that he made for me.

We talked of America and the social and mental phases of our people as presented not only by "A Hoosier Holiday," of which he had come to speak, but also of his own life and experiences. He had never been poor, he said. His family connections had been of the best. He had attended Harvard or Yale or Princeton, I forget which. But there were frustrations which the nature of his body had more or less forced upon him, and these, of course, had taught him so much more than could any college. Frankly, and because of them, he understood me and my work, and had come to say so. We passed into a warm, sympathetic understanding, and then, strangely enough, I saw before me and ever afterward, not a dwarf at all, but a tall, strong, powerful man, whose body matched the fine mind that occupied it.

It is an absolute truth that, look at him as I might, I never again saw him as I had first seen him. I could not. Be he where he might—and I encountered him on various occasions, usually with the most interesting or attractive men and women—I could only sense him as a major mind encased in a minor body, but which last, in its turn, was again encased in a larger one that walked with him, took its time from his own, and perfected the figure which, for some mystifying reason, I envisioned. And then one of the things I said to myself was, how wonderful it was that mind, the essential constructive force that occupies the body, could perform this miracle, not only for me but for all the others who knew him. For, when I encountered him once in a restaurant, he was entertaining the editors of two of the principal weeklies of the country. And another time, under similar circumstances, I saw him the centre of the enthusiastic interest of three as youthful and attractive girls as one would wish to see. And yet another time, when I took tea with him in his own bachelor quarters, I found the service of the place in charge of as engaging a type as the most fastidious male might require. He was not lacking for attention on that score and, better yet, as I felt in at least two cases, it was based on sure appreciation of his real worth.

But not so long after that, word was brought to me that he was seriously ill, and likely to die, as he did. The moment I had the news, I hastened to his door, but at the time he was too ill to be seen. I then sat down and wrote a letter, reciting my appreciation of his friendship, his character and his critical worth, hoping that before he died, if he did, he might read it.

For some reason, I had slightly misdirected the letter, and it was only after he had been dead some time that the letter was returned to me by the post office, and I realized that the strongest and best impulse in me in regard to him and his friendship had failed of its mark.

That which was crooked
Straightened.
That which was defeated
Joined
With that which was
Victorious.
And that which was beautiful
Blended
With that which was ill-planned.
To be separated
And made crooked
Or straight
Again.

You, the Phantom

What to me in life achieves the ultimate of the fantastic as well as the ridiculous, is the exaltation of the human as opposed to, or set over against, the natural or creative forces by which man finds himself surrounded. When he is not busy overestimating his own significance and powers as compared to these others, he becomes fearful and falls down before them—and more—in the past at least, proceeded to symbolize them as Gods—10,000 or more. When he was not doing that, he, where he possessed any of the mental significance he was so ready to ascribe to himself, was to be found, prying or peeping through chinks and mouse holes such as microscopes and telescopes, at the vast illimitable processes of nature or the universe without and about him. Yet these, in turn, he described, and still does, as "mechanistic" and so decidedly not *mental* like himself, either in their content or result! Imagine! Indeed the stone, or plaster, or wooden images that he set up, and at the feet of which he too often worshipped— and still does—were, as he sensed them, better symbols of the forces above him than all their illimitable and quite visible reality about him. The image he could grasp. The other not.

But how odd, considering that a man comes into the world via these processes and mechanisms at which he so blindly peeks! And how still more odd, that after centuries and centuries of peeping and prying and arguing with this earthly authority and that; reading what has been or is being written by this or that or the other so-called *mind* and examining and copying as many of the natural processes as he can, and testing their accuracy for himself, or a process, or a theory that no more than duplicates some already functioning process of nature, proceeds to celebrate forthwith not the wonder of the natural and creative forces about him, but the wonder and originality and power of his own mind.

For instance, an Anaxagoras (B.C. 400) decides that the atom alone must be the basic unit of the universe. And forthwith how

Esquire 2 (November 1934): 25–26. Reprinted by permission of Esquire Magazine,© 1934 (renewed 1962) by Esquire, Inc. *The Bedside Esquire,* ed. Arnold Gingrich (New York, 1940).

astounding is the mind of Anaxagoras. Or a Leonardo, after puzzling over the flying of birds, succeeds in suspecting that some day man must fly. How astounding the mind of Leonardo! Again, a Newton seeing an apple fall to the ground discovers the law of gravitation! How supremely great Newton! But before Anaxagoras, were atoms. And before Leonardo, birds flew. And before Newton, there was the law of gravitation.

And what was it that arranged and maintained all these? A non-thinking, non-reasoning mechanism? If not, then what becomes of the so-called amazing mental distinction of these individuals who did no more than observe the seemingly changeless and hence, as they would say, highly *mechanistic* processes of nature which they copy? Yet today—and day after day—whenever any one individual here on earth finally senses (and that owing wholly to a sensitive equipment provided by this other so-called "mechanistic" process of force, operating not only outside but through him) we hear other men exclaiming in admiration and awe: Hearken! Behold! How great is the mind of man! He has discovered that apples fall to the ground, that birds, because of this or that mechanical form, and this or that metabolism or chemism fly. But can it be that he and not his universe is the mechanism? And that by it he has been definitely limited to a state this side of reason? It is not possible—even in many ways self-evident.

At least for myself, finding myself an extension of these same "mechanical" mysteries which the great mind of man has for so long stared at and pondered over and spied upon, as might any cat at a mouse hole, or any rat peering out upon infinite mystery from the entrance to its petty shelter, I can find nothing that is not mind, neither myself, nor any lesser or greater thing. But some is free moving mental energy, or impulse, or both, and some, as in the case of men, animals, trees, etc., is but the implementation of the same. But with energy connections with the whole which permit of partial movement.

Take myself for instance. I am a minute assemblage of other more minute and yet amazingly coordinated beings—or energy containers (none so small but that if disarranged or disordered, may, and even will, end me—my so-called being.) More, as a part of myself—a somewhat larger mechanism than themselves yet of which they may or may not be conscious—they function quite well in me as a part of my structure, as one of me and I, because of them and other forces above them and which same controls all of us, function fairly well among other such mechanism as myself, so

287

much so that at last I am convinced that I am not so much an individual force but a mechanism for the mind and the intention of some exterior and larger mental process which has constructed me and these minor entities which help to make me what I am, but not, probably, for any individual purpose of my own, but rather, and quite obviously to me, for some purpose of its own. In other words, I am not wholly and individually living—but being lived by something else that has constructed me and is using me, along with all other forms and creatures and elements and forces, for purposes of its own. So much so that I am but the minutest fraction of some process of living which, in turn, is a product of this other exterior as well as interior reality and power, and which same (thanks be) has, for some infinitely small fraction of its much larger and more mysterious life, included me as some minute part, or movement, of its immensely greater life. Yet its relation to me is what?—Its process of functioning through me and so using me as a minute expression of itself how? Well, let us see what that is like.

A man is painting a house, or a picture. The man either is or is not an extension of an idea of a man, emanating from somewhere and definitely characterized as an idea by the fact that endless billions of men, like the one under discussion, have come and gone, are coming and going, and will come and go. This makes the *man idea* the only reality or actual man, the physical man whom we see painting the house or picture being nothing more than an extension, nay, even a mimeograph copy of the man model above described. Yet both are, if you choose, the invention, or possibly accident of something desiring to express itself, for the time being at least, in the man form. That this something seems also to desire to express itself in bird, flower, fish, insect, rock, gas, planet, and other forms is obvious and goes without saying. In short, a universe (and of those there are many) seems to be one of its (in a very immense sense) forms or extensions.

None the less, this replica of the man form, who is painting the house or picture, is moved by emotions or impulses which he does not create. They are created in him by other things, both internal and external—usually external. More, the materials with which he works, the wood of the house, the cloth of the canvas, the metals and elements of the paint he is using, are all alive and are also extensions of this universal creature. And now we know that all things are composed of identically the same vital atoms or their component parts—electrons, protons, neutrons, etc., etc. But how many? We are unable to calculate. The main thing is that all

288

are alive, active, busy forming (for what reason—by what command?) new matter, or gases, or nebulae, or suns, and yet all are an extension of creative energy, the very energy-body of the universe itself, they having no life or being apart from it. Not only that, but they are, accurately or indifferently, as you will, disposed of by the larger creative force or energy wheresoever and, seemingly, howsoever it wills.

In the present instance they are of course only partially subject to the mood or impulse of the man extension—the replica man—who in turn is obviously an extension and a part of the mood of the universal creative will or force. Yet also they are partially independent and are therefore only partially, not totally, at the disposal of the mood or intention of the man.

To be sure, he will put the paint on the house, or the canvas, and arrange it according to his mood of the moment, thus seemingly fixing certain atoms or protons or neutrons, for the time being, in a given place. Actually, however, if one can accept the latest developments in connection with electro-physics and thermodynamics or chemics, or what have you, not any single atom is definitely and permanently fixed anywhere—all are moving and changing—one electron of an atom packing its bag and departing for where we do not know, the while another electron is entering and taking its place. None the less, there is this present arrangement of them on the part of the man replica—his mood or desire, which, in turn, is imposed upon him by something outside him. Indeed, insofar as these atoms are concerned, there remains a probably total unconsciousness on their part of the use that the replica man is making of them, just as in our personal lives and instances where we are arranged as employees of, let us say, the Standard Oil Company, the General Electric Company, or the Bell Telephone Company, we have no least notion of the plans, of say, the Electric Company and the real use it is making of us, any more than it has of the details of our private lives or minds. It can only guess what we are thinking or doing, just as we can only guess what it, via its executives and their business arrangements, is doing. Yet there both are, being moved and fixed by the replica man, just as he is being moved and fixed by the creative process of which he is an expression. In other words, the creative process, or something behind it again, is thinking, planning, doing something important in connection with all of its manifestations, or it is idling and dreaming. And we replica men, like the rest of the creatures of the world we know, and of the other worlds we see but do not know, and the universe, are, or may be, important or not important—mere shadow or foam, sound and fury—signifying nothing.

Yet one thing more. A secondary phase of this universal thinking is the man painting. A tertiary phase—if we men mimeographs want to be vain—are these same atoms which constitute his paint, and colors, and which, in the arrangement he is moved to give them, serve to illustrate his ideas or moods on the canvas or house, as may be. Also the atoms in us. A fourth phase is the electrons in them. Yet no doubt all of those things, men, atoms, electrons, gases and what not, are, as I have said, acting according to mathematical laws which are plainly the concealed and directed orders or thoughts or intentions of a universal creative energy at the very same time that they appear to be responding to lesser laws of their being and their environment. In short, while they are seeming entities and "on their own" as we say, still they are subject to the moods and the movements not only of the man mind, but, beyond him, of the universal creative mind. All either are an integral part of the universal mind, or they are differentiated portions of it—either itself—or superiorly differentiated by the whole of which they are still an integral part.

To my thinking, the great creative energy seems to wish to bloom forth or breathe itself outward into all of the endless forms that we see. Their actions and counteractions and reactions are no more than conditions of its nature—not theirs—yet all together being in some larger way conditions (perhaps) of universal thinking or being. Who is to say? Yet all to one purpose, namely, the fell and important or idle and unimportant desire or mood on the part of something, which is *the all,* to express itself either meaningly or meaninglessly. (A fine thing to be thinking as one goes home on the five-fifteen.)

I Find the Real American Tragedy

The first in a lengthy, five-part account which Dreiser published in Mystery Magazine *on the Robert Edwards murder case of 1934. Other cases mentioned by Dreiser are the Patrick-Jones-Rice case of 1900, the Colonel Thomas Swope-Dr. Bennett Hyde case of 1909–1910, the Carlyle Harris case of 1894, the Gillette case of 1906 [not 1905], the Roland Molineux [not Molyneux] case of 1899 [not 1907 or 1908], the William Orpet case of 1916 [not 1909 or 1910], and the Avis Linnell-Clarence Richesen [not Richardson] case of 1911.*

It was in 1892, at which time I began work as a newspaperman, that I first began to observe a certain type of crime in the United States. It seemed to spring from the fact that almost every young person was possessed of an ingrowing ambition to be somebody financially and socially. In short, the general mental mood of America was directed toward escape from any form of poverty. This ambition did not imply merely the attainment of comfort and the wherewithal to make happy one's friends, but rather the accumulation of wealth implying power, social superiority, even social domination. It all struck me as anomalous, in a supposedly Christian democracy dedicated to the principle of brotherly love.

Of course, in my school days I had swallowed innocently enough those stories of patriots who had devoted their lives unselfishly to the upbuilding, development and defense of their native land. They had fought and died for liberty as against privilege, and for the right of every man to life, liberty and the pursuit of happiness. But a few years later, on seeking to place myself economically, I found that there were some contradictions not to be overlooked. Most men, as I found, were neither patriots nor advocates of liberty for others, nor were they even fair-minded. Life was a struggle for existence, and a cruel struggle. To be sure, there was operating a so-called social system which sought by law

Mystery Magazine 11 (February 1935): 9–11, 88–90.

at least to enforce some measure of honesty and fairness. But as to the working of the same, how different! In every town and city with which I came in contact, the well-to-do dominated the less well-to-do, and to the general disadvantage of the latter. The rich controlled whatever industries there were and fixed all too often the most exacting and not infrequently slave-like hour and wage terms. Altogether, pride and show, and even waste were flaunted in a new and still fairly virgin land—in the face of poverty and want, and not poverty and want on the part of those who would not work, but the poverty and want of those who were all too eager to work, and almost on any terms.

In other words, I was witnessing the upbuilding of the great American fortunes. And once these fortunes and the families which controlled them were established, there began to develop our "leisure class," the Four Hundred of New York and the slave aristocracy of the South, plus their imitators in the remainder of the states. And this class, as I studied it, presented the very interesting thought that all of its heirs and assigns were not so much interested in work or mental or national development in any form as they were in leisure and show—the fanfare and parade of wealth without any consideration for the workers from whom it was taken or the country as a whole. I saw also that the maintaining of those privileges was likewise the principal business of those who were not heirs to anything—the young and ambitious in nearly all walks of life. In fact, between 1875 and 1900 it became an outstanding American madness which led first to the great war of 1914–18 and culminated finally in the financial debacle of 1929.

Indeed, throughout this period, as I found, it was the rare American heart that was set, for instance, on being a great scientist, discoverer, religionist, philosopher, or benefactor to mankind in any form. True enough, a man might start out to be a doctor, a lawyer, a merchant, an inventor, perhaps even a scientist, but his private obsession, due to the national obsession which I have just described, was that the quick and sure way to do this was to get money. And one of the quickest ways to get money was to marry it, not develop oneself and so have money come honestly. In short, we bred the fortune hunter de luxe. Fortune-hunting became a disease. Hence my first notice of and interest in the particular type of crime first mentioned.

In the main, as I can show by the records, it was the murder of a young girl by an ambitious young man. But not always. There were many forms of murder for money. The Albert T. Patrick case

292

in New York presented the picture of a shrewd attorney murdering his rich old client. For this crime Patrick was sentenced to life imprisonment. Another case—guilt not finally proved—related to the millionaire Swope family in Kansas City. A doctor son-in-law was charged with bringing about not only the diseases but the deaths of Swope and several heirs to his fortune. The doctor was acquitted, but the evidence presented a very arresting picture of the mental mood of many Americans in regard to money.

A third variation was that of the young ambitious lover of some poorer girl, who in the earlier state of his affairs had been attractive enough to satisfy him both in the matter of love and her social station. But nearly always with the passing of time and the growth of experience on the part of the youth, a more attractive girl with money or position appeared and he quickly discovered that he could no longer care for his first love. What produced this particular type of crime about which I am talking was the fact that it was not always possible to drop the first girl. What usually stood in the way was pregnancy, plus the genuine affection of the girl herself for her love, plus also her determination to hold him. This the conventionally-minded usually acclaimed as reasonable and right (this determination, I mean), while the more sophisticated looked upon it as a futile and stupid reason for holding that which is not to be held, or if so held, is worthless.

Nevertheless, these murders, based upon these facts and conditions, proved very common in my lifetime and my personal experience as a journalist. One of the most tragic of them I contacted in 1894, when I first arrived in New York. It was the really tragic case of Carlyle Harris, a young medical student, an interne in one of the leading New York hospitals, who seduced a young girl poorer and less distinguished than he was, or at least hoped to be. No sooner had he done this that the devil, or some anachronistic element in the very essence of life itself, presented Carlyle with an attractive girl of a much higher station than his own, one who possessed not only beauty but wealth. The way Carlyle finally sought to rid himself of the other girl was to supply her with a dozen powders, four of which were poisoned, and so intended to bring about her death. One of them did. Result: discovery, trial and execution. In this case I chanced by reason of a strange contact to know his mother, a rather fine and loving, if overly-determined and ruling one. She was a widow and had little money. But she was utterly devoted to her son's welfare and bent on bringing about his success, socially as well as professionally. She wanted him to get up in the world, be famous,

293

marry money. She told me so. In part I blame her for her urgency and insistence on what was the proper type of life for him. In part I blame America and its craze for social and money success.

After that, this particular type of tragedy, as it seemed to me, became more and more common. As a matter of fact, between 1895 and this present year there has scarcely been a year in which some part of the country has not been presented with crime of this type. For instance, there was one in San Francisco in 1899. In 1900 came a Charleston, South Carolina, case, wherein a girl was shot by her lover because he wanted to better his social position by marrying a Charleston society girl.

In the Summer of 1905, at Big Moose Lake in the Adirondacks, the murder which I wrote about twenty years later and which I named *An American Tragedy* was committed. It concerned one Chester Gillette, a young collar worker at Cortland, New York, and Grace (better known as Billy) Brown, who came from a farm near Otselic, New York, but worked in the same factory with Gillette at Cortland. The first America heard of it was when the press in a small dispatch from Old Forge, a small town not far from Big Moose Lake, announced that a boy and girl who had come to Big Moose to spend a holiday had gone out in a boat and both been drowned. An upturned boat, plus a floating straw hat, was found in a remote part of the lake. The lake was dragged and one body discovered and identified as that of Billy Brown. And then came news of the boy who had been seen with her. He was located as a guest of a smart camping party on one of the adjacent lakes and was none other than Chester Gillette, the nephew of a collar factory owner of Cortland. He was identified as the boy who had been with Billy Brown at the lake. Later still, because of a bundle of letters written by the girl and found in his room at Cortland, their love affair was disclosed, also the fact that she was pregnant, and was begging him to marry her. In one letter, the last, she even threatened that unless he came to her at once at Otselic (where, because of her condition, she had retired), and would take her away and marry her, she would return to Cortland and expose him "before all his fine friends." He was indicted and charged with murder. The upturned boat, his straw hat (a duplicate of the one he usually wore), a wound over the girl's forehead—which he said was caused by the overturning boat but which the District Attorney charged was made either by an oar or a broken tennis racket found hidden under a log in the woods nearby and which was proved to have been purchased by Gillette—were sufficient to convince a country jury that he had committed the crime. And he was electro-cuted at Auburn Penitentiary, a final confession, it is said, having preceded his death.

After that, and cited here in order to show my reason for naming this crime *An American Tragedy,* came others of the same nature. I will list them as briefly as possible.

In 1907 or 1908 the Roland Molyneux case of New York City. In 1909 or 1910 the Orpet case, in Chicago. In 1914 or 1915 the Avis Linnell-Richardson case of Hyannis, Massachusetts. In this case the facts equally warranted the title: *An American Tragedy.* For here was a young preacher, Richardson, with a small church in Hyannis. He had come up from nothing, learned little or nothing, accumulated no money, and was struggling along on a small salary. Of course, he was good-looking, socially agreeable, a fair orator, and so on. From all I could gather at the time, Avis was a charming and emotionally interesting and attractive girl, but of circumstance and parentage as unnoticed as Richardson's. Alas, love, a period of happiness, seduction with a promise of marriage, and then Mephis-topheles, with nothing more and nothing less in his hand than a call to one of the richest and most socially distinguished congregations in Boston. There followed his installation as pastor, and soon after that one of the wealthy beauties of his new congregation fixed her eye on him and decided that he was the one for her. Yet in the background was Avis and her approaching motherhood. And his promise of marriage. And so, since his new love moved him to visions of social grandeur far beyond his previous dreams, he sought to cast off Avis. Yet she in love and agonized, insisted that he help her rid herself of the child or marry her. Once more then, poisoned powders and death. And at last Richardson dragged from his grand pulpit to a prison cell. And then trial, and death in an electric chair because he had killed Avis.

But then on July 31st of this year, at Harvey's Lake near Wilkes-Barre, Pennsylvania, occurred what was immediately an-nounced by the newspapers as an exact duplicate of *An American Tragedy.* It was a murder said to have been committed by Robert Allen Edwards, a resident of Edwardsville, a part of Wilkes-Barre. His victim was Freda McKechnie, daughter of Mr. and Mrs. George McKechnie of Edwardsville. And by various newspapers I was shortly asked to say whether or not this was a duplicate of my story and whether in my opinion the novel had brought about the murder. My answer was that without much more evidence than was available at that time I could not say, but that because of many

295

related cases which had occurred before this one, I doubted very much that the crime was inspired by the book.* It seemed to me rather one inspired by conditions in America which produce, or at least have produced up to this time, exactly that sort of crime.

My reason for saying this was that by the time I had reached the place where I wanted to and did write *An American Tragedy*— that is, 1924–1925—I had concluded that the facts outlined in the introduction to this article were the real cause. Furthermore, in my examination of such data as I could find in 1924 relating to the Chester Gillette-Billy Brown case, I had become convinced that there was an entire misunderstanding, or perhaps I had better say non-apprehension, of the conditions or circumstances surrounding the victims of that murder *before* the murder was committed. From these circumstances, which I drew not only from the testimony introduced at the trial but from newspaper investigations and information which preceded and accompanied the trial, I concluded that the murder was not one which could either wisely or justly be presented to an ordinary conventional, partly religious, and morally controlled American jury and be intelligently passed upon. Rather I concluded that there were too many elements of a social and economic, as well as moral and religious, character to permit a jury (themselves the representatives, one might even say the victims, of these same financial conditions and social taboos) to judge fairly the guilt or innocence of the alleged murderer.

In the case of Chester Gillette, I soon decided, after examining his background, that he was in the first place not sufficiently developed mentally to be the deliberate author of a truly anti-social murder. He was too young, too inexperienced in the ways of life, to calculate a crime which would be sufficiently anti-social to warrant his destruction. His parents had been exceedingly poor, victims really of their inability to devise even a moderate physical subsistence for themselves and their children. They were street preachers, running small and unprofitable missions. In short, social pariahs. They had moved about a great deal, forming no connections of any worth, and being ambitious, Chester Gillette had obviously been over-impressed by what he considered the superior state of others. Furthermore, and to complicate his illusions in connection with all this, there were rumors of an uncle, the brother of his father, who was a well-to-do collar manufacturer in Cortland,

* Dreiser reported the Edwards trial at some length for the New York *Post* from October 2 through October 6, 1934.

I Find the Real American Tragedy

New York. Chester Gillette seemed to have built up the notion that if in some fashion he could connect himself with the superior life of this uncle, he would naturally pass from a lower to a higher social and financial state. And that, as you see, ties up with the general social and financial attitude of Americans—their dreams of grandeur, all based on financial advancement.

Furthermore, as I said to myself, this was really not an *anti-social* dream as Americans should see it, but rather a *pro-social* dream. *He was really doing the kind of thing which Americans should and would have said was the wise and moral thing for him to do had he not committed a murder.* His would not ordinarily be called the instinct of a criminal; rather, it would be deemed the *instinct of a worthy and respected temperament.*

However, when Chester reached Cortland, he found that his better state was not to be as easily come by as he had dreamed. In other words, he was placed in the anomalous position of being at once the nephew of a man who was socially and financially secure and at the same time a mere eight-or-ten-dollar-a-week collar worker. His future seemingly depended on his personal skill. And this he did not possess, for he was by no means gifted technically. He was romantic and to a degree vain, but not constructively acquisitive.

Next, his position as a collar worker forced upon him the social opportunities which conditioned the workers themselves. For companionship he had to look to his fellow-workers and among them he found Billy Brown, a girl of a beautiful and sympathetic temperament who was drawn to him by his looks and the fact that he was related to the family which owned the factory in which they both worked.

At the trial it was not denied by him that he loved her at first. The general picture seemed to indicate that he was happy enough in this companionship, until, by reason of his reputation as a nephew of a rich man, he came to be looked upon finally as worthy of the attention of girls of a higher station than Billy Brown. And finally, one of these girls paid him considerable attention and quickly inflamed him, not only with love for her but with the thought that by marrying her he would be stepping up into the social world represented by his uncle, and which he considered ideal. This fact, which I found to be the oustanding one in the prosecution's effort to establish and prove motive for murder, was the one which proved to me that it was not a desire for murder that was prompted by that dream of his but rather the reverse. For if it proved anything, it proved that he desired to reach a social state in which no such evil thing as murder could possibly be contemplated. In short, as I said to myself at the time, it cannot be true that this boy is unsocial in his mood or tendencies. It is just the reverse. He is pro-social.

The fact that he aspired to a better social state with this other girl proved, if anything, that he had no desire to go against the organized standards of the society of his day. In fact, having made what he considered a social mistake in connecting himself with Billy Brown, his hope and desire was to rectify that by a conventional marriage with this other girl. And that at first by no means indicated or suggested as existing in his mind any thought, let alone determination, that he would or should be required to murder anybody in order to achieve it. He merely wished to divest himself of the poorer relationship in order to achieve the richer one. And you may depend upon it that if he had had money and more experience in the ways of immorality, he would have known ways and means of indulging himself in the relationship with Billy Brown without bringing upon himself the morally compulsive relation of prospective fatherhood.

But he did not have the money. And the lack of it, however inimical to his dreams of a happy marriage with the richer girl, was no crime in itself. What crime there was entered at the point where, finding himself frustrated on the one hand by his desire to marry the richer girl and on the other hand by his inability to extricate Billy Brown from her predicament, he thought of murder. But even here it was impossible for me to say that at any time murder was his desire. What he really desired even to the very end was escape. And up to the moment that he upset the boat and struck her with a tennis racket (if he did), his desire was not to go against the ideals of society, but to go with them. Frustration was not anything which he criminally planned. It came upon him without any desire on his part, and decidedly against every wish of his being. When he found that he could not free himself from this girl, then there entered the thought of escape: murder.

But there again, I was compelled to ask myself: "Was it murder for murder's sake?" Anyone with a grain of sense knows that it was not. He did not wish to murder. He sought every lane of escape before murder came as the last sad resource. For he was confronted by a state to which he was socially and emotionally fearfully opposed, one which was sufficient, probably, to have affected his powers of reason. It could, and probably did, absolutely befuddle and finally emotionally derange a youth who because of his romantic dreams, and more, because when subject to them he was also subject to those dreadful economic, social, moral and conventional pressures about him, was finally driven romantically mad and brought to the point of committing a crime that was so terrible to the world.

But why so widely heralded at the time? Why the sorrow, sympathy, pain really, to the hearts of millions not only for Billy Brown but for him? Why? I will tell you. Because the emotions, so much more quickly than the far more commonplace scales of the brain, register the essential truth. That is why.

Not Chester Gillette, as I said to myself at the time, planned this crime, but circumstances over which he had no control—circumstances and laws and rules and conventions which to his immature and more or less futile mind were so terrible, so oppressive, that they were destructive to his reasoning powers. No more and no less. He was not seeking murder. By no means. To the very last analysis, even when he struck the blow, he was seeking to escape—striking to escape. If at the moment when he stood in the boat and was ready to strike Billy Brown with the tennis racket, a voice had called: "Stop! You don't have to do that in order to escape. Take the girl to a doctor. Have an operation performed. Give her this money and tell her how deeply you desire to be released and why, and she will release you!"—there is no question in my mind, and none in yours, that he would have dropped the racket and gladly gone about the business of giving this girl her life and freedom. Is there any sane person on the face of the earth who will honestly deny the validity of this? But life—circumstances—would not have it so.

And yet in spite of these conditions and circumstances which were plainly to be seen by anyone who could see, the boy was fearfully denounced, tortured with public obloquy and even hatred. It was suggested that he be lynched, and once the case was given to the jury he was quickly convicted of murder and sentenced to death. And although the case was carried to the Court of Appeals and afterwards to Governor (later Chief Justice) Hughes, neither the court nor the governor could trace out these truer reasons for the deed which he committed. He must die.

*   *   *   *   *   *

Lessons I Learned from an Old Man

Once when I was working for a certain Western daily, famous and powerful in its region, I was sent by the city editor to ask a retired manufacturer of great wealth certain questions concerning a terminal project which was then being planned and which involved millions.*

Was it a good thing? Did the city need it? Would it be easy and profitable to finance?

In telling me what to ask he had not told me whether my man was old or young—simply that he was retired and that I would find him at his home.

I was a mere boy at the time, not more than twenty-two, and much more interested in life as a spectacle and the whyfors of it in its entirety than in anything relating to finance or commerce. Still the questions I had to ask were well in mind and I was prepared to bring back very definite replies, assuming that my manufacturer would answer them.

En route, partly because of his great fame and by reason of my being a stranger in the city, I built up an interesting picture of what the man I was to interview would be like.

He would be middle-aged, being so wealthy, rather stern and dogmatic, probably indifferent to all reporters. I would have to be very formal, say quickly and clearly what I wanted, note sharply his replies and make durable mental notes, since probably he would resent my penciling his replies in his presence. So many, as I had noted, were begrudging of the least time given to a reporter.

As I drew near the vicinity in which he lived and saw the great houses, I was by no means reassured. His was situated, with perhaps as many as seven others, in a great enclosed "place," huge wrought-iron gates at either end, a porter in charge to demand who it was one wished to see, wide lawns and pathways on either hand, a spacious and decorated double drive in the center.

Your Life 2 (January 1938): 6–10.

*Dreiser's article on the terminal, "Greatest in the World," appeared in the St. Louis *Globe-Democrat,* December 11, 1892, p. 28. This article, however, does not contain a report of a statement by a "Mr. Y——"

The house in its turn was so large and impressively designed that it overawed me. Oblong, of yellow stone, with a red-brown tile roof, a noble frieze, sunken French windows, decorative chimneys, a handsome, deeply recessed door, it seemed just the abode for a rich and powerful and forceful man.

As I approached it I felt that one must be very important indeed to be worthy of it. I braced myself spiritually, as it were, to endure the weight of its massy claims.

Once at the door I was greeted by a portentous footman in knee-breeches and spike-tailed coat of blue, with polished brass buttons and white velvet cuffs, who wished to know what I desired. I told him. He disappeared, leaving me outside, but presently returned.

I was then conducted up a grandiose stair that turned twice in wide sweeps, great rugs lying on the landings, bronze statuary facing one at every turn, hangings, carved furniture and great spaces giving one a sense of lavish and yet discriminating expenditure. A deeply cut door opened into a huge library, with its richly-carved shelves and its more richly-bound books.

In front of a great open fireplace and confronted by a white wolfhound on a rug sat, to my surprise, an old and thin and feeble man, whose hair was so white, whose shoulders so narrow and whose hands and face so thin and sunken, that I was shocked. His eyes, blue and still, had receded deep into their sockets. His skin was leathery and seamed.

"Mr. Y——?" I inquired.

He nodded slightly.

I proceeded at once to explain as succinctly as may be all that had been told me to ask, marveling betimes at his age and weakness. He listened gravely, his hands lying flat on a black woolen blanket that covered his knees. Now and then he crooked the fingers of one or the other of them.

"Yes," he said slowly and with difficulty, as it seemed to me, from time to time as I talked. "Yes."

When I had done he paused and staring more at the floor than at me said, "Yes, my boy, I will answer all your questions, only my interest in all these things is now so slight that it seems scarcely worth while. I do not know why they trouble to ask me."

I stared, impressed by the meaning of his words. He was so old, so feeble. Life—the great life force of which he had been a part—was a thing of the past.

That fire which had been inside him, that lust which had built

301

this great house, his great business, which had surrounded him with servitors and beauty and fame, was now so thin, so pale a thing, that one wondered why any one should bother about him any more. And still, so great were his wealth and fame that his name was of the utmost import.

Although he personally was no longer of this world, really a mere shadow, still what he had to say, was, seeing that it could be proved that he was still alive. Slowly and painfully, it seemed to me, he answered each of my questions, folding and unfolding the fingers of one or the other bony hand and occasionally and feebly clearing his throat.

Somehow, as I wrote, and afterwards as I walked away, the true import of my visit seemed not so much that this huge terminal might or might not be profitably built and operated (he seemed to think it might), or that one of the wealthiest men of the city had so said, but that age and enfeeblement should relentlessly overtake a man of obviously once such great power and strength.

Life must go on, to be sure, and this terminal must be built, and thousands—millions, no doubt—would profit by it once it was. But this once young and now old man! What of him? This great house with all its luxury, built to enshrine so fading a spark! What did all this amount to to him? The uselessness! The futility to him now of all he had done!

This, far more than his carefully noted replies, or how much the paper desired them, was what I was carrying away, and that quite filled my mind to the exclusion of everything else.

Once I was near my office again I began to speculate (most vaguely, I must say, at the time, being so young) as to the curious import of all this to me and the difference between this in which I was really interested, and the other in which the city editor of the newspaper was interested, and concerning which, and which alone, I would be expected to report.

His age, the greatness of the house, the lapse of all his strength, as I now realized, would be of no least import to the man who had sent me out, and yet it was so fascinating to me. *Why was it that a newspaper must entirely ignore that which interested me now? What did one do with such things, such facts as I had seen?* I asked myself.

Here was something, as I now noted, that I had discovered for myself, which was not journalism and yet which was more important to me than the purely journalistic facts wherewith I was supposed to return—more appealing, beautiful—a fact so stupendous that it moved me deeply.

This old feeble man, once so powerful physically no doubt and still so significant as a name and a holder of wealth who, now, amid the trappings of his wealth could only feebly open and close the bony fingers of his hands, stare at the floor, and say, "My interest in all these things is now so slight that it is scarcely worth while"—a spectacle for God and Men. . . .

Around me was swirling the life of the city. Trolley cars clanged, wagons rattled. Hundreds of thousands, young, vigorous, new to life, as zestful as ever he had been, pushed and jostled in the ways. But he who had once been so vital a part of it was out there alone before his fireplace, in his great house, empty-handed, forgotten, a silent white dog for a companion.

I bustled into the office.

"Well, what did Y—— say?" my city editor asked.

I told him the answers he had made.

"Fine! Fine!" he said. "Just what we want! That'll make a lead, all right. Write it just as you tell me, the questions and his answers."

"Shall I tell anything about how old he is?" I ventured, being still intensely interested in my idea. "He is very old, you know, very feeble. He could scarcely talk to me." These other facts seemed so huge, so sad.

"No, no, no!" he almost shouted, being interested in other things by now. "Can that stuff! Write only his answers. Never mind how old he is. That's just what I *don't* want. Do you want to queer this? Stick to the terminal dope and what he thought. We're not interested in his age."

I proceeded and wrote as he said, avoiding all reference to what I had seen and thought, and the next day the first page carried a ringing, clear approval of the terminal idea, by one who was apparently as much alive and as forceful as ever and intensely interested in it as a great and needful improvement as any man in the city.

No doubt the vast majority of the people thought of him even then as young, active, his old self. But all the while this other picture was holding in my mind, and continued so to do for years after. I could scarcely think of the city even without thinking of him, his house, his dog, his age, his bony fingers, his fame.

The city editor who wanted only the vital, momentarily valuable replies as to whether or no he approved of the terminal idea had raised in my mind, once and for all, the question as to what one was to do with these larger questions—a picture like that, a tragedy like that. What did one, or could one, do with such facts, such pictures, if not publish them in a newspaper?

Finally, after several years of meditation really, the answer came.

It became plain to me then that journalism was not the field for this, that it required a different type of thought from that which was holding at any moment in any newspaper office anywhere, or ever would, a different medium of presentation; namely, that which is concerned with life in the round, at large, its more evanescent and yet less current phases, its greater and sadder contrasts.

Those particular matters about which the city editor had wished to know concerned, as I now saw, only such things as were temporary and purely constructive in their interest, nothing beyond the day—the hour—in which they appeared.

Literature, as I now saw, and art in all its forms, was this other realm, that of the painter, the artist, the one who saw and reported the non-transitory, and yet transitory too, nature of all our interests and dreams, which observed life as a whole and drew it without a flaw, a fact, missing. There, if anywhere, were to be reported or painted such conditions and scenes as this about which I had meditated and which could find no place in the rush and hurry of our daily press.

Then it was, and not until then, that the real difference between journalism and literature became plain.

Presenting Thoreau

Dreiser's introduction precedes his selection from the work of Thoreau in the Living Thoughts series.

When I think of philosophy and philosophers as they range through the centuries from earliest Greece to this hour, I am impressed with the fact that all are men of genius, temperamentally and deeply moved, like poets, by the phenomena of life by which they find themselves surrounded. And in that sense, and in that sense only, that is temperamentally, wrestling with the *why* as well as the *how* of it all. For we know, of course, that science in its technical or practical approach toward the phenomena of existence has long since abandoned almost every hope of an answer to the *why* of things, and has concentrated on the *how* of what it sees going on about us. So Galileo, for instance, as early as sixteen hundred, troubled by the until then unsolved problem of whether the earth attracts all bodies with the same force or speed, made a test by dropping things of differing weights from a tower and found that one arrived as quickly as the other; also, that to arrive at the same time, none required that it be either pushed, pulled, or acted on in any way other than by the one force attracting it to the earth. Simple, seemingly; and yet thousands of years of observations by men of their environment had passed before these primary facts were arrived at. Then, too, the fact of gravitation as a law was only established by Newton as late as 1666.

From then on science has proceeded almost exclusively to concern itself with the *how,* not the *why.* At the same time, the philosopher and dreamer or poet, while profiting by science, has never ceased to concern himself with the thought of, or as I see it, he has unceasingly reacted to, the mystery of *why.* For there is, of course, this matter-energy which fills all space. There are these various laws by which the different forms of matter-energy are regulated, or by which they describe their inherent nature and therefore to which they voluntarily conform. In other words, they

The Living Thoughts of Thoreau (New York: Longmans, Green, 1939), pp. 1–12.

are either regulated by something (God is one word often used to describe that something, also Spirit, Brahma, Divine Essence, or Force) or, being all in all in space and time, they are, *collectively,* the equivalent of this imaginary something. And whether self-regulatory or not, they still conform to laws which are the equivalent of self-regulation and hence of the essence or spirit otherwise assumed to inhabit or inform them.

Through what they are and do, they express its uttermost character and being. And by us, as reacting evocations of the same, they can only be spoken of as the universe. And only such laws and actions as have been scientifically verified can be ascribed to them. All else must be shunned or ignored. For, nowadays, the scientists insist that philosophical generalizations must be founded on scientific results. All talk of any supreme regulating and hence, legal or directing force or spirit is *out.* There is no known God or Spirit. He cannot be scientifically described *in toto,* if even in part. Hence the unconscious confession of scientific defeat and even confusion in the title of the verified and so staggering body of evolutionary and historic biological, chemical and physical data which Ernst Haeckel included in his truly great work, *The Riddle of the Universe.* Hence also the tentative, noncommittal comment by scientists anywhere of the seeming universality of law, or state or condition, physical or chemical, maintained in any portion of space, as in a sidereal system for instance. Even time-space, which is now assumed as relative, is therefore more or less of an illusion. Yet side by side with all this, in all branches of science, is constant and non-changing reference to creative thought or deduction via increased nervous sensitivity to already long-existing data, as though man, an evocation of this non-understandable universe or matter-energy-space-time, could individually and mentally be creative, whereas that from which he derives could in no wise be.

It is at this point that the *why-asking,* scientifically informed but mentally non-creative philosopher, parts company with the *how-limited* scientists of the laboratories and the mathematically-minded calculators of the libraries and universities. For he continues to ask *why.*

For all its knowledge of *how,* science cannot say *why.* And furthermore, it starts nervously at the faintest suggestion that man, powered as a chemical and physical contrivance of exterior forces, in responding to and synthesizing these inpouring and down-pouring stimuli, may be nothing more than a radio or television device—and that the same may be true with animals, insects, vegetation. In short, that as a television station distributes voices, colors, forms, motions, and ideas or thoughts via sounds and gestures—so some extraplanetary forces may be broadcasting man and human life to this planet.

That, of course, carries to a logical conclusion the vast mass of data which tends to demonstrate that man is a cosmic implement or tool. But to that point our scientific mechanist refuses to proceed. He has not, as yet, he says, assembled sufficient data to warrant so esoteric a deduction. We must wait. None-the-less, the idealist believes in cosmic law—and the mindlike processes which accompany it—in the engineering or technical genius which accompanies the construction, operation, continuance and dissolution of everything on this planet. He assumes that this could be the work of some superior force in the matter-energy-space-time continuum, something for instance that inhabits and directs that which everywhere appears as directed matter-energy; something, in other words, that plans what matter-energy does and is to do. Alas, there's the rub. For that would be a God, name it as we choose. And if good or evil be introduced into the picture, as man assuredly feels both to be in the picture or process, as he finds it here, then, in his thought, at least, this super-force or intellect or mind would be the author of both.

But here one crosses again to the realm of the speculative philosopher, the idealist or dreamer or visionary, who chooses, in at least some cases, to study carefully what science has assembled and who, from that vantage point, insists that the data already assembled indicate the existence and rule of such a master, that its nature and its spirit are fully written or set forth in that which man senses of himself here, as well as through the tools and guides his creator has evolved for him. But of course, there is a third conclusion, that all our questioning is only too meaningless. There may be in the universe only a process. An eternal equation may be the very nature of things.

The most recent individual who has interested me in connection with this problem is Henry David Thoreau, the recluse of Concord, who for so long a time was thought of not at all as a philosopher but rather as a naturalist, essayist, prose poet, and nature lover, with at best, some eccentric views of the society by which he found himself surrounded and who, for the most part, he chose to ignore.

As a matter of fact, in the strict or academic sense of the word, Thoreau cannot be looked upon as a philosopher at all. He appears never to have once thought of arranging or compiling his ideas in relation to the problem of things and their causes here on earth or in space-time after the fashion of Spinoza, or Kant, or Hegel, or Spencer. That he had thoughts, as well as most definite deductions in connection with most of the matters that engage the speculative thinkers of even our day, is very clear from the fourteen published volumes of notes that he left, to say nothing of *Walden,* or *A Week on the Concord and Merrimack Rivers,* or his letters, and essays. Although his thoughts are scattered higgledy-piggledy through these volumes and the twenty-two years of his writing life, and run the gamut of most of the by now stereotyped problems of life or matter-energy in space-time, still, if you are enough interested, you can piece them together for yourself, as I have done or attempted to do in this volume. And here, as you may see for yourself, you find him dwelling on mind in nature, form in nature, time, change, knowledge and its source and limitation, beauty and art, truth and error, reality and illusion, the problem of morals, of free or controlled will, of the emotions, of good and evil in the cosmic sense, of sorrow and joy, mercy and cruelty, society, religion, justice, death and even a future life!

* * * * * *

For myself, I am free to say that of all my philosophic and scientific reading of recent years from Democritus to Einstein, these scattered notes of Thoreau impress me as being more illuminative, not of the practical results or profits of science (which have in our time so led to an increasingly complicated mass of material as well as to mental or ideational structures, with their accompanying compulsions to greater physical as well as to so-called "mental" dexterities, that they well nigh befuddle if not wreck the man-mechanism which has to deal with them) but of the implications of scientific results or cosmology. For Thoreau as well as Loeb, and at this hour Einstein, in fact, all up-to-the-hour science, look upon man and life, chemical and physical, as directed but in the purely mechanical sense. Immutable law binds us all. Only, he was not, as so many are, willing to label the process as mechanical and stop there. He preferred, or rather, as I should say, he was compelled by his sensory reactions to all things, to view them as but dimly conscious mechanisms directed by a superior and pervasive something which has not only evolved them, but, like the centripetal force or essence in the heart of an atom which keeps its revolving electrons from flying tangentially outward and away, holds them in place and order. Thus in *Walden* you find him asserting, "We are not wholly involved in Nature. I may be either the driftwood in the stream, or Indra in the sky looking down on it." And again, on the same page, "However intense my experience, I am conscious of the presence and criticism of a part of me, which, as it were, is not a part of me, but spectator, sharing no experience, but taking note of it; and that is no more *I* than it is *you*." (Italics mine.) And again, same page, "I only know myself as a human entity; the scene, so to speak, of thoughts and affections; and am sensible of a certain doubleness by which I can stand as remote from myself as from another"—which, as you can see, is far from looking upon himself as a will-less, thoughtless machine, but rather, possibly, as the inhabitant *in part* of a machine or instrument built by another—the manufacturer let us say of all man-known machines—in which one is permitted to dwell but not to direct, since one is there, as he says, only as a "spectator, sharing no experience." And, as if to clinch this man-machine conclusion he adds (the *Week,* p. 408), "Our present senses are but the rudiments of what they are destined to become." Which is not unlike Henry Ford saying, "Wait till you see my 1940 model. It will have everything."

I am sure that I shall appear to be imposing on Thoreau an ultra-modern and ultra-mechanistic approach to the problem or mystery of nature, but this is because I am selecting at this point a few of his most essential comments relating to this particular problem and ignoring the endless ramblings of his exploring mind through all phases of philosophic speculation from will-lessness to free-will, from almost divine guidance to accidental mechanistic sufficiency.

Really, having read about 2,400,000 words of this selected material, I feel as though Thoreau lived a kind of cycle, going from the one extreme of colorful concrete natural description to a most vaporous, enormous profundity. The only figure which occurs to me is as if some god who was alive at the beginning of the world should break through in Thoreau, and remember something of what Nature's mind is. Now it seems to me that almost all his comments on men, society, the vindictive and critical side of his nature, his moral views, are not really essential to his greatness at all, but only necessitated by the superficially physical bounds of his being. I feel as if he were tapping some marvelous, musical, lyrical source, which *was* life, which *is* a dream. It is the same sustaining assumption that is in poetry, in music, the same figure as comes to one from a consideration of archaic art, like the figures of the animals in the caves in France and Spain, the Greek myths—the optimism, the grandeur of the vision of an unconquerably limitless universe, rushing and sounding furiously and noiselessly at once.

This suggestion of force, of something cloudy and beautiful, fearless, not taking thought—all in one thing—that it is which he intimates of nature. That is where his inconsistencies count for nothing, because, as I see it, his *source* is inconsistent. That is why he rejects with more than necessary fervor for a god all the doings of men which obtrude themselves on his vision. He seems to have hold of something when he sits on his hillsides and watches the sky and the sun and stars, trees and birds. It is the source of them all which he is feeling, a passion for what is in another sense, pure relativity. Where he seems foolish, it is only a denial of this nature-feeling in himself or others. Although at times he seems so, or asserts that he is, he is not sad, nor does his vision crucify him, because he seems more than man, and at the same time is perfectly content to know *his* universe to be only what *he* can see. He is saying over and over, the universe exists for me; he instinctively knows this, and he will milk every ounce of sensation out of it that he can. And because he is more primitive than modern he is more sensate than social, more optimistic than pessimistic. I mean by *primitive* someone who is less dependent on men than most are today, and can see beyond a race, a time, or today, and praise the whole.

* * * * * *

[I Believe]

Substantially, my feeling about life amounts to just what it did when I first tried to express it for this series.* And so this essay will be more of the same, only, apropos of mechanism, I will try to meet some of the arguments which have been suggested to me.

It seems to me in the first place that although many find something intrinsically displeasing in the very idea of a mechanical universe, there is nothing unesthetic about it. The ugliness of a machine in a special sense is apparent only because of a limited idea of a machine. A man who is repelled by the concept of machinery is not considering universal machinery but something like a factory—with goods which are known going in one end and coming out the other, reformed. Yet it should be obvious that nothing like the end or the beginning or the whole utility of the universal machine is known. All we think we know is some process, however small, but definitely a mechanical process, and of this we are a part. There is nothing unesthetic to me in this idea, nothing degrading to man, nothing to besmirch or belittle the grandeur and mystery of life which is the direct evidence of sense.

Invert the analogy of the machine which comes from science and think of the special form as derived from the general form, and this cloak of pettiness falls off mechanism. In any case, the word "machine" implies a misunderstanding of it.

Thus, a flower is as much a mechanism as a sewing machine; a rainbow as a dynamo; the mechanical processes in all are easily traced or diagrammed. Given elements and moisture, heat and light, and the chemisms that can function in this environment do function. Remove light, or heat—establish what we look on as cold or dark—and nothing that our limited senses can register appears;

I Believe: The Personal Philosophies of Certain Eminent Men and Women of Our Time, ed. Clifton Fadiman (New York: Simon and Schuster, 1939), pp. 355–62.

*The *I Believe* collection was a sequel to the 1931 *Living Philosophies* collection, also published by Simon and Schuster. Dreiser's 1929 article "What I Believe" had been republished in *Living Philosophies.*

though that there are many things registering themselves *on one another* beyond our limited sensory reactions, we know.

But law! It governs everything from the speed of light and the spaces between island universes, to the floating of the minutest mote of dust in any space—the accurate physical and chemical laws accompanying these same being as mathematically deducible as those governing the floating of a battleship in water or an airplane in air (the limits of experimental science ever broadening). More, the chemical and physical accuracy and finish that go into the designing, coloring, and functioning of a beetle's wing, a fly's eye, a spider's web, a stalk of grass or a bird's feather, involve what we have come to look on as mind or science or knowledge as those are expressed in invention, designing, and constructing here. So that what one sees everywhere in nature or space suggests endlessly more of genius than man has ever achieved or is likely to.

And beauty! Involved in all things! Beauty of design, beauty of color, beauty of motion, beauty of sound, and beauty of finish, as recognized by the five senses—though how, in ourselves, we come by this sense of or reaction to "beauty" in ourselves, we cannot know, since we are plainly mechanisms designed to respond in the way that we do.

Which brings us back to the problem of mind or individuality, or individual thinking, since none of these things to which we respond are in use other than as processes, designs, compulsions, necessities, reactions, which cause in us the illusion of what we call mind, individuality, individual thinking. But plainly these are illusions only. All derive from various embodying or governing forces and conditions and materials, which, in their totality, we variously refer to as the Universe, God, or the Vital Force.

But, having said so much, where are we? Back to the Creator or God of the Bible? Or Brahma of the Hindus? Almost, if not quite, I should say. But with these exceptions. For into the speculations or reactions of humanity in regard to creation or God, has come science which has resolved the one-time "supernatural" so-called, into the natural, although not entirely. A vast body of data as to substances and forces has been assembled and is now known to many men, and by not a few of them used to advance their own functions and purposes. Science suggests that what we see or sense as the universe is not the instantaneous sum or result of a creative will, but an evolutionary process, which is none the less creative in a relative sense, in that it involves change. That it may or may not always have been as man senses it—even in its totality—is not

312

necessarily to be apprehended ever—even by an evolving mechanism such as he is. He may retrograde and disappear. What has appeared through science is that, with man on this planet, plus all the protoplasmic chain of creatures, animal and vegetable, that have either preceded or now accompany him here, special environing conditions have been necessary, and that as these have changed so has he. Thus a little more heat or cold either develops or destroys at either end of the measure.

That man has improved and is even the epitome of the solar if not universal creation is the belief or reaction of some. That man is an evolved mechanism peculiar to this solar system and its environment and is likly to improve or decay with it, is the chemic reaction of others. That man is no more than a balanced equation between various forces, and that he cannot possibly exist save in a world which presents and must present endless and opposing contrasts or variations, is the profound conviction of others; i.e., that there is not and cannot be, if we are to have life *as we know it,* either absolute good, or absolute evil, but only relative good and relative evil—in other words, the new reigning description of relativity. So too with strength and weakness, as this applies to the various creatures that inhabit the earth, for an all-powerful creature could not possibly be opposed by another all-powerful creature. The result would be deadlock, stalemate, no suggestion of life whatsoever. So again with truth and error or falsehood, for in order to know truth there must be that by which it can be measured. For without the existence of relative error, or illusion, how could truth be known? What would there be to set opposite in order that its truthfulness should be plain? Hence for the possibility of life, here, *as we know it,* there must be relatively (not absolutely) good and evil, courage and fear, love and hate, joy and sorrow, beauty and ugliness—a balanced or fairly proportional quantity of each, even though it be true, as Christ said, "Woe to him by whom the evil cometh."

My personal reaction to all this, and to all science, as it relates to life on this planet, not elsewhere, is that this is true, and that from it there is no escape. What there is elsewhere, we, balanced mechanisms, so organized to respond, are in no position to say. For, in order to have wisdom we must have ignorance. For what or where would wisdom be without its contrary? The enlighteners of ignorance would do what? Whom would they enlighten? Where?

And just here a word as to progress. For "progress" or

change there is of sorts—a relative progress or change merely as I
see it, although others are sure that the "progress" that brought us
into being, playing and enjoying or suffering at this interesting or
miserable game as each sees it is far superior to the force—their
state or mentality—which brought us into being.

Yet how can that be?

Is the creator less than the created? Or merely different?

As a child I wondered at houses, tents, lampposts, wagons,
sidewalks, and the whole array of mechanically devised implements or utensils with which we have surrounded and aided ourselves (principally in numbers or masses) the better to pleasure
ourselves. Later, because in connection with the coming of these
and our use of them I heard of progress, I wondered why. Why
progress? From what to what? One already carefully balanced condition to another. For before ever my day was, were endless others
crowded with wonders, as stupendous as any I was witnessing. So
where the progress? Was not Egypt as amazing as America, or
China, or India? And before ever they were, the entire evolution of
man, beast, fish, flower, bird, tree; compare our airplane to a
bird—a gull or eagle. Our rate of speed to that of light, or the
earth. We laugh at or commiserate the savage; but he neither
laughs at nor commiserates himself. He is adjusted to his environment, just as we are to ours, just as the Egyptians were to theirs,
just as every living or physical and mental (so-called) thing is adjusted to its. So to talk of progress instead of change would be to
assume that so stupendous a process as Life, Nature, the Universal
Creative Force, could or had to learn something, from something
else! Us, for instance? Whereas it makes us.

The point of all this is that I have been awakened to and
convinced of the unity of all processes, forms, variations, motions,
and activities of matter, or matter energy, the staggering wisdom
and care or fixed condition that evokes, directs, controls, and
maintains their presence, harmony, beauty, order, or seeming dis-
order, as some rearrangements sometimes seem. Also, that both
relativity and mechanism are but processes of this immense creative something which, if not compelled so to function, still does
so. Also that for all this seeming cruelty and brutality of some of
the creative processes, real enough to the subjects or victims of the
same, there is still holding in this governing synthesis called Life,
some balancing good; and this is a necessity by reason of which
what we see here on earth—and all the sensations we experience—
can be. Without this dualism, this mechanism, and this relativity of

all things, this altogether dramatic and glorious force that, for any or no reason, involves and evolves, would not be what it is—the multiple and thrilling, or pleasing or painful, series of sensations called life.

To be sure, this poses the question as to what can be the value of our lives if all this should be so. How are we to evaluate anything, since everything seems to depend ultimately on some unknown, but inevitable, source? Do not the values of all things fall away? Civilization and the products of all thought and human effort? Nevertheless, at this point I wish to show that in spite of this devaluation, we are ourselves organisms, and we are as helpless to cease desiring or not desiring, as ever we were. Hence, we cannot be solely the *contemplators* of all this, as Schopenhauer would have us be, or ride roughshod over life, constantly aware of its valuelessness, as Nietzsche proposes, or even adhere to any standard of values set up arbitrarily by and through us, or our religionists, with knowledge that they cannot have any absolute meaning.

For law, the precepts of religion, and art, and creeds, and directions of all kinds, appear thus to have been set up in vain, and as we all know, quite all of them give way before one another. And so that which is outside of us, goading us to one action or another, comes to have no meaning in itself; that is, the individual items of the universe outside of us do not always have the same effect on us. In other words, possessions, people, travel, art, the vision of nature and knowledge, leave us with different feelings at different times. They are seen to be alternative to each other in producing what is, I must finally conclude, *our* only reality. And that is the succession of states of mind, of moods, of emotions, which all must undergo.

However, as you can see, it is this succession of contrasts in our own reactions which means *life* to us, joy and sadness, pleasure and pain, courage and fear, desire and indifference, etc. Life is what it *seems*. We inevitably *feel* these things. The equation of the universe—the fact of contrasts outside of us—corresponds to this interior cycle; but no individual item outside or inside of us can assure us of the perpetuity of any single reaction. It is for this reason, it seems to me, that if there is any practical value to philosophy at all, we might *feel* better, in the course of ages, perhaps might even come to a scale of values—no different in the absolute equation than what we have now—but which would relate solely to a consideration of *reactions* as such, without any relatively meaningless considerations of what may be done in the exterior world of causes and actions.

The larger my conception of it, if it can be called large, the more I am able to fit what might seem conflicting evidence into one whole pattern. All the contrasts of life—good and evil, beauty and ugliness, joy, sorrow, big and little, knowledge and ignorance—all these fall away as evidence of any inherent dualism or cross-purpose in nature, just as does the idea of the individual or the importance of the individual, or of life, or of any special aspect of the universe which men have from time to time singled out for their egotistical attention. It will be seen that we, men, or any one of us, cannot be regarded as ends in ourselves, or for that matter, there does not seem to be anything that can be singled out as a "purpose." It will be seen at the same time that the illusions of value which make up the cycle of our life must be necessary and evidently are functional to some other end, unknown to us. It will be seen that our wildest dreams such as perfectibility, free will, progress, love, justice, truth, goodness, God, the importance of man, of intelligence, are not created by us but are mere derivations suggested by partial evidence—I say partial because not one of the above but has its "enemy" so-called—its opposite in degree, at least—some other dream inconsistent with it. Even mechanism, which seems to me the fruit of as disinterested contemplation as I am capable of, depends entirely on the existence of illusions which oppose it, and but for which I would never have considered the proposition seriously!

[Statement on Anti-Semitism]

Dreiser's somewhat jaundiced contribution to an "Editorial Conference" on Jews, in the American Spectator 1 *(September 1933), had stimulated a belief that he was anti-Semitic. See in particular Hutchins Hapgood, "Is Dreiser Anti-Semitic?" Nation 140 (April 17, 1935): 436–38. The Nazi attack on European Jewry led the League of American Writers to publish in 1939 a collection of statements by eminent public figures on the subject of anti-Semitism.*

Today world society, because of the illuminating data furnished by thousands of years of social experience as well as the more integrated and clarifying knowledge of life and how to live it gathered by science, should at least have arrived at, one would hope, the place where it could function without barbarism—these constant resorts to persecution, individual and social murders, or war—and the endless forms of physical and mental cruelty that come from religious and racial prejudices. Personally I do not believe in social torture of any group, or race, or sect for reasons of difference in appearance or creed or custom. Where these latter involve what other sects or creeds look upon as inequities of social procedure, these same should be dealt with civilly via equitable legal procedure.

But how to overcome or dissipate these extensions of ancient ignorance, delusions, illusions, prejudices and what not that protrude from ancient days into our bright new realm of knowledge. Cannot the sects or races be cured of their sometimes aggravating, sometimes savage determinations to preserve or extend themselves by war or boycott or persecution or robbery? It is quite plain, of course, that no social or religious or racial problems can either humanely or equitably be solved that way. It is not a question of an eye for an eye or a tooth for a tooth—but an eye for no eye, a tooth for no tooth. Mostly the alleged crimes relate to passing differences in language, dress, information, beliefs, customs. You do not eat as

We Hold These Truths . . . (New York: League of American Writers, 1939), pp. 45–47.

I do; pronounce my native tongue as I do; dress, walk, talk or respond as fast or in the same way to this or that, as I do. Hence you are accursed. You should not live in the same world—at least the same land or city with me. Out! I cannot endure you and I cannot wait for you to change. Is not that the mood of many races, tribes, groups, creeds, sects, nationalities at this hour—or at least of their leaders?

Yet the social, religious, national or racial problems are never really solved in, by or through such a mood. Instead, wars, persecutions, cherished hatreds and social and legal inequities of all descriptions follow. Consider the warring sects in India at this hour. The social and religious hatreds in Europe, America and Asia. And all of this in the face of modern science—the verified realities of political, social, economic law!

Just now it is the Jews in Germany; the Negroes in America, the democratic-minded Loyalists in Spain, the backward in China, the swart Fellaheen in Egypt, the Moors in Africa, the Czechs in Czechoslovakia, who are being seized upon and exploited, restrained, oppressed or murdered—each according to some theory as to their unfitness on the part of some other nation or group as often as not, really more often than not, for economic purposes; the desire and hope of profit on the part of the exploiters.

But how to overcome all this? By urging the victims to fight back and helping them so to do. Of course. By advertising said inequities and iniquities to the entire world, and propagandizing against them and their perpetrators? Of course. That more equitable governments or nations and races should be asked not only to protest but to bring such pressure as they can—make war even on the authors of inequity or iniquity is also right.

But—at this point—the equitable individual continuing to do his best to bring all equitable peoples and governments into active opposition against the inequities and iniquities, can he do more? No—nothing. Improvement from there on depends on the collective mass results of his respective individual energies. But so far these have not been sufficient to stop these several outrages. They are still with us. I am, of course, for the general abolishment of these outrages, wherever. And I so urge and have urged. If all will do as much there is at least the hope that these various ills will be ended. A majority must combine to bring it about. And I am strong for such a combination in all of these cases. The record of my personal appeals over many years proves this. What more would you have me say or do?

Concerning Dives and Lazarus

*From late 1939 through 1942 Dreiser issued a number of privately
printed broadsides and pamphlets in which he stated his opinion on
contemporary social and political events. He sent these publications
to prominent figures and also enclosed them in letters to friends.
Several of them were initially printed in the San Francisco* People's
World, *a Communist newspaper.* Soviet Russia Today, *an English
language magazine published in America by the Soviet Union, was
soliciting Dreiser for a "friendly" comment on the Russian-Finnish
War, which had just concluded and which had aroused much sympathy in America for Finland. The Russian-German non-aggression
pact of 1939, followed by the invasion of Poland by both countries
and the invasion of Finland by Russia, had placed American Communists in the uncomfortable position of defending a Communist
alliance with Nazism. The party-line response to this difficulty was
to stress that the major world struggle was not between specific
nations but between capitalistic imperialism wherever it was found
and the working class, and that the actions of the Soviet Union in
1939 contributed to its ability to defend itself in the coming struggle.
Dreiser's attack on England and France in this broadside is in accord with this official Communist Party position.*

TELEGRAM

THEODORE DREISER   MARCH 15, 1940

1426 NORTH HAYWORTH

HOLLYWOOD, CALIFORNIA

WOULD YOU JOIN A NUMBER OF LEADING AMERICANS IN WRITING
SEVERAL HUNDRED WORDS FOR PUBLICATION SOVIET RUSSIA TO-
DAY IN ANSWER QUESTION QUOTE DO YOU BELIEVE THE CAUSE OF
INTERNATIONAL PEACE HAS BEEN FURTHERED AND THE POSSIBIL-
ITY OF SPREADING THE WORLD WAR REDUCED BY THE OUTCOME OF
THE SOVIET FINNISH CONFLICT UNQUOTE   WOULD APPRECIATE
RECEIVING YOUR ANSWER NOT LATER THAN MARCH EIGH-
TEENTH   114 EAST 32 STREET   JESSICA SMITH EDITOR

Broadside, March, 1940. *Soviet Russia Today* 8 (April 1940): 8–9, with title, "The
Soviet-Finnish Treaty and World Peace."

No, I do not believe so,—not as long as England can get any additional sucker countries or enslaved colonies to do her fighting and her money furnishing for her. India supplied her the money for her war against Napoleon. India and all her other colonies, plus Imperialistic Russia, Monarchial Italy, Capitalistic France, Royal grafting Belgium, plus untutored savages from Africa, untutored Americans from the United States and the sane, self-seeking Japanese won her purely Empire saving first war with Germany. So far in this World War II Democratic Spain, Democratic Czechoslovakia, Capitalistic Poland and would be Democratic Finland have bled and died to save her and yet she is not saved. But she still has hope, if not absolute faith, that her colonies covering one fifth of the world,—Africa, dominated Canada, Australia, New Zealand, South Africa and Arabia along with Capitalistic France and her Capitalistic associate and servile admirer, the United States, will furnish the men and the money to keep her alive and going. The poor Finns undoubtedly thought they were once more saving the world for Democracy when they allowed England and France and Germany—before this new world war started—to build and furnish her Mannerheim line for her. But she was mistaken. This kind service on the part of England was another little trick to use Finland as a corridor through which England could attack Russia and at the same time bring the United States running.

Poor little Finland!

Enormous, horrible, imperialistic Russia!—the only country in all the history of the world that has given the working mass—not the loafing class—a break. And the ignorant Finns, led by a bought and paid for governing group, had to die for that.

For as anyone with even failing sight can see, the planning and building of such an immense defense mechanism as the Mannerheim line by small Finland—population 3,400,000—is not to be explained by either the fears or the resources of such a population. What! 3,400,000 Finns fight or hold at bay 180,000,000 Russians! You might as well think of Denmark building a Dannerheim line to keep Germany out. Or Holland, a Hollandaise one. Or Belgium, a Belgianheim line. Belgium allowed England to build one for her in 1912, '13 to keep the Germans out and spent four years under Germany's heel for her pains and with no more than a thank you kindly from the dear British. But Belgium is not building another, you notice. Once was enough.

But why should England wish to attack Russia? And why does she hate Germany for not attacking Russia? For, as you know, Russia is kind to the Jews; gives them the best deal they have ever had in their history. And as you know, Germany has not. And, whereas Russia is truly democratic, Germany, according to England, is not. And yet England proclaims itself democratic and hates Russia.

The real reason, of course, is that Capitalism or the power that springs from the possession of money, oppresses, and always has, unorganized labor, and so today fears and fights this recent development in Organized Labor, Russia. If you don't believe this, read history and look around you. The profit system, or that other term for it, the Capitalistic System, fears and hates the non-profit or equal break for all system now holding in Soviet Russia. And England, which represents the Capitalistic System wishes to destroy the non-profit system. If you doubt this, see how our multimillionaires and their banks and associated business groups hate and fight organized labor as well as the complaining unemployed here in America. And in England see how labor is sweated and starved there, as well as in India, Egypt, England's African colonies and where not else? Read a history of India, of Egypt—of the Boer War and our own Colonial War. And the reason for this is that accumulated money and the power crazed upstarts who come into possession of it always wish to dominate millions of slaves so that they will look like something which they really are not—creatures of superior minds, instincts, wisdom and judgment. If you doubt this, read, for one thing, the history of Rome. For another, the history of our great American fortunes by Gustavus Myers. This last presents an unbroken chain of American robber barons. In England, my Lord this and the Duke of that is nothing more than a robber business man or commercial slicker presented with a title, or he or his son or grandson or heir. Without money, as you can find out for yourself in England, he is nothing,—discarded by his associate lords and dukes for the want of it.

To get money and keep it and rule the less clever in the matter of money getting has been the business of England ever since it started. And to get it and keep it[,] it has assailed and sought to conquer every other power that it has contacted adjacent to its ever enlarging realm. And in England—the British Empire— my Lords this and that, ever since money got them their titles, have oppressed and cheated the masses not only of England but of each and every one of the colonies which she founded or the realm which she conquered. You need only to read the histories of India and Egypt and British Africa, north and south, or that of the Brit-

321

ish West and East Indies and of Canada, Australia, British Guiana and where not else.

But in the Russian Soviet system now (since 1918) rapidly expanding in wealth and strength, England, and for the first time in all her history, has met a new power that she truly fears and wishes to destroy. And to achieve this destruction she has attacked her in every conceivable way since the close of the first great war. In fact to achieve this she has joined with her, since 1919, so called "Democratic France" but really Capitalistic France, to say nothing of Italy, Germany, Poland, Belgium—indeed the entire capitalistic wage slave system the world over. For her chief concern, as quite every informed person today knows, is India, which is adjacent to Russia, and which is the next logical country to turn from its England imposed slavery to the Communistic System. For India is England's chief earthly gold mine. Its simple, hard working, religious minded and just millions, nearly 400,000,000 of them, have kept the titled classes of England in leisure and comfort for the last 300 years. And what is more, since the beginning of her conquest of India, she has drawn from those slaves the money to battle and destroy Napoleon in Europe, the Dutch and the French in America and the Boers in South Africa and the Germans in Europe in 1914–18. With Indian money she was able to explore and colonize America, the West Indies, Australia, New Zealand and Africa including South Africa and Egypt. Their work—that of the simple Hindu—has served to pay the dividends on the shares of the so called capital which England is said to have invested in "developing" these various countries and colonies. Alas "investing" in England, as in other capitalistic countries, means tricking and taxing the natives and even the English colonists of her extending realms of their original inheritances or labors, and doing so by maintaining mixed and native soldiery (always captained by English officers) in order to battle and slay any who failed in obedience, and so thus establishing peace and British colonial "loyalty." Only now, Russia, by growing in power and wealth, has tended to threaten all this—to communize India. And that is why England will not end this war if she can help it, without first fighting, and, if possible, destroying Russia.

And to that end she has already sacrificed Democratic Spain, Socialist Austria, Democratic Czechoslovakia, Capitalistic Poland and Democratic Finland—and all under the guise of once more saving the world for Democracy. What she really wants to do, as all who know anything know, is to save her own imperial control of the world—and for no other purpose. To this end she is still ready to sacrifice France and Germany and the Balkans and Turkey and the remaining Scandinavian countries, if only she could. And already she has called upon all her colonies for money and men to help her—but not for the sake of her colonies—but solely for the preservation of the imperial group that inhabits the south of England and no other place. For England, as you know,—Imperial England—counts on every colonial,—black, brown, yellow, red or white to fight and die for her. It has, by now, become an old and honored English custom as well as tradition. She even looks to the United States, as she did in the last war, to at long last, rescue her from destruction. She openly says so and we ought to know. For we are the only ones who could possibly save her. But "the Yanks are not coming."

"You shall not press down upon the brow of labor this crown of thorns: You shall not crucify mankind upon a cross of gold."

William Jennings Bryan,
Democratic Convention, Chicago, 1896

My Creator

Many, many times in my semi-industrious life I have been asked by one person or another what I thought of life(!) or whether, if ever, I sought to interpret the Creative Force by reason of which all of us find ourselves present—numbered among the living. At that time my brash and certainly most unpremeditated reply was that I took no meaning from all that I saw unless it was some planned form of self-entertainment on the part of the Creative Force which cared little if anything for either the joys or sorrows of its creatures, and that, as for myself, "I would pass as I had come to be, confused and dismayed,"—a very definite statement, which for some reason or other, seemed to register sharply on the minds of many, and which since, and up to this very day, has been thrown back at me whenever I have chosen to claim any clear understanding of any of the amazing processes that I see in full function about me in the world. And yet here they are—a minute number of them.

War and peace, mercy and cruelty, sorrow and joy, love and hate, change and stability, youth and age, ignorance and knowledge, humor and the lack of it. Also, the disrupting factor called chance, memory and forgetfulness, courage and fear or strength and weakness. Also beauty and ugliness. Death or an immaterial life after this, as well as the evidence of plan and design in all things everywhere from time immemorial. Thus mountain to rock to pebble to sand or water to snow to ice to hail to vapor and return. Or flower to vine to tree to bush to weed to grass—even the bryophyllum plant which actually grows while you wear it—absorbing its nourishment from the air and needing neither water or earth to cause it to thrive! As for the purpose of all this—good, bad or indifferent. Ah, there! as in endless other instances, I found myself staggered by its import or a lack of the same—the why of it?

For certainly bryophyllum is not a numerous resident of this earth any more than was the great Auk, which disappeared from this earth a century or two ago.

Unpublished manuscript, November 18, 1943. Copyright the Trustees of the University of Pennsylvania.

324

Truly the endless variety of life, from amoeba to man; the three toed dog-sized horse to his present day, heavily hoofed descendent; the one time sea going mammal of minute size that descended or ascended to be a whale, and so on ad infinitum, puzzled me to the point of reading Darwin, Haeckel, Spencer, Loeb, Lodge, Crookes and who not else—Freud, Menninger—a long list. In fact I spent three solid years informing myself as to their views and conclusions, as well as those of many, many others, which same, in my case, led to the making of the above list and my personal conclusion in regard to the same. As to that conclusion it was that contrast, however attractive or disagreeable,—joyful to many, or terrible to others—as for instance, extreme wealth as opposed to extreme poverty; extreme beauty as opposed to extreme ugliness, extreme strength as opposed to extreme weakness, extreme wisdom as opposed to extreme ignorance—that was apparently indispensable to this life and world process if we are to have life, as we know it.

* * * * * *

However, while in awe and wonder, I study the various constructive processes of nature, and witness, as I say, not only the very necessary contrast, in so far as all thinking or reacting creatures are concerned, between all things,—tree with fish or bird or animal or flower or man or worm or germ or gnat or elephant, with any or all of the same, I am really most awed, and to a very great degree, made reverent by the all prevailing evidence of not only an enormous and all pervasive subtlety and skill in the construction and arrangement and operation of all of these obviously endless forms which now either are here, or are still, at this time, coming into being, and only now are beginning their evolution, or have been and have passed, and, or have never been entered in the records of the knowledge of man, who, himself, in earlier and seemingly almost unrelated forms, has come and gone—whether ever to return or not, who is to say? The hairy ape! pre-eocene man! The Piltdown man, etc. etc. etc.

And now as to these,—the mechanical and chemical genius of their construction and operation! Also the amazing variety and, what is more, the almost invariable esthetic appeal of their design! We think of design as an art and praise this and that creature of the Creator,—painter, sculptor, poet, architect, designer, inventor as geniuses, even, in some instances, superlative geniuses, but solely because of the examples of design that they have furnished us.

Phidias and Praxiteles for their forms in stone, Michaelangelo's tombs of the Medici,—or his slaves; Leonardo's conception of the Last Supper or the aeroplane. Botticelli's suggestion of spring and youth in paint—yet copied from where? Nature?

And yet, do but open your door and walk into your garden or the fields—or even into the hard streets of a city with its shop or house windows!

Design! Design! Design! In each and every instance copied from a previous design in nature somewhere, and what is more arresting, by a creature—male or female—itself a design of nature, itself chemically and mechanically repeated these endless millions of years.

In my garden is an orange, a lemon, an avocado, a walnut and a banana tree, to say nothing of a variety of flowers. As to the trees, I have this long while, been overawed and made most profoundly respectful—really, in a sense reverently, and if I did not dislike the current connotations of the word—religiously so. For my avocado is planted in a hard packed body of dust covered earth which extends earthward some twelve feet and requires a by no means large quantity of water to cause it to flourish—build itself an eighteen inch thick trunk,—at least a half dozen three to four inch branches—and branching from those, a score of two of lesser branches bearing in their season heaven only knows how many smooth and shiny leaves—graceful as a warrior's shield is graceful, and bearing in its season, which endures through October and November, all of two hundred or more round ebony skinned avocados—which begin, each and every one, as a green bud and end, in November, as a soft and buttery fruit or vegetable which, for flavor and taste, has nothing that out rivals it.

But what interests me in this, to some possibly commonplace, process, is not the fact that this particular process and result is annually undertaken by this tree and successfully completed, but by mankind in general—if they happen to know of it, and by some thought little of.

An avocado tree? What of it? It bears avocados after the manner you describe and they are very good. What of that? I can buy them for ten or fifteen cents a piece, depending on size. So what? Only my answer is plenty what.

For here is one of these miracles of my Creator—Nature—which confounds me completely. For I have been thinking this long while that insofar as man is concerned, at least—also as to many animals and birds and even fishes and insects—that each is

326

equipped with a brain—that particular organism on which we pride ourselves.

But, whether they have or not, here is this particular tree, which, out of millions of important trees and plants, arrests my attention and will serve to pose a quite amazing problem well worth thinking of. For, in the sense that we know the animal, insect or human brain, the tree or plant or flower family has no such mechanism. Examine any one carefully and you find that it has many things,—roots, bark, a powerful wooden post of varying height which it very carefully erects in order, in due course, to carry the varying and increasing weight of many branches, which, in their turn, are to be equipped with twigs, which, in their turn, are to be equipped with buds and later, leaves, which, in their turn—the buds first, the leaves last, are to be fed with a chemical fluid or sap extracted from the ground by the roots—an imitative tangle duplicate of the branches of the tree above which, before ever the latter were, were shot forth by some creative force in the comparatively minute seed which same, by some process, known only to the Creator, extracted from the soil, the chemical and fluids—which, with sunlight and rain from above, were to make this beauteous thing with its artistically polished fruit, not only lovely to look at but helpful in the matter of sustaining many creatures—birds and animals, as well as men.

But this process, thus arbitrarily selected by me as an illustration of the supreme genius of this Creative force that so overawes me, is, as all know or should, but one of possibly endless billions of such processes which have resulted in the endless variety of forms or creatures,—animal, vegetable, mineral—which have come and gone since first this particular planet became, or was made habitable for any type of form plus any type of movement.

It is true that as to design, as well as utility—as predatory man has been developed to register design and utility—not all are possessed of the same esthetic or practical appeals or values as are many others. The frog is by no means possessed of the same esthetic appeal as the humming bird or the nightingale. Yet like the kangaroo, the giraffe, the rhinoceros and the elephant, it serves at best apparently to provide the always arresting value of contrast, by reason of which man—and very likely many other creatures—find life interesting—or at least endurable.

The fact is, however, that more than anything else in connection with the Creative Force which brings us and all other phases of life into being—at times for so little a time as (in the instance of

327

some flowers or insects) an hour or a day; in the case of some trees or vines, for hundreds of years,—is this matter of design. For design, however one may feel concerning some of it, is the great treasure that nature or the Creative force has to offer to man and through which it seems to emphasize its own genius and to offer the knowledge of the same to man. Design! Design! Design! And with each astounding variation, either of beauty or practical wisdom or both. And what is of greater import to some than even beauty, there stands forth to the eye, as well as to the practical physical tests of any one who chooses to imitate the same, the most brilliantly informed and carefully exercised engineering knowledge that somehow nature or the Creator has seen to it, *ever*, that man should see it. For whatever the height or breadth or thickness or weight of trunk or branches or roots, or the fruit or flowers of either tree or flower, as well as the wind and heat and cold forces of any particular area, which may tend to strain or injure or destroy the same, the Creator of the tree, the flower, the vegetable, the animal or man—and whatever his or its beauty or homeliness, has seen to it that each is so constructed or engineered, as well as chemically and sensitively equipped, within and without, to withstand the same,—at least to an arresting degree and for a given period—be it one day, one hour, one year or three score years and ten, or a thousand years!

And yet, in addition to that, there seems to have been thought out the advantages or disadvantages of a given soil or climate area where each may flourish, or at least may test its strength. And although all varieties of advantage or disadvantage may prevail—now here and now there—and although bitter or sweet may be the lot of this or that created thing, that often enough (after the fashion of the soldiers of a contending and yet well clothed and well equipped army) is now here and now there, and seemingly arbitrarily at times set down to make its way as best it can, yet—and again it is not often, as you will note, that flower or tree or what you will is alone anywhere, or that it is not (more rather than less) well fitted to make its way in the realm to which its Creator has called it—suffering or no suffering—cruelty or no cruelty. For, plainly, if one will but trouble to look and study, it has not only been thoughtfully and considerately, devised and equipped for the task to which it is called. For, for instance, behold the savage and yet stately lion, forced by want to lurk and kill— and yet which same is kind to his kind. Again, but see the beautiful and yet anachronously awkward flamingo, or his fellow, the ibis or the wading birds, in general—how carefully constructed and equipped for the lives they must lead.

Or, and again, if one turns to the sea, behold the endless variety of creatures from whale to shark to crab or petty minnow, or jelly fish, yet each so carefully designed and constructed for the world in which it is to find itself. Yes, everywhere, from pole to pole, design, as well as efficiency and chemical energy, are ever harmoniously present so as to fit in each creature not only with a chemo physical world without but another within so as to produce beauty, as well as hunger and desire and pursuit and defeat or victory—the intricate and interesting, and yet often enough, trying, and worse, terrible and yet not wholly unbeautiful structure or game we call life.

And so, studying this matter of genius in design and beauty, as well as the wisdom of contrast and interest in this so carefully engineered and regulated universe—this amazing process called living—I am moved not only to awe but to reverence for the Creator of the same concerning whom—his presence in all things from worm to star to thought—I meditate constantly even though it be, as I see it, that my import to this, my Creator, can be but as nothing, or less, if that were possible.

Yet awe I have. And, at long last, profound reverence for so amazing and esthetic and wondrous a process that may truly have been, and for all that I know, may yet continue to be forever and forever. An esthetic and wondrous process of which I might pray—and do—to remain the infinitesimal part of that same that I now am.

1015 N. King's Rd.,
Hollywood, 46, Calif.
Nov. 18, 1943.

Theodore Dreiser Joins
Communist Party

Dreiser's letter appeared in the same issue of the Daily Worker *which announced that the just concluded convention of the Communist Party of America had replaced Earl Browder with William Z. Foster as chairman of the Party. Browder had been hostile to Dreiser, but Foster was an old friend; hence the timing of Dreiser's request. [It was of course known some time before the convention that Foster would replace Browder.] The prose style of the letter is not characteristically Dreiserian, which suggests that the letter was ghostwritten or severely edited.*

As a testament to his deep faith in "the common people, and first of all, the workers," Theodore Dreiser, one of the outstanding novelists of the world, applied for membership in the newly reconstituted Communist Party and was admitted unanimously by the delegates to the convention held in New York City over the weekend.

* * * * * *

Dreiser's letter to Foster follows:

Hollywood, Calif.,
July 20, 1945

William Z. Foster
New York, N.Y.

Dear Mr. Foster:
˜ I am writing this letter to tell you of my desire to become a member of the American Communist organization.
This request is rooted in convictions that I have long held and

Daily Worker, July 30, 1945, p. 5.

330

that have been strengthened and deepened by the years. I have believed intensely that the common people, and first of all the workers,—of the United States and of the world—are the guardians of their own destiny and the creators of their own future. I have endeavored to live by this faith, to clothe it in words and symbols, to explore its full meaning in the lives of men and women.

It seems to me that faith in the people is the simple and profound reality that has been tested and proved in the present world crisis. Facism derided that faith, proclaiming the end of human rights and human dignity, seeking to rob the people of faith in themselves, so that they could be used for their own enslavement and degradation.

But the democratic peoples of the world demonstrated the power that lay in their unity, and a tremendous role was played in this victory by the country that through its attainment of socialism has given the greatest example in history of the heights of achievement that can be reached by a free people with faith in itself and in all the progressive forces of humanity—the Soviet Union. The unity of our country with the great Soviet Union is one of the most valuable fruits of our united struggle, and dare not be weakened without grave danger to America itself.

Communists all over the world have played a vital part in welding the unity of the peoples that insures the defeat of Fascism. Theirs were the first and clearest voices raised against the march of aggression in China, Ethiopia and Spain.

Dr. Norman Bethune, the great pioneer in saving war wounded through the use of the blood bank, died in China helping the free peoples of that country withstand the Japanese hordes years before the democratic countries came to their aid. His dying request was that it be made known that since many years he had been a Communist.

Out of the underground movements of tortured Europe, Communists have risen to give leadership in the face of terror and all-pervading military suppression. Tito of Yugoslavia won the admiration of the world for his leadership of his people to victory. The name of Stalin is one beloved by the free peoples of the earth. Mao-Tse-tung and Chou En-lai have kept the spirit of democracy and unity alive in China throughout the years that divisive forces have split that country asunder.

In the United States, I feel that the Communists have helped to deepen our understanding of the heritage of American freedom as a guide to action in the present. During the years when Fascism

331

was preparing for its projected conquest of the world, American Communists fought to rally the American people against Fascism. They saw the danger and they proposed the remedy. Marxist theory enabled them to cast a steady light on the true economic and social origins of Fascism; Marxism gave them also a scientific understanding of the power of the working people as a force in history which could mobilize the necessary intelligence, strength and heroism to destroy Fascism, save humanity and carry on the fight for further progress.

More than 11,000 Communists are taking part in that struggle as members of the armed forces of our country. That they have served with honor and patriotism is attested to even by the highest authorities of the Army itself.

More and more it is becoming recognized in our country that the Communists are a vital and constructive part of our nation, and that a nation's unity and nation's democracy is dangerously weakened if it excludes the Communists. Symbolic of this recognition was the action of the War Department in renouncing discrimination against Communists in granting commissions. A statement signed by a number of distinguished Americans points out that "the Army has apparently taken its position as a result of the excellent record of Communists and so-called Communists, including a number who have been cited for gallantry and a number who have died in action."

It seems to me that this ought to discredit completely one of the ideological weapons from the arsenal of Fascism that disorients the country's political life and disgraces its intellectual life—red-baiting. Irrational prejudice against anything that is truly or falsely labeled "Communism" is absurd and dangerous in politics. Concessions to red-baiting are even more demoralizing in the field of science, art and culture. If our thinkers and creators are to fulfill their responsibilities to a democratic culture, they must free themselves from the petty fears and illusions that prevent the open discussion of ideas on an adult level. The necessities of our time demand that we explore and use the whole realm of human knowledge.

I therefore greet with particular satisfaction the information that such leading scientists as the French physicist, Joliot-Curie, and the French mathematician, Langevin, have found in the Communist movement, as did the British scientist Haldane, some years ago, not only the unselfishness and devotion characteristic of the pursuit of science, but also the integration of the scientific approach to their own field of work with the scientific approach to the problems of society.

I am also deeply stirred to hear that such artists and writers, devoted to the cause of the people, as Pablo Picasso of Spain and Louis Aragon of France, have joined the Communist movement, which also counts among its leading cultural figures the great Danish novelist, Martin Anderson Nexo, and the Irish playwright, Sean O'Casey.

These historic years have deepened my conviction that widespread membership in the Communist movement will greatly strengthen the American people, together with the anti-fascist forces throughout the world, in completely stamping out Fascism and achieving new heights of world democracy, economic progress and free culture. Belief in the greatness and dignity of Man has been the guiding principle of my life and work. The logic of my life and work leads me therefore to apply for membership in the Communist Party.

Sincerely,

THEODORE DREISER

INDEX

Index

Index

Index

*Donald Pizer, Pierce Butler
Professor of English, Newcomb
College, Tulane University,
received his B.A. (1951), M.A.
(1952), and Ph.D. (1955) degrees
from the University of California,
Los Angeles. He is the author of
several books and many articles in
scholarly journals and has edited
the works of Hamlin Garland,
Frank Norris, and Theodore
Dreiser. His most recent work is*
The Novels of Theodore Dreiser:
A Critical Study *(1976).*

*The manuscript was edited by
Marguerite C. Wallace. The
typeface for the text is Times
R~~~~~~~ ~~~igned under the
~~~~~~~~~ ~f Stanley Morison
~~~~~~~~~ The display faces are
~~~~~~~~ ned by R. Hunter
~~~~~on in 1938, and Helvetica,
designed by M. Miedinger in 1957.
The text is printed on Kingsport
Press B & W cream white paper,
and the book is bound in Columbia
Mills Fictionette cloth over
binder's boards. Manufactured in
the United States of America.*